ANARCHY
ONLINE

ANARCHY ONLINE
by Charles Platt

 HarperPrism
An Imprint of HarperPaperbacks

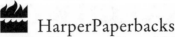
HarperPaperbacks
A Division of HarperCollins*Publishers*
10 East 53rd Street, New York, N.Y. 10022-5299

HarperPrism is an imprint of HarperPaperbacks.

HarperCollins®, ⬛®, HarperPaperbacks™, and HarperPrism®
are trademarks of HarperCollins*Publishers* Inc.

HarperPaperbacks may be purchased for educational, business, or sales
promotional use. For information, please write:
Special Markets Department, HarperCollins*Publishers,*
10 East 53rd Street, New York, N.Y. 10022-5299.

Printed in the United States of America

Cover design by Designed to Print

A hardcover edition of this book was published in 1996
by Black Sheep Books

First printing: March 1997

Designed by Erico Narita

Some portions of this book previously appeared in a different form in
Wired magazine; these portions appear here with the permission of *Wired*.

Photographs credited to the author are copyright © 1996 by Charles Platt.
Copyright on other photographs resides with the photographers.

This book contains many excerpts of text from online sources. These
excerpts are reprinted with permission, except in cases where the authors
were anonymous and could not be found.

Feedback: Charles Platt can be reached at cp@panix.com.

Library of Congress Cataloging-in-Publication Data is available
from the publisher.

Visit HarperPaperbacks on the World Wide Web at
http://www.harpercollins.com/paperbacks

❖ 10 9 8 7 6 5 4 3 2 1

Dedication

To John Battelle,

Kevin Kelly, and

Louis Rossetto

For the opportunity,

the inspiration, and

the support.

Acknowledgments

Sections describing the H.O.P.E. conference, Bruce Fancher and Patrick Kroupa, video pirates, Scott Charney at the Department of Justice, and the crackdown in Cincinnati were commissioned originally by *Wired* magazine. Much of the text has been radically revised for inclusion in this book. Interviews with Ann Beeson of the ACLU, David Chaum of DigiCash, Bill Joy of Sun Microsystems, David Lawrence of UUnet, and Phil Zimmermann (creator of PGP) were originally commissioned by the *Los Angeles Times,* which used only very brief excerpts.

Writing nonfiction entails bothering a lot of busy people, asking questions, and then asking them to check that I didn't make any mistakes when I wrote down their answers. I received generous help from the online community and a high degree of trust. I have tried hard to live up to the expectations of everyone who talked to me.

I'm especially grateful to Bruce Fancher, Mike Godwin, Patrick Kroupa, Declan McCullagh, and Jim Thomas, who provided me with a lot of primary source material and told me where to find more. Godwin in particular was amazingly generous, freely sharing source material that he had already gathered for a book that he was writing himself.

Thanks to all my other sources and advisors: Joseph Allen; David Bannisar; Ann Beeson; Stuart Beraha; Tom Betz; Steve Brown; Dave Buchwald; Scott Charney; David Chaum; Conchy Joe; Eric Corley; Barry Crimmins; Lewis De Payne; Jeff DelPapa; Philip Elmer-DeWitt; Bob Emerson; Dan Farmer; Joel Furr; John Gilmore; Charles Glasser; Scott Greenwood; Katie Hafner; Henry; Keith Henson; Donna Hoffman; Steve Jackson; Bill Joy; Kevin Kelly; Peter Kennedy; Susan Kim; Cameron Laird; Geoff Langdale; David Lawrence; Ron MacDonald; Scott Madigan; Fred Martin; David McClure; Brock Meeks; Michael Mehta; Stevens Miller; Muffy; Douglas Mullkoff; Lee Noga; Greg Ombrewski; Cleo Paskal; Bret Pettichord; Rose Platt; David Post; Joshua Quittner; Christopher Reeve; Brian Reid; Jack Rickard; Donna Riley; Martin Rimm; Lance

Rose; Alexis Rosen; Louis Rossetto; Shabbir Safdar; Seth; Lorne Shantz; Robert Steele; Bruce Sterling; Brad Templeton; Peter Trei; David Voght; Yuri; Phil Zimmermann; and the writers of anonymous Usenet posts that are quoted in my text.

Thanks also to the nice people who have published me, edited me, copy-edited me, fact-checked me, and issued checks for me at *Wired*: Louis Rossetto, Kevin Kelly, John Battelle, Martha Baer, Kim Heron, Mandy Erickson, Rod Simpson, and Inja Lowenstein, among others.

I dug up a lot of data and acquired my early online experience with the help of MindVox, still the freest and most entertaining Internet site, featuring an iconoclastic attitude and unique archives chronicling the early days of the modem world. To reach MindVox, telnet phantom.com or dial (212) 989-2418 (voice) or (212) 843-0801 (modem, N–8–1).

I did most of my Net research through Panix, a Unix site that provides reliable unlimited access at a fraction of the cost imposed by large services such as CompuServe or AOL. To reach Panix, telnet panix.com or call (212) 741-4400 (voice) or (212) 741-4444 (modem, N–8–1).

Dave Buchwald offered sober critical analysis at crucial junctures in the ongoing creative process. He also suggested some really silly book titles.

Russ Galen persuaded me to use e-mail years ago when there was hardly anyone to write to. Bruce Fancher gave me an Internet account when I still wasn't sure what the word *Internet* meant. I would have arrived here eventually, but the two of you shortened my journey.

John Silbersack facilitated this book, wittingly or unwittingly, and John Douglas permitted it. Erico Narita designed it with her usual meticulous attention to detail.

Thank you all.

Contents

Introduction

Searching for middle ground among Net extremists————1

Part 1: Net Crime

A typical hacker bust————7

Phone phreaks before the age of hacking————9

Origins of the "fuck-you" hacker attitude————11

Early hacker acts with the Apple][————13

Kids open up the world of computer bulletin boards————15

How copy-protected game software was pirated————16

Hack and counter-hack among 1980s New York teens————19

Law enforcement launches BBS sting operations————25

Operation Sundevil terminates the first hacking era————26

Some hackers go legal————33

Software piracy on a BBS in the 1990s————34

The Internet becomes a new hacker playground————38

Hanging out at a hacker conference————41

"Dark Fiber" describes the hacker ethic————47

Darkside hackers who do it for the money————50

Hackers spoof journalists; journalists fight back————52

How hacker Kevin Mitnick acquired mythic status————57

Markoff, Shimomura, and the ethics of hacker journalism————59

The hacker witch hunt————65

Katie Hafner defends Mitnick————69

"Roscoe" spoofs journalists and hassles the FBI————70

True darkside hackers are seldom profiled————74

Contents ■ *continued*

Satellite video: an opportunity for darkside hackers————76

Background color in the Bahamas————80

Meeting Fred and Ron, video pirates of the Caribbean————83

A garage workshop where video codes are cracked————84

The amazing history of satellite video piracy————86

How pirate dealers sell their service————90

Video piracy benefits hardware manufacturers————94

A pirate is invited to a sting operation————95

Hot gossip from the pirate underground————98

Helpful hints for amateur pirates————102

Two men who have put video pirates in jail————104

One pirate who got busted—but still won't quit————106

New encryption systems, and new ways to crack them————110

Is satellite video piracy technically legal?————112

Video piracy offers lessons for all computer users————113

New satellite systems open a new hacking era————116

Introducing Scott Charney of the Justice Department————118

How the Justice Department controls law enforcement————121

Scott Charney speaks out on netcrime————124

Other perspectives on Scott Charney————133

Robert Steele's plan for better Net security————134

Dan Farmer's SATAN program tests the Net————141

Case history of a virus attack————143

Fighting viruses, now and in the future————145

An overall assessment of the hacker threat————153

Introduction

Doomsayers and Technophiles

So much conflict!

So much confusion!

So little common ground!

On one side stand the doomsayers. The Net, they claim, is a lawless sewer infested with criminals and perverts. If your child logs on, he'll be depraved by pornography or seduced by a pedophile. If you download some software, a virus will eat your hard drive. Supposedly the Net corrupts decent people, destroys communities, and degrades human values. In the words of Mark Slouka, author of *War of the Worlds: Cyberspace and the Hi-tech Assault on Reality*, we must turn away from cyberspace and "align ourselves with physical reality now, before it's too late."

On the other side stand the technophiles, promising a virtual utopia. The Internet, they say, will undermine authoritarian governments, generate wealth, empower minorities, and revolutionize society. "I used to think that it was just the biggest thing since Gutenberg, but now I think you have to go back farther," says John Perry Barlow, cofounder of the Electronic Frontier Foundation. He seriously suggests that establishing a global network will be "the most transforming technological event since the capture of fire."

With such extremes of horror and hype, it's no surprise that the online environment has turned into a battleground.

So far the doomsayers have won some major victories, aided by conservative legislators and hysterical news stories about hackers and netporn. The press, in fact, has gone out of its way to make the Net seem as frightening as possible.

Well, hackers *do* interfere with other people's computers, and sexually explicit material *does* exist where unsupervised children can find it. But laws to protect us from these threats have been hastily drafted by politicians who are mostly uninformed and in some cases hostile toward the Internet. As a result, there has been a stream of legislation to throw people in jail if they merely trespass in someone's computer or say "shit" online.

Naturally, the libertarians have fought back. The Secret Service has been sued for seizing systems containing private e-mail. Local police have been sued for violating the constitutional rights of computer bulletin board owners and their customers. The federal government has been sued by citizens' groups claiming that Net decency laws are unconstitutional. Some hard-core libertarians insist that *any* form of legislation controlling cyberspace is unwanted, inappropriate, and unworkable.

And so it seems there is still no room for compromise. Neither side will give an inch. Freedom online has joined the list of issues, such as abortion, flag burning, or drug use, that can never be happily resolved.

I think a large part of the problem is caused by misinformation. Many conservatives seem so shocked by media reports that they don't bother to investigate the Net for themselves. They don't want to know about it; they just want to control it. Conversely, some technophiles suffer from their own form of myopia, refusing to admit that anarchy online does create some real social problems.

The purpose of this book is to fill the information gap. Part 1 assesses the real dangers of netcrime. Are hackers and data thieves a real danger to home computer users and corporate networks? What are their motives and their techniques? Will new laws really do anything to protect us from intrusion, vandalism, and viruses? What can we do to protect ourselves?

Part 2 looks at problems caused by netspeech. How much pornography really exists online? How much of it is legally obscene? Should it be controlled? *Can* it be controlled? Should we be concerned about other forms of free expression, such as threats, libel, or hate speech, now that every Internet user can reach a potential audience of millions?

Net fears and freedoms are directly linked. When we yield to our fears and ask the government to take control, we automatically sacrifice some liberty. This is the challenge posed by anarchy online: to find ways of civilizing cyberspace without turning it into an Orwellian nightmare of government surveillance where free expression is stifled and people think twice before speaking frankly.

So long as we have only a simplistic view of the Net, we can't possibly address these complex issues. We need to see cyberspace clearly, understand how it works, assimilate its history, measure its dangers, and consider the consequences of trying to control it. Only then can we make smart, sensible choices about the future of this unique and vitally important communications medium.

Charles Platt
New York City, June 1996

Part 1

Net Crime

The methods and motives of
system crackers have
barely changed since phone
phreaks started manipulating
long-distance networks
in the 1970s. The scale of
activity, though, has grown
enormously despite vicious
federal penalties. Today
computer crime is a lucrative
topic for journalists and
a fertile area for lawmakers,
both groups being eager to
emphasize horrifying potential
dangers. When we look for
actual damage or criminal
profit, however, we find a very
different story.

Hackers: Threat or Menace?

A beefy guy like a football coach steps cautiously onto the porch of a house on a Los Angeles back street. He's wearing white sneakers, blue pants, and a navy windbreaker with POLICE in big white letters across the back. He closes his right hand around the gun holstered at his hip. Birds are singing. Trees rustle in the breeze. It's 9:30 A.M. on a bright California morning.

"Police!" the man shouts. "Open the door! *Open the door!*" His voice is loud enough to wake sleeping dogs a block away. In his left fist he clutches a search warrant. He thumps the thin paneling of the front door.

Another cop joins him, keeping his shoulders against the wall. He's younger and slimmer, with curly black hair hanging down the back of his neck and a ruggedly handsome face. His square jaw moves rhythmically as he chews gum. Wearing a white sweatshirt and sunglasses, he looks more like an actor than a law-enforcement officer. He holds his badge in one hand and his 9 mm automatic in the other. The gun is aimed directly toward the line between the door and its frame.

The door opens six inches, and the cops charge forward, throwing it wide. Inside, a shadowy figure stumbles back, looking horrified. The cop in the white sweatshirt jams his gun in the man's face. "Hands up!" he shouts.

"Against the wall!" shouts the other cop. They grab the man and whirl him around. "Hands up! Don't move! Is anyone else in here?"

Meanwhile, a couple of gray-haired, fortyish, corporate-looking gentlemen in neatly tailored suits come strolling up the front walk as if they just happened to be in the neighborhood and decided to drop in. They're Secret Service agents. As they step into the house the first cop is still holding the terrified homeowner at gunpoint while the second cop prowls from room to room, checking behind furniture and peering into closets.

And now here comes the news team. They were tipped off about this bust in advance. They bring their camera into the living room while more police arrive and start pulling cushions off the couch, peering behind pictures on the wall, and turning over ornamental vases to see if any evidence falls out.

The Secret Service guys quickly find what they want: an old Leading Edge computer, a cheap Epson dot-matrix printer, and a couple of plastic caddies full of floppy disks. But no one's in a hurry here. The cops wait till the news team finishes shooting and relocates outside. *Then* they carry out the computer. They parade it past the camera as if it's a homemade bomb or a kilo of cocaine.

Finally they bring out the owner: a timid, thirtyish guy with a mustache and glasses. He tries unconvincingly to look defiant as they march him away in handcuffs.

What did he do? Well, he used his computer to make a phone call to another computer, and then he copied some files. Maybe that doesn't sound like much, but unauthorized access is a federal crime, and theft of data is another federal crime, and either one can be punished with jail time.

In other words, the guy was a *hacker,* and we all know what that means. He could probably cripple the AT&T long-distance network,

Charles Platt

paralyze the 911 emergency response service, or cut off communication in and out of the White House.

It's just as well that he's been taken away. The Net is that much safer, now, for law-abiding citizens.

Isn't that right?

The Phreaks of Tap

Back in the early 1970s I hung out with a bunch of phone phreaks. They used handles such as Al Bell or Mr. Phelps; I never knew their real names. Once a month I went to a crummy little office on Broadway near 28th Street in Manhattan and helped them stick mailing labels on envelopes for their newsletter, which was called *Tap*.

These ragged, paranoid, hairy weirdos looked like archetypal anarchists as they sat around on broken furniture and traded tips on how to exploit quirks of the telephone network. Sometimes they shared recent mail from John Draper, better known as Captain Crunch, the most notorious phreak of all. Draper was serving time in jail for his bad habit of using a blue box to make free long-distance phone calls. I took my turn reading the mail, and then maybe I'd make a beer run with Al Bell, who warned me not to walk too close to the buildings in case security personnel working for the telephone company tried to drop file cabinets on our heads.

Was he serious? He obviously thought he was. Like most phreaks, Bell was smart, neurotic, rebellious, and full of melodrama. I don't think he ever tried to get rich from his knowledge of telephones and electronics, but he could have if he'd wanted to. One time a shifty-looking guy dropped in at the office and hunkered down in a corner with Bell, talking about component values in a badly photocopied circuit diagram. Later I asked what the circuit was for. "Burglar alarm system," Bell said. He shrugged. "I guess some business in midtown is going to get knocked over next week."

Phone phreaks of the 1970s rented office space in this building (right) in midtown Manhattan, where they traded codes to manipulate the long-distance network. [Photo by the author.]

Was he concerned? He didn't seem to be. He had simply provided some information; if someone chose to use it for illegal purposes, that wasn't Bell's responsibility.

At another meeting I met a grouchy old guy who had spent many years working for the local utility company. We all sat around listening while he told us how to short out electric meters or remove rollersmith locks from gas meters. His attitude was just like Bell's: He passed along some information, and if we used it to commit crimes, that had nothing to do with him.

Two decades later Stewart Brand, founder of the *Whole Earth Catalogue,* came up with his famous phrase, "Information just wants to be free." Of course, information isn't capable of wanting anything; *people* want it to be free. But why? What motivated the subversives of *Tap* to spend time and money holding meetings and printing a newsletter just to spread their knowledge around?

Refugees from the Straight World

Phone phreaks of the early 1970s were descended from Yippies of the late 1960s. Al Bell had worked with Abbie Hoffman, and Hoffman had mentioned the phreaks in his Yippie manifesto, *Steal This Book* (which was how I first heard about them myself).

According to Yippie ideology, capitalist society is dominated by unscrupulous corporations and corrupt politicians who lie, cheat, and steal to maximize their own well-being at everyone else's expense. Consequently, we should screw the system before it screws us first.

Most phone phreaks seemed uninterested in radical politics, but they shared the underlying mind-set. They didn't trust business or government and felt alienated from the status quo. They were loners, the kind of guys who never tried out for the football team, didn't score with girls, and had a hard time fitting in. Most of them weren't even successful academically, because they refused to waste time learning stuff that didn't interest them.

As a result, they acquired a grudge against the straight world and an all-purpose "fuck you" attitude. In an earlier era they might have turned into smarter-than-average juvenile delinquents, but the long-distance telephone system saved them from that. It enabled them to find each other, and it also served as an environment where they *did* fit in.

They literally lived in the lines, exploring phone switches and setting up open-ended conference calls where people dialed in from all over the country and talked for hours. This was the first true electronic community, a primitive preview of what would later be known as virtual reality.

The community was small because it imposed some formidable entry qualifications. To make your own blue box, you had to interpret badly printed schematics that were usually full of errors, and you needed sufficient manual dexterity to solder electronic components to a piece of perforated board without overheating them. Even after you had assembled your hardware, you still couldn't use it till you learned undocumented technical features of the long-distance telephone system.

Tap was the primary public source of this special knowledge. From a law-enforcement perspective, the newsletter looked like a subversive document encouraging people to become electronic criminals, but that wasn't the real purpose. The phreak subculture felt threatened and vulnerable, operating out beyond the boundaries of conventional society. Naturally enough, like any oppressed minority, they wanted to attract more members so that they could feel more secure.

That was why they wanted information to be free: so that it could infect outsiders with the meme of nonviolent technorebellion.

The Dawn of Microcomputers

The information that appeared in *Tap* was gathered in two main ways: social engineering and trashing.

Social engineering was a euphemism that basically meant conning people by impersonating telephone installers or repairmen, demanding information from telephone company employees, and tricking engineers into setting up useful configurations at a local exchange.

Trashing, on the other hand, meant wading through Dumpsters outside telephone switching stations or business offices, slicing open garbage bags, and delving through junk-food leftovers, napkins, and dirty paper cups, searching for documentation or internal memos that might contain some nuggets of technical information.

Trashing was clearly a low-class occupation, but with their love of melodrama, the phreaks made it sound like international espionage. "Dress all in black," advised a primer on the subject by a group calling themselves the Phoenix Force. "Always carry two razor blades, a penlight flashlight, and a small black boot knife laced to your calf or thigh. The razor blades are often used to slice through plastic bags, etc., and the knife can serve many purposes . . . the majority I hope you will never need it for."

In reality, for some phreaks, trashing was a humdrum chore. "It was just part of my routine," recalls Bruce Fancher, who now runs a legitimate Internet service provider but spent some of his teenage years exploring the phone system. "I'd always go through the phone company Dumpsters on my way home from high school. I didn't think twice about it."

Fancher didn't fit the rebel stereotype. He was clean-cut, good-looking, and well-mannered, wore oxford shirts and good leather shoes, and kept his hair parted neatly at the side. He seemed to be a respectable young man from a good East Coast family, and indeed he was: His father had cofounded a highly successful New York newspaper, *The Village Voice,* and young Bruce grew up in a home where there was no shortage of either money or culture.

Still, he was bored at school and easily seduced by technology. In the late 1970s, when he started learning about the phone system, phreaking was being revolutionized by an exciting new tool: the microcomputer. An Apple][could be programmed to control a modem, and the modem could speak the language of the telephone network. It just so happened that one brand of modem, the Apple Cat, could broadcast tones that were normally used for purely internal purposes in telephone switches. Why did the Apple Cat have this interesting feature? Maybe because it had been designed by John Draper, aka Captain Crunch, now out of jail and making an honest living, more or less, collaborating on projects with Steve Wozniak, the designer of the Apple][.

Microcomputers opened up possibilities for phone phreaks that had never existed before. On the most primitive level, "war dialing" was a standard technique to locate interesting phone numbers. Basically it meant trying a vast range of possibilities (such as 555–0000, 555–0001, 555–0002 . . .), just hoping to hit something useful. This chore could now be handled by an Apple running a BASIC program that would work unattended for hours or days and would automatically log the results.

But the phone system was no longer an end in itself. It was becoming a means to an end. By 1980 thousands of mysterious, powerful mainframe computers were linked into the national phone network at locations ranging from a teenage phone phreak's high school to government research labs scattered across America. Better still, most of these computers were poorly protected against smart kids with a lot of free time. Here was a new environment far bigger than the long-distance lines, and the phreaks quickly taught themselves the skills that they needed to explore it. Soon they were hacking computer code.

They had become hackers.

Electronic Eden

Hackers were freeloaders, seizing telephone lines and stealing processor cycles from systems that didn't belong to them. But the load that they put on data networks and computers was really very small, and in any case they soon started creating places of their own to hang out in.

A microcomputer with a modem wasn't just a tool for cracking other people's sites. It could be a site itself. Suitably programmed, the computer would automatically receive phone calls, accept electronic messages, and store them. People could "log on" by dialing the computer and stating their name and password. Once they had done that, they could read the messages that other people had posted and post new ones of their own. This was the basic concept of a bulletin board system, or BBS.

The first BBS was created by Ward Christensen and Randy Suess, a couple of computer nerds who wanted a convenient way to swap and share technical information with their colleagues. At this time teletypes were still the main tool for sending text via telephone lines, running at 110 data bits per second (bps), which worked out to around 140 words per minute. Christensen and Suess went beyond this and used 300-bps modems—archaic by today's standards, but revolutionary at the time.

A man named Bill Blue wrote his own version of the BBS program in a language that would run on the Apple][. Now almost anyone could set up his own board.

The concept was slow to catch on. By the end of 1978 there were maybe half a dozen boards across the nation. In 1980 there were still only about fifty. Modems were still very expensive, and the hardware and BBS programs weren't entirely reliable. Everyone was expected to pitch in and help make things work, as in the early days of ham radio, when hobbyists spent more time wrestling with their equipment than actually sending or receiving messages.

Patrick Kroupa became involved with the modem world during this period. His father was a physicist at the National Center for Atmospheric Research, where they used the largest, most powerful systems in the world. "They had the first Cray ever built," Kroupa recalls. "I used to watch people feed punched cards into a reader. I learned how programs work, and when I was nine my father bought me an Apple][Plus. A little after that I started interacting with phone phreaks. I went to the first Applefest in Boston, where people were trading software on cassette tapes. I started writing programs of my own in 6502 assembly language. But then I got a modem and my interest shifted to the people at the other ends of the networks."

At first, Kroupa recalls, the chat on a typical BBS was usually technical and boring. "Most of the conversation tended to focus on things along the lines of, 'How do you hook an 8-inch drive onto an Apple][?' and '*Any* idiot can see that setting the seventh bit high on the xdef ref is the *wrong* thing to do. Of *course* it'll make the program crash—are you stupid or something?'"

But by 1982, by his estimate, there were close to a thousand bulletin boards up and running, and the modem world was evolving as a rich, multilevel subculture. People could now transfer data at the heady rate of 1,200 bps. In other words, for the first time ever, you could send and receive text *faster than you could read it.*

But text wasn't the only information being traded online. Programs also were being freely shared.

Pirates

Almost every BBS soon offered its users free archives of entertainment software. Some of it was legitimate "shareware" . . . and some of it wasn't. Video games were a hot item, and kids started collecting them with the same intensity that a previous generation had collected baseball cards.

Unfortunately, the games were expensive, and they were copy-protected, meaning that the disks were encoded in such a way that a computer would refuse to copy them. Consequently, cracking copy protection schemes become a necessary and valuable skill.

This was not a simple business. The cracker had to understand machine language and be familiar with the lowest-level internal workings of a computer (usually an Apple][). Using a separate

Bruce Fancher (left), also known as "Dead Lord," makes a rare appearance with a co-conspirator thought to be the elusive "Lord Digital." [Photo by Erico Narita.]

program called a machine-code monitor, the cracker would read the protected disk one byte at a time in an operation known as "boot tracing," mapping the sequence of instructions that was executed when the game took control of the computer. At crucial points in the sequence, new instructions had to be inserted.

After a game was liberated from its copy protection, the cracker usually added his own "page": a preliminary text screen that appeared automatically when the game started, mentioning the cracker's online handle to enhance his status as a cool dude in the community. The game was then freely distributed, usually via bulletin boards run by kids who couldn't crack games themselves but enjoyed playing at being pirates.

"I am a computer PHREAKER and PIRATE," wrote DJ the Pirate in a short confessional describing his trade. "I sit down in front of my computer for hours and hours calling AE's [ASCII Expresses— bulletin boards] all across the country getting new WAREZ [computer software] every day. Most WAREZ I get before they are even sold on the market. . . . How do WAREZ get from the Company to the Pirate World you say? . . . Some new company makes the mistake of coming out with some new software. Usually an employee will have connections (usually stealing), and end up bringing the WARE home with him. . . .

"Now he gets to work and begins to 'CRACK' it. . . . No WARE is safe from crackers. Any disk can be CRACKED. Sometimes it can take 10 minutes and sometimes weeks. To be a good CRACKer you would know ASSEMBLY LANGUAGE very well. Ok, now that he is done CRACKing he will either distribute it himself across the country or give it to some friends to distribute. . . . The entire country gets it within a few days and the software company (which hasn't even released it yet!) gets some whopping financial losses and most probably goes OUT OF BUSINESS! Not to worry though because someone else will be a fool and start his own software company."

This, of course, was just another dose of the usual teenage melodrama. But dozens of "pirate boards" did exist, purely for trading bootleg software. And once again, everyone was eager to swap information—which in this case consisted of the software itself. No money was ever involved; it was still just a matter of sharing the bounty and bringing more people into the subculture. And now that fewer technical skills were required, the subculture was growing fast.

Jousting Online

The early 1980s saw a wild proliferation of amateur-run bulletin boards offering free access to anyone who felt like dialing in. The boards had exotic names such as Gremlin's Lair, Mysterious Island, Temple of Chaos, or Pirate's Prison. All communications were in plain text, often capital letters only, with no more than forty letters per line, because cheap microcomputers were often plugged into television sets, and text on a TV screen wasn't legible if there were more than forty columns.

Despite these limitations, each BBS established a unique identity and atmosphere. A typical log-on message might run something like, "Welcome, traveler! State thy name if thou darest venture into the Crimson Castle. Your sysop, the Iron Baron, will cast miscreants into the fetid dungeon. Be warned!"

"The boards were like oases in the desert," says Bruce Fancher, who used to get up at 5 A.M. each day to monopolize his parents' phone line with his Apple][before he went off to school. "Different travelers would meet up with each other. A lot of legend and storytelling went on. I wasn't just Bruce Fancher, limited to things that teenagers could do. I was a notorious hacker dude with associates in California."

Fancher found it intoxicating, but when Patrick Kroupa looks back at the period he sees a darker side. "As romantic and wonderful as this seems," he wrote in a reminiscence that he posted on his own system years later, "a lot of the people involved had been brutalized by life, and much of this new reality was born out of a tidal wave of pain and dissatisfaction. . . . My early understandings of what this 'place' was were shaped by a handful of people whose skills I admired and sought to emulate, yet whose lives I felt great pity and sadness for. . . . Most of the pioneers were guys who . . . had given up on finding joy in the 'real world' and were constructing a rocket ship called cyberspace to get them out of here as fast as possible."

The modem world truly brought out the best and the worst in people. On the plus side, everyone was equal online; age, gender, race, and nationality were totally irrelevant. No one was in it for the money. People shared their knowledge freely, and they enjoyed a refuge that was uniquely safe and innocent, truly an electronic Garden of Eden—because the rest of the world didn't even know that it existed.

Still, as Kroupa says, many BBS users were refugees from reality. Some of them—including himself and Fancher—suffered from the same all-purpose "fuck you" attitude as the early phone phreaks. They gave themselves baroque, sinister names, like comic-book villains: the Marauder, Sharp Razor, Doom Prophet, or Lex Luthor (who founded the legendary Legion of Doom). The names were self-satirical, but at the same time they created a sense of playful menace that sometimes crossed the boundary between fantasy and reality. Some hackers felt it was all part of the game to impersonate each other, copy private mail and password files, and try to crash each other's systems. Secret alliances were made and betrayed, and there was jousting online.

"There was a gamelike element in being a hacker back then," says Fancher. "There was less threat of law enforcement and more freedom to create a character and act out with your peers and brag. There was no hacker hysteria then. What was going on was a secret to most people. They had no idea."

Fancher and Kroupa both became known as loose cannons in the modem world. Kroupa's online handle was Lord Digital; Fancher called himself Dead Lord in a tribute to one of his favorite writers, H. P. Lovecraft. Dead Lord and Lord Digital were both located in New York and became friends online, although they didn't know each others' names and didn't meet in person until many years later.

Kroupa enjoyed tantalizing the hacker community with farfetched yet plausible descriptions of a program he had allegedly written named Phantom Access, which he claimed could crack any system anywhere. He refused to share it with others in the modem world because, he said, they were "unworthy to receive such a gift." Kroupa's whole shtick was outrageous hype and insufferable elitism, and it worked: He acquired a reputation as one of the "hacker elite," while Phantom Access acquired a mythic status, the holy grail of the hacker community.

Years later, when another hacker calling himself The Plague finally got hold of a copy, he modified it and passed it to Fancher, who circulated it among friends in New York. The pearls had finally been cast before the swine; but of course there was a hidden catch. The modified version contained a routine that counted how many times Phantom Access was used, and on the twelfth time it trashed the victim's hard drive.

Looking back, Fancher still finds it hard to take any of this seriously. "If you wanted to run a hacking program," he says with a shrug, "you had to be prepared to pay the consequences. Of course," he adds, "this all happened before viruses were illegal."

The New York segment of the modem world was rife with plots, counterplots, and scandal. A member of the scene who called himself Seth took the trouble to immortalize the online community in typically melodramatic terms:

"You've probably heard of The Plague at some point in your 'modem career.' He was second only to Dead Lord in the utter fear that he commanded from the NY pirate community. . . . Whereas Bruce was more daring in his assaults . . . The Plague always seemed to do things more covertly, pulling the strings in the background, staying invisible, striking utter terror into his prey. The Plague did as many evil deeds as Bruce, however very few of those deeds ever ended up being attributed to himself."

New York hacker Seth is captured in a rare photo with a friend who remains anonymous.

According to this account, The Plague was instrumental in releasing CyberAIDS, a virus designed to trash the hard drives of pirate BBS owners, most of whom were marginally technoliterate, which placed them at the bottom of the intellectual pecking order.

But Seth stopped short of portraying The Plague as being 100 percent evil. "Whatever others thought of him aside, The Plague did do several really cool things. One of them was writing a multitasking operating system (actually an extension of ProDos) for the Apple //GS. It was unreal. It had full process control and made Unix System V look like something out of the stone age. Priorities for processes could be set, I/O could be redirected. For graphics programs, the graphics screen could be split (if two programs were running at the same time). A process could be suspended, then restored later at exactly the point that it stopped. It also had a unique feature of interprocess communications. That is, processes could send information to each other, to optimize execution time and to provide more flexibility."

In fact, this multitasking operating scheme never existed. It was just another boast, a technomyth to tantalize the gullible teenage proletariat.

Still, CyberAIDS did exist, and Fancher says he uploaded it to all the pirate boards he could find. "It was a disaster," he says cheerfully. "Everyone got nailed."

CyberAIDS later became the basis for Festering Hate, an even more vicious virus. According to Seth: "The primary purpose of Festering Hate was not so much to destroy thousands of hard disks full of ill-gotten warez, which it did quite nicely, but rather to gather the screaming and ranting of those stricken pirates as they foamed at their keyboards on their elite boards. Both The Plague and Patrick have several megs of these buffers [raw transcripts], which I must say are just incredible. I would call these files a sadist's bible. In trying to summarize The Plague, all I can say is that never has any single person wrought so much damage and destruction on the modem community in so short a space of time."

And if this all sounded childish and foolish—well, it was. The kids spoofing each other and crashing each other's systems were no different from kids surreptitiously tying each other's shoelaces together, putting goldfish into toilets, or slipping thumbtacks onto the principal's chair. All you needed was a sense of humor and a sense of proportion to see that these wicked hackers with their scary names were no worse than trick-or-treaters wearing Halloween masks.

Unfortunately, some people viewed the masks as if they were the real faces of the kids underneath. Police, in particular, lacked the humor or the technical background to see the harmlessness of what was happening. They equated teenage rebellion with juvenile delinquency, vandalism, and petty theft.

Festering Hate, a virus program that trashed pirate boards in the 1980s, spawned spinoffs that seemed too far-fetched to be true—although who could be sure?

The Festering Hate world tour has come to Cambridge. See this awesome punk band live in concert at MIT. Lead guitarist David Whitney will be playing solo works as well as some of the band's top hits like "Z-Link Infector", "Brooklyn Blues", and "Tell 'em Rancid sent ya" and many many more. Don't miss this great show. Call 225-0540 for ticket information. Sponsored by the Kool/Rad Alliance and the Harvard Square Boys.

(c) 1988 Kool/Rad Alliance Inc.

Worse still, when police learned that these teenage hackers liked to crash each other's systems, it took only a small leap to imagine the same kind of thing happening to large government computers or even the long-distance telephone network. An organization with a name such as Legion of Doom sounded like a terrorist group, and when someone calling himself Lord Digital claimed that Phantom Access could open up any computer in the known world, this sounded like a threat from a saboteur.

The age of innocence online had lasted for maybe five years. Now, it was about to end.

Sting Operations

Spurred by exaggerated fears of computer crime, Congress passed the Computer Fraud and Abuse bill in 1984, making it a felony to trespass into someone else's computer without permission. This statute even made it illegal merely to trade *information* describing how to crack a system.

Many states passed their own laws against trespass, and local police started penetrating the modem world in haphazard fashion. At first there were some small-scale busts of boards where hackers swapped data. Then, on March 5, 1986, seven hackers were arrested in the first-ever sting operation mounted against a bulletin board.

The Phoenix Phortress, located in Fremont, California, just across the bay from San Francisco, consisted of one Apple //e computer on a telephone line rented under the name "Al Davis." Over a period of five months, Davis offered his computer to hackers as a free meeting place where they could pool information on access codes and other tools of the electronic trade.

After accumulating a regular clientele of about 130 users, Davis revealed himself as Sergeant Daniel Pasquale of the Fremont Police Department, and seven local hackers were placed under arrest. Their online names were the Adventurer, the Highwayman, the

Punisher, the Warden, Lasertech, Doctor Bob, and Captain Hacker. In real life, they were just a bunch of kids. One was nineteen, one was seventeen, two were sixteen, and three of them were fifteen years old. They were charged with stealing telephone service, trafficking in access codes, and various misdemeanors.

The bust shocked the hacking community. The modem world had been a private realm, totally free from the strictures of real life—and one of its oases now turned out to have been poisoned. One hacker at the time said that the bust had broken "the sacred barrier between the phreak/hack community and the rest of the world."

This was only the beginning. Five months later a three-line BBS in Detroit turned out to have been set up by a TV journalist who used it to gather information on hacking activities for a muckraking TV documentary. He conned many of the users into revealing their real names, and included this information in his show.

One month after that, an Arizona board named Metalland South, run by sysops (system operators) calling themselves Iron Man and Black Lord, was quietly busted, and control was transferred to law enforcement, who continued running it as a sting operation.

Writing for *Phrack* (a hacker newsletter that was freely distributed online), Knight Lightning warned that "today's phreak/hacker must learn to be more security conscious. What makes anyone think that they can trust someone just because they are running a bulletin board? This blind faith is what will be the downfall of many a hacker. . . . The stakes in this game are a lot higher than no television after school for a week."

Sundevil

By the end of the 1980s the modem world was enormous compared with the old phone phreak community. As of August 1988, there were maybe 10,000 boards nationwide, spawning countless affinity groups. Knight Lightning listed 125 hacker clans that he knew of personally, and their names read like a roster from some imaginary cyberwar:

The Administration ... Advanced Telecommunications, Inc./ATI ... ALIAS ... American Tone Travelers ... Anarchy Inc. ... Apple Mafia ... The Association ... Atlantic Pirates Guild/APG ... Bad Ass Mother Fuckers/BAMF ... Bellcore ... Bell Shock Force/BSF ... Black Bag ... Camorra ... C&M Productions ... Catholics Anonymous ... Chaos Computer Club ... Chief Executive Officers/CEO ... Circle Of Death ... Circle Of Deneb ... Club X ... Coalition of Hi-Tech Pirates/CHP ... Coast-To-Coast ... Corrupt Computing ... Cult Of The Dead Cow/- cDc- ... Custom Retaliations ... Damage Inc. ... D&B Communications ... The Dange Gang ... Dec Hunters ... Digital Gang/DG ... DPAK ... Eastern Alliance ... The Elite Hackers Guild ... Elite Phreakers and Hackers Club ... The Elite Society Of America ... EPG ... Executives Of Crime ... Extasyy (Elite) ... Fargo 4A ... Farmers Of Doom/FOD ... The Federation ... Feds R Us ... First Class ... Five O ... Five Star ... Force Hackers ... The 414s ... Hack-A-Trip Hackers Of America/HOA ... High Mountain Hackers ... High Society ... The Hitchhikers ... IBM Syndicate ... The Ice Pirates Imperial Warlords ... Inner Circle ... Inner Circle II ... Insanity Inc. International Computer Underground Bandits/ICUB ... Justice League of America/JLA ... Kaos Inc. ... Knights Of Shadow/KOS ... Knights Of The Round Table/KOTRT ... League Of Adepts/LOA ... Legion Of Doom/LOD ... Legion Of Hackers/LOH ... Lords Of Chaos ... Lunitic Labs, Unlimited ... Master Hackers ... MAD! ... The Marauders ... MD/PhD ... Metal Communications, Inc./MCI ... MetalliBashers, Inc./MBI ... Metro Communications ... Midwest Pirates Guild/MPG ... NASA Elite ... The NATO Association ... Neon Knights ... Nihilist Order Of The Rose ... OSS ... Pacific Pirates Guild/PPG ... Phantom Access Associates ... PHido PHreaks ... Phlash ... PhoneLine Phantoms/PLP ... Phone Phreakers Of America/PPOA ... Phortune 500/P500 ... Phreak Hack Delinquents ... Phreak Hack Destroyers ... Phreakers, Hackers, And Laundromat Employees Gang/PHALE Gang ... Phreaks Against Geeks/PAG ... Phreaks Against Phreaks/PAP ... Phreaks and Hackers of America ...

Phreaks Anonymous World Wide/PAWW ... Project
Genesis ... The Punk Mafia/TPM ... The Racketeers
... Red Dawn Text Files/RDTF ... Roscoe Gang ...
SABRE ... Secret Circle of Pirates/SCP ... Secret
Service ... 707 Club ... Shadow Brotherhood ...
Sharp Inc. ... 65C02 Elite ... Spectral Force ... Star
League ... Stowaways ... Strata-Crackers ... The
Phrim ... Team Hackers '86 ... Team Hackers '87 ...
TeleComputist Newsletter Staff ... Tribunal Of
Knowledge/TOK ... Triple Entente ... Turn Over And
Die Syndrome/TOADS ... 300 Club ... 1200 Club ...
2300 Club ... 2600 Club ... 2601 Club ... 2AF ...
Ware Brigade ... The Warelords ... WASP ... The
United Soft WareZ Force/TuSwF ... United Technical
Underground/UTU

Law enforcement saw this proliferation as an ominous trend that
had to be stopped. They responded with Operation Sundevil.

Early in 1989 Robert Riggs (whose online handle was Prophet),
Frank Darden Jr. (called Leftist), and Adam Grant (known as Urville)
accessed the Bellsouth telephone network, discovered a computer
that interested them, and browsed through its data files. When
they found two pieces of documentation describing a program to
control the 911 emergency response service, they copied the text
and exited discreetly, leaving the originals undisturbed.

All three hackers belonged to the Legion of Doom, which often used
a public-access Unix system named Jolnet in Lockport, Illinois, to
store, disseminate, and discuss interesting information. Riggs posted
the 911 documents to this system and also sent a summary of them
to Knight Lightning, the editor and publisher of *Phrack*, whose real
name was Craig Neidorf. Neidorf wasn't a member of the Legion of
Doom and wasn't especially interested in the 911 information, but
he published it anyway on the well-established general principle
that information wanted to be free. For him it was just a minor item
of no great importance, soon forgotten.

At first nothing happened. But Rich Andrews, the system operator at
Jolnet, found the illicitly copied Bellsouth text files and decided he
should notify AT&T that their security had been compromised. AT&T

referred the matter to the Secret Service, and the Secret Service got back to Rich Andrews, who cooperated with them.

A full-scale investigation began. Agents started quietly logging onto boards where hackers were known to hang out. All e-mail in and out of *Phrack* was monitored. Finally Riggs, Darden, and Grant were arrested and charged with theft of proprietary information worth $79,449, while Neidorf was charged with disseminating information to enable other hackers to achieve illegal access, abuse computer systems, and thwart police action.

The indictment listed the Bellsouth document as a "highly proprietary and closely held computer program that controlled and maintained the E911 system." So here was the threat: The juvenile mind games and role playing of hackers had gotten totally out of hand, and these sociopathic kids had started doing the kind of thing that law enforcement had always feared. They were screwing around with a program that provided emergency response system for a nine-state region in the South.

It was time to send a message to the so-called hacker community, and the best way to do that was to make an example of someone. Riggs, who was twenty years old and lived in Decatur, Georgia, found himself faced with a maximum jail sentence of thirty-two years and a maximum fine of $220,000. Neidorf, a student at the University of Missouri, who was nineteen years old, faced a maximum sentence of thirty-one years and a fine of $122,000.

It's important to remember that Neidorf wasn't being charged with hacking a system; his only alleged crime was receiving some text and putting it into an electronic newsletter. Even Riggs wasn't accused of doing any damage. He had merely copied two documents from a phone company's computer. Moreover, contrary to what the indictment said, these documents were *not* computer programs. They were plain text describing administrative duties relating to the 911 system. Nor was this information "closely held." Nor was it worth $79,449. In fact, Neidorf's defense attorney proved that Bellsouth had already offered it for sale to the general public in printed form for $14.

These facts should have put the whole thing in proportion, but they didn't get much exposure in the national media. Journalists didn't know enough about computers to reach their own conclusions, so they believed what they read in press releases from the Department of Justice. They also showed no scruples about playing up the "hacker threat." After all, a bunch of people calling themselves the Legion of Doom had started breaking into the 911 network. That sounded like a story that would move some newspapers.

Meanwhile, federal agents were arresting other hackers who had any connection with the case. On March 1, 1990, the Mentor, a member of the Legion of Doom, was woken at 6:30 A.M. by a Secret Service agent pointing a gun at his head. Agents then spent several hours searching his apartment, seizing his computer equipment and hauling it away.

Chris Goggans, who called himself Erik Bloodaxe online, found himself woken by federal agents, who confiscated his hardware.

The Phoenix Project BBS in Austin, Texas, announced that it would start using an encryption scheme to protect users' e-mail from the kind of federal surveillance that had been used on e-mail to and from *Phrack*. "I have personally phoned several government investigators and invited them to join us here on the board," one of the system operators told his users. "If I begin to feel that the board is putting me in any kind of danger, I'll pull it down with no notice." He never got the chance; the BBS was promptly raided and its equipment was seized.

The Illuminati, another BBS in Austin, was owned and operated by Steve Jackson Games. It too was raided—apparently because a sysop from the Phoenix Project was a company employee. But this marked the end of the government's uninterrupted rampage. The Secret Service had failed to do their homework on Jackson, who turned out to be a legitimate businessman. He successfully sued for damages, humiliating agents who had violated the Electronic Communications Privacy Act by seizing computers containing private e-mail. The Electronic Frontier Foundation was created largely in response to publicity about Jackson's case, and they funded his lawsuit.

Steve Jackson's legitimate business was raided by Secret Service agents—who paid dearly for their blunder.

Still, it took him well over two years to win, and by that time the hacker world had changed forever. Twelve different members of the Legion of Doom were ultimately busted on various charges, and the age of innocence was officially over. The great, glorious game of cracking systems and browsing through data files had turned out to be far more hazardous than anyone had ever imagined.

The case against Neidorf was dropped when Bellsouth admitted that their $79,449 document could be purchased by anyone for less than the price of an average hardcover book. But Riggs, Darden, and Grant were not so lucky. Riggs was sentenced to twenty-one months; his companions got fourteen months each. In addition, the three were told to pay $233,000 in restitution, although since they had caused no damage, this penalty didn't seem to make much sense.

Writing in *Phrack*, Chris Goggans willingly agreed that Riggs, Darden, and Grant "had basically total control of a packet-switched network owned by Southern Bell [as it was then named] (SBDN). Through this network they had access to every computer Southern Bell owned, ranging from COSMOS terminals up to LMOS front ends. Southern Bell had not been smart enough to disallow connections from one public pad to another, thus allowing anyone who desired to do so, the ability to connect to, and seize information from, anyone else who was using the network."

In other words, the hackers did have a huge amount of *potential* power. But they hadn't used it, and according to Goggans, they had never intended to. He wrote: "No member of LoD [the Legion of Doom] has ever (to my knowledge) broken into another system and used any information gained from it for personal gain of any kind—with the exception of maybe a big boost in his reputation around the underground."

Also writing in *Phrack*, Neidorf painted the same picture. "LoD members may have entered into systems numbering in the tens of thousands," he wrote. "They may have peeped into credit histories, they may have monitored telephone calls, they may have snooped into files and buffered interesting text, they may still have total control over entire computer networks." Still, he went on: "What damage have they done? None, with the exception of unpaid use of CPU time and network access charges. What personal gains have any members made? None, with the exception of three instances of credit fraud that were instigated by three separate greedy individuals, without group knowledge."

Maybe this seemed self-serving, coming from a hacker with an obvious need to justify his activities. But Jim Thomas, a professor of sociology and criminal justice at Northern Illinois University, felt so concerned by the crackdown on hackers that he started publishing his own online newsletter, *Computer Underground Digest* (which has maintained an almost uninterrupted weekly schedule to the present day). In his editorial in the first issue, Thomas referred to "draconian anti-computer abuse laws," "media hysteria," and "witch hunts" by law enforcement. He concluded: "Yes, crimes are committed with computers. But, crimes are also committed with typewriters, cars, fountain pens and—badges."

Patrick Kroupa was less willing to view his fellow hackers as being totally benign. He wrote: "What had begun with the best intentions, as the ultimate extension of human curiosity, had devolved into a cultural movement that had very little to do with the ideals that had inspired it. The term 'hacker' had become synonymous with 'criminal,' and taking a look around at the state of the underground, it looked as if much of it had in fact degenerated into crime cartels composed of angry teens. . . . It was no longer the exhilaration of knowing that you could actually reach out and touch a satellite . . . it had come down to the negative power trip of fucking with something for the sake of pissing people off or just showing the world how much power you really have at your disposal if you ever decided to throw a tantrum."

Maybe Kroupa was speaking from his own experience more than from that of others, but either way, the online euphoria of the 1980s was gone. Kroupa himself escaped the LoD busts; he had retreated to New Mexico to try to find new purpose in life, taken up body building, dropped acid, achieved enlightenment, and ceased using his computer for anything other than word processing.

Transitioning to the Straight World

Bruce Fancher had also escaped the heavy hand of law enforcement. He had graduated from high school and gone to prestigious Tufts University, near Boston, where he studied history. He didn't stay there, though. "By the second year," he says, "I was intentionally wasting my time. I joined a fraternity and got stoned or drunk every day and partied all the time. But there's only so much partying you can do. So there I was, bored out of my head, and someone says, 'Hey, let's go back to where we were when I was fifteen years old and try to make money at the same time.'"

The "someone" was Kroupa, who returned to New York in 1991 and suggested starting their own legitimate BBS as a site for a role-playing computer game. Fancher dropped out of college in December of that year, and the two ex-hackers raised $20,000 from their families. With associates such as The Plague and Phiber Optik (another former member of the Legion of Doom), Kroupa and Fancher built their new BBS. The parent company was named Phantom Access Technologies (a sly reference to Kroupa's semimythical hacking program), while the BBS itself was named MindVox.

By the time the system was fully functional it was 1992, and the Internet was showing the first faint signs of becoming a national media event. MindVox became an Internet site, and today it serves several thousand users. It also functions as a unique storehouse for hacker history, with archives transcribed from old Apple][disks chronicling the infighting, plots, and counterplots of the New York modem world in the 1980s.

Other hackers looked for similarly legitimate lines of work. Many learned Unix and became system operators or programmers, and in this way the rebellious hacker spirit was recycled into the emerging environment of the Internet, adding a streak of nonconformity that persists today.

In Houston, Chris Goggans and two others from the Legion of Doom formed Comsec, a computer security consultancy company. Their press release claimed, "We were all the cream of the crop of the computer underground and know precisely how systems are compromised and what actions to take to secure them." Today Goggans is still involved in the same business.

Hacking in the Nineties

Thousands of bulletin board systems still exist, scattered across the country, but almost all of them are now run as legitimate businesses. Pirate boards have mostly disappeared; the kids who used to maintain them as game exchanges are more likely, these days, to be buying Nintendo cartridges. Only a few pirates still deal in warez—just for the fun of it. In the following case history, the pirate's real name has been changed at his request.

"My handle was Axeman," says Mike Wollenski. "I used to run a BBS called the GrindStone. I started it when I was fifteen. It was a good ol' boys board, meaning that it only served people I knew by reputation, or personally. I had one phone line and eighty megs of storage."

According to Mike, he never charged anyone for membership or downloads. The operation was just a hobby. "Making money off stolen software is a fantastic way to have the feds come gunning after your ass," he says.

The board ran without trouble for three years, serving a maximum of 150 users. In 1994 Mike went to college and set up a new version of his BBS from there. Still there were no problems, even though he was now dealing more heavily in stolen software. "I got back into the pirate scene big time," he says. "I loved getting uploads, especially uploads that were less than three days old. I used to have a contact at IBM who would be able to get us the latest OS/2 beta source codes for device drivers and utilities. He'd send it up and some guys would download it and it would spread from there."

At Christmas break, Mike moved the BBS back home again and took things one notch farther. "Right around this time," he recalls, "in my AC [area code], 914, an interest in H/P/V/C/A started." H/P/V/C/A stands for Hacking, Phreaking, Viruses, Cracking (or Carding, depending on who you ask), and Anarchy. "Me, being the information hound that I was, decided to join a mail network called MOBNet."

This was an informal store-and-forward message system. Mike would accumulate a bunch of BBS messages or other data, reduce their size with a file compression utility such as PKZip, then pass them to another BBS. He received material on the same basis.

"On a good day," says Mike, "I would get in a couple hundred messages, all dealing with hacking into systems, how to crack password files on Unix hosts, how and where to find credit card numbers, and, more importantly, how to protect yourself from these things happening to you. So here I was, a pirate board in 914—rather successful, as far as this area code goes—getting pretty new files, and a ton of information daily about the 'darker sciences.'"

On Christmas Eve Mike received a warning. "I get a call from a friend of mine, telling me, 'Dude, shut it *down!* Kill it! Nuke everything, and close everything up! Some kid just got popped for credit card fraud, and he's telling the cops that he got it from *you.'* Needless to say, I freaked. I immediately took it down."

Foolishly, though, after a couple of days he put everything back online. A couple more days after that, he was raided.

"I'd been to the movies with my younger brother and a friend of ours from school. I think it was at ten-thirty or so. On our way back to my house, the car phone rings. Understand, it was my parents' car; I had to raid the change bin for the money to see the movie. My bro picks it up, says, 'Yeah? Uh-huh. Hmmm. Uh . . . okay. Bye.' He turns to me and says, rather loudly, 'You're going to *jail!* The cops came over to the house with a search warrant and took your computer and stuff. Mom and Dad are pissed!'"

When Mike got home he found that state police had taken his 486SX/33 IBM-compatible computer, the monitor, keyboard, modem, mouse, and all his software—"including the stuff I had bought!" he says with a tone of wounded disbelief. "They also took most of my parents' software. They tried to take my mom's computer as well; I gather yelling ensued, and that computer never left the house."

Mike was only a few days over eighteen. The police promised that if he cooperated, he'd be charged as a juvenile, there would be no felony charges, and his identity would be kept secret. This sounded like a good deal, so he supplied the password to unlock his system.

According to Mike, the cops then proceeded to betray him. In February 1995 a local newspaper ran a two-part article on hacking in which Mike was the only person identified under his real name. A few months later, when Mike came home from the spring college semester, he found himself charged as an adult, with two class-E felonies carrying more than ten years of potential jail time. He was horrified. "In the end," he says, "my lawyer talked them down to a violation—disorderly conduct—with a $250 fine and twenty-five hours community service. But I had been so worried about the case, I couldn't finish my semester at school. The cops had lied to me outright in front of me and my lawyer, so I had no idea what they were going to do next, and I basically panicked."

He regrets now that he cooperated. "I should have told them to go fuck themselves silly. But I gave them access to my files, and because of that, a good friend of mine also got busted. For all I know he went to jail; I don't really want to know."

The main reason for police action against Mike's board was not the software but the file containing credit card numbers. "Most of them I got from a friend," he says, "but some of them came from carbon copies in trash bins outside the mall. It's easy to get them; you just go down there at two A.M. when all the rent-a-cops are enjoying their doughnuts."

He insists, however, he had no interest in the numbers. "Once I had them—okay, great, now what? I never used any of 'em, because I have parents. They are better than any credit card I know of. I don't have to pay interest, I don't have a spending limit—hell, I don't even have to pay them back! So did I sell card numbers? No. Did I give them to people? No. Were they available if people left a message on my board? Yes. Just like they are available anywhere else in life. What it comes down to is that I was busted because I let people do what they wished with my hard-drive space. I think that what people did with my board was their own business. The police came in and violated that right."

Mike's parents imposed some limits for a while: no modem usage, and he had to ask permission to make phone calls. Eventually he got his computer system back from the police—everything except the hard drive—and computers are still his main interest. He's hoping to make a career out of them as a network technician.

Meanwhile, he says, pirate boards are scarcer than ever. "After I was busted, all the local boards disappeared. As far as I know, there's only one board left in 914. There are still boards in other areas with a couple thousand people on 'em, but most are in the Midwest, where people are naturally closemouthed and don't go out of their way to make trouble for each other. Overall I think there's less activity than there used to be, and there's been a general decline in the pirate community as a whole."

Sites Unseen

Has hacking experienced the same decline as software piracy? Definitely not. Even though federal laws provide a massive disincentive, a whole new generation has emerged. Hackers of the 1990s show much less interest in the phone system and hardly any interest in setting up their own bulletin board systems and jousting with each other online. They have a powerful new toy to play with: the Internet.

Back in the 1950s, computers were monsters that filled large rooms and required massive air-conditioning systems. Their processing power was limited; one computer could work on only one task at a time.

By the late 1960s, timesharing became possible. In other words, one computer was now powerful enough to be shared by many people using terminals wired throughout a building, forming a very rudimentary network. This was a great way for scientists or students to get easy access and process their data.

But each college and laboratory was still an island cut off from the others. The Defense Advanced Research Project Agency started the Internetting Project, which aimed to link all the mini-networks into a big, nationwide system. The result was ARPAnet.

Right from the start it was a "distributed" network. In other words, there was no central switching office. Instead, each node in the network was smart enough to operate independently, routing messages to other nodes on its own initiative. Electronic mail followed an unpredictable zigzag path, skipping from one site to the next, using any connection that happened to be lightly loaded at that particular moment.

The system was more elaborate than this, because messages were broken down into "packets" of data. A long piece of text could be sent as many separate packets, which might follow different routes to the same destination, where they were reassembled in their proper sequence. This sounded like a hopelessly inefficient and risky way of doing things, but computers now worked so fast and reliably, the system was practical. Moreover, it was *fault-tolerant*, meaning that it would function even if several computers in the network stopped working. When a node in Chicago went down, messages could just as easily pass through Detroit. Since the system was supposed to be usable in a national emergency (such as a nuclear attack), this was an important consideration.

For many years ARPAnet served its purpose in a low-key, utilitarian way. In 1983 the net still linked fewer than 500 primary sites, mainly because it was reserved for government research. But as computers continued to get cheaper, civilians saw a need to link their systems, too, and they created smaller-scale networks, such as CSNet, for transmitting nonmilitary science data.

Eventually the National Science Foundation created NSFnet, which formed a "backbone" linking the other networks, and this ultimately became the Internet. By 1987 it served 28,000 host computers. Soon after that, it established links via regular phone lines with commercial service providers such as CompuServe and America Online. Today the Internet is open to anyone who owns a modem and can pay maybe $10 a month for access through a service provider.

In mid–1995 the first statistically reliable survey of Net use (sponsored by O'Reilly and Associates, a publisher of computer books) showed that there were almost ten million U.S. adults with online access, including four million using the new commercial service providers. According to O'Reilly, the total number of users worldwide was probably about twenty million.

Despite this amazing growth, the basic setup of the Net has remained the same. It is still decentralized, with no central switching station. All users are equal; no one is in control (except for the owner or operator of a computer that serves as a node on the Net, who sets the terms for users who subscribe to his service). And the whole network is dedicated to the idea that information should be free.

This makes it unique in the history of human communication: a nonprofit, decentralized system without any formal rules and regulations, entirely controlled by the people who use it. This also means that it's extremely vulnerable to being manipulated by anyone willing to spend a few days learning the command language that is shared by most computers on the net.

That language is named Unix. Created almost thirty years ago, Unix was intended to provide maximum power and flexibility. If you give the right password, Unix allows you to look at any data, write your own program and run it on the host computer, or wipe out millions of files. Worse still, many Unix utility programs have flaws in them—which are easily exploited by hackers.

Moreover, no one needs the technical knowledge or mastery of hardware that restricted entry to the phone phreak community. Today the hardware is prepackaged, the software is cheap and easily available, and you can learn to use it by shopping at your local bookstore. Linux, a freeware clone of Unix, will run on a PC. And *Unix for Dummies*, at your local bookstore, teaches the basic concepts in a series of simple steps.

Once you've acquired your basic skills, you'll have little trouble learning how to use them for illegal purposes. *Tap*, the newsletter, is long gone, but a bigger, better publication has taken its place. *2600* magazine appears quarterly, sells around 20,000 copies, and has national newsstand distribution. Its title derives from the tone frequency that phone phreaks once used as a can opener on the long-distance telephone network, but its focus extends far beyond phreaking. A typical issue contains articles on how to write computer viruses, listen in on cellular phone calls, and exploit Unix bugs. There's also an online discussion group (alt.2600) where you can seek help in your hacking activities, and there are local meetings on the first Friday of each month. These meetings are not so different from the old Tap gatherings of the 1970s, except that they take place on a mind-boggling scale, in public spaces such as shopping malls and city parks scattered across thirty-three American cities and five foreign countries.

2600 is owned and edited by Eric Corley, who prefers to use the pseudonym Emmanuel Goldstein (the name of a subversive character in Orwell's *1984*). Corley promotes his magazine and its hacker readership as a positive phenomenon: a healthy outlet for harmless teenage curiosity. He believes wholeheartedly in the so-called hacker ethic, which holds that information should be freely shared and systems should be freely accessible, so long as no damage is done. Corley promotes this outlook not only in his magazine but on a regular New York radio show.

In 1994 he took his crusade one step further. For the first time, he presented a hacker conference that promised to teach people the fundamental techniques of system cracking. Called Hackers on Planet Earth, or H.O.P.E., the conference was held on the twenty-fifth anniversary of Woodstock—which, according to Corley, stood for the same spirit of freedom.

I was interested in H.O.P.E. as an opportunity to find out how much the scene had changed since the days of those Tap meetings in the dusty old office on Broadway. Would the hackers of the 1990s be substantially different from the phreaks of the 1970s? There was only one way to find out.

Where's the Crime?

On the eighteenth floor of New York City's Hotel Pennsylvania is a dowdy old ballroom with many burned-out lightbulbs in bent brass chandeliers. A beat-up sound system at one side of the room makes scratchy noises while a skinny guy in a

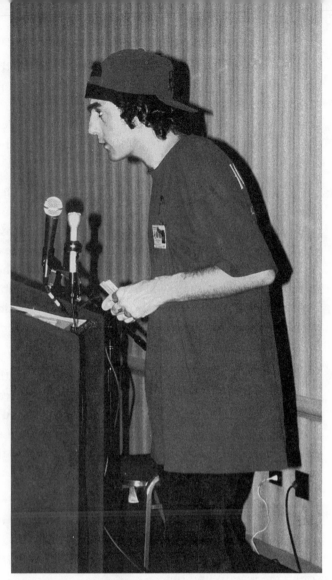

Eric Corley, editor/publisher of 2600 Magazine
(under the name Emmanuel Goldstein),
greets hordes of hackers at the Hotel Pennsylvania.
[Photo by the author.]

tie-dyed T-shirt sorts through a stack of CDs. Meanwhile, bearded sysop types try to link a bizarre mix of antique computing equipment into a local-area network with Internet access. The hardware is scattered around on tables. There are no formal exhibits, no booths, no buffet, no coffee, and no bar.

CNN and NBC are here, prowling like starved alley cats in search of tasty leftovers. They cluster around a teenager wearing a black jumpsuit with flames hand-painted across his shoulders. He's soldering components onto a tiny piece of perf board. "What does it *do?*" a journalist asks, although there's a sense that his real interest may run a little deeper. Is the gadget *illegal?* Is it *scary?* Can it paralyze vast computer networks with a single pulse?

This is, after all, Hackers on Planet Earth. There have been other hacker conventions, but this is the first to come right out and offer educational seminars on subjects such as:

■ **Cracking the MetroCard, a magnetic-stripe fare card recently introduced for subway travel in New York City. "We will read the cards, duplicate them, and make every attempt to defeat the system," says the conference program.**

■ **Lockpicking. "Everything from picks to rakes to electric drills to Simplex locks."**

■ **Boxing (i.e. free phone calls via blue/red boxes). "Contrary to popular belief, boxing is not dead. We will have some top phone phreaks on hand to show you what works, what doesn't, what used to work, what never did, and what probably might."**

■ **Cellular phones. "We will show how cloning is not just for criminals and how you can clone a phone on your own PC!"**

It all sounds titillatingly wicked. So where's the action? *Where's the crime?*

The conference was scheduled to start half an hour ago, but so far the only action is out in the lobby, where hundreds of would-be attendees are squished together, back to belly, waiting patiently for nifty customized photo badges, each of which unfortunately takes about sixty seconds to come out of a laser printer. There are maybe 600 attendees, so if you multiply that number by the time per badge, it'll take *ten hours* just to check everyone in.

A friendly Dutch hacker with long golden hair and a tie-dyed T-shirt devises an impromptu solution. He goes around selling red numbered pieces of paper as temporary badges, takes $25 per person, and stuffs the cash in a brown paper bag. No one has any problem with this. No one questions the Dutch guy's authority or doubts that he'll pass the money to the organizers. He could steal it—but he chooses not to.

An hour later, the conference is up and running and a throng of hairy teenagers in sneakers, T-shirts, and dirty jeans listens attentively to an opening address from a well-fed, tough-looking character wearing shiny black shoes and a suit and a tie. He's Robert David Steele, an expert on computer crime who worked on

Red-box circuits can be soldered while you wait at Hackers on Planet Earth. [Photo by the author.]

the clandestine side of the CIA for nine years, was an advisor for Marine Corps Intelligence, and now runs an annual conference on the protection and dissemination of information. He exudes an air of authority as he spits out sound bites with swift, mechanical precision. "You can cripple a nation very easily with just a few individuals," he says. "Wall Street is hiding major losses. Cyberspace is not safe right now."

He paints a scary picture of terrorist infocriminals, businesses that don't even know how much data they're losing, and banking networks that could be gutted overnight. Then, switching smoothly

CONFERENCE RULES

1. Do not hack, phreak, or mess with hotel property, wiring, or fire alarms.
2. Do not enter non-public hotel areas.
3. Do not go beyond the toilets on the 18th floor.
4. Do not enter rooms or areas marked "HOPE Staff Only!"
5. Wear your badge at all times.
6. Do not remove any tape or signs.
7. Do not grafitti any surface.
8. Do not open any windows.
9. Smoke only legal substances and only in designated areas.
10. Assume you are being watched at *all* times by your worst nightmare.

Anarchy reigns at Hackers on Planet Earth—or does it? [Photo by the author.]

to a kinder, gentler mode, he asks the audience to help him fight these threats. "Hacking is not a criminal act," he says. "You represent a critical national resource. . . . I think of you as law-abiding citizens who have immense potential to contribute to society."

The misfit Net-heads and rebel code crunchers give him a loud ovation. They like being told that they're law-abiding citizens. But

Robert Steele, formerly with CIA, tells an audience of hackers that they're a critical national resource.

aren't some of them also the outlaws whom Steele was talking about a moment earlier? Don't they have the power to steal business secrets, manipulate bank accounts, and plant destructive viruses?

Well, yes, they could do stuff like that, but supposedly they choose not to.

A few hours later, in a hallway outside the main ballroom, half a dozen hackers gather around a small, thin man wearing a yarmulke. He says he's affiliated with the Anti-Defamation League of B'nai B'rith, and he came here to hand out fliers denouncing a BBS run by white supremacists who claim that the Holocaust never happened. Several hackers are holding these fliers and looking at them doubtfully.

"You see, the phone number is right there," the Jewish man says, pointing to the bottom of the broadsheet. "Now, you people, with your technical skills"—he gives them a sly smile—"you could *do something* with that number, couldn't you?"

A hacker glares at him. "What are you trying to say?"

"These people are spreading hate!" the Jewish man cries. "This is the worst kind of anti-Semitism. They should be stopped!"

"You mean," said the hacker, "you want us to crack this board and *take it down?*" He steps back. "Hell, no. I wouldn't do that. Not under any circumstances."

There's a murmur of agreement from the others. "Freedom of speech!" one of them shouts. "That's the whole basis for the hacker ethic. If you don't understand that, you've got no business here!"

"But this is *hate* speech," the Jewish man protests.

No one even hears him. The crowd is united in moral outrage. They could do what he wants them to do, no doubt about that. But they adamantly choose not to.

Face-to-Face with Dark Fiber

At the end of the first day of the conference, around 2 A.M., standing outside the hotel on Seventh Avenue as a steady drizzle comes down, I'm introduced to a man in his late twenties who calls himself Dark Fiber. By day he runs an office network, but he still hacks in his spare time, invading Unix sites on the Net, just looking around. This, of course, is now a felony. Even if you do no damage, you're still not allowed to enter someone else's computer—because it's a violation of privacy, and because the *potential* for damage is there.

I ask Dark Fiber how he feels about that. Do hacker intrusions pose a real threat?

"People have destroyed system files, wiped out password files," he says. "Others just blunder in and corrupt data by accident. But if data is properly backed up, there's no physical loss, just a large amount of inconvenience."

Inconvenience, however, is not the whole story. The hacker habit of copying interesting data—while leaving the original untouched— means a corporation has no way of telling whether its privileged information is still secure.

Dark Fiber himself has a penchant for walking off with stuff that doesn't belong to him. He shows me a loose-leaf binder containing a certain document that he claims is a system administrator's guide to New York City's MetroCard electronic fare collection ystem. When I inspect it closely, I find that his claim is true: There are complete schematics, right down to the part numbers. Needless to say, this rare item has not come into Dark Fiber's possession via legal means.

What does he plan to do with it?

"I'll probably run it through a copying machine and distribute it to a select few hacker friends."

Sell it?

"I won't *sell* it." He sounds offended. "A true hacker never does that. One of the overriding tenets of hackerdom is that information wants to be free, and a lot of us take that very seriously. You have to understand, my motivation isn't to ride free on the subway. I was born and raised in this city, and I've always paid my way. I'd just like to understand the system a little bit better. It's a purely intellectual interest on my part."

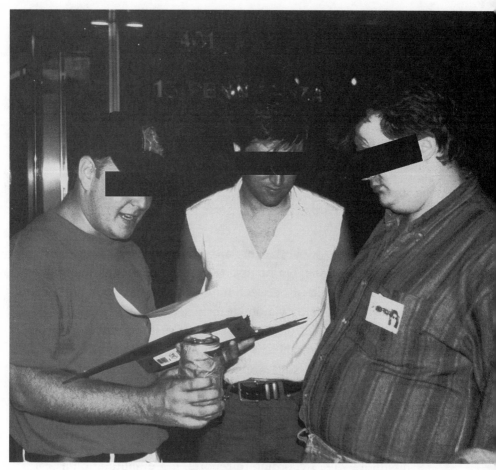

Dark Fiber peruses purloined schematics for the Transit Authority's new farecard system while two underworld associates watch with undisguised indifference. [Photo by the author.]

But if he shares his information widely, that could cause the MetroCard system to be hacked.

"I think the system will be hacked, and eventually it will have to be improved to make it more secure. Nevertheless, I think this information should be available."

If details of the improvements are also stolen and shared, electronic fare collection will never be feasible, I point out.

"I see the paradox, but this is a central theme in hacking in general. Where do you draw the line? Every hacker has to wrestle with his conscience."

So the conscience of individuals is our only guarantee of security. Should the functionality of computer installations across the country depend on the goodwill and self-restraint of some unpredictable rebels with a "fuck you" attitude?

Tales from the Darkside

Most hackers aren't in it for the money—but there are exceptions. On August 18, 1995, court documents were unsealed showing that between June and October 1994, $10 million was transferred illicitly via about forty separate transactions using Citibank's electronic funds transfer system. Vladimir Levin, a twenty-five-year-old biochemistry graduate employed by AOSaturn, a Russian software company, was charged with using a legitimate customer's password and identification to access Citicorp's computers at 111 Wall Street in New York City. Levin allegedly transferred some of the customer's funds to a bank account in Finland, where an accomplice began making personal cash withdrawals. According to reports, more multinational transfers followed over the next four months, involving at least five other hackers—two in the United States, two in the Netherlands, and one in Israel.

Citibank's press release naturally tried to put a good face on it. No clients had suffered a loss. All the transactions had been blocked or reversed. There was never any cause for alarm.

The subtext was embarrassingly obvious: *No need to close your accounts at Citibank, folks! Your money has never been safer!*

How do intruders penetrate such a secure system? The techniques today are no different from when teenagers of the Legion of Doom broke into computers just for fun:

■ **Impersonation.** Usually this means stealing a password. Passwords may be kept on the system itself, usually in encrypted form. A user may have chosen an obvious password, such as the name of a pet or a date of birth, which a hacker can guess via trial and error. Or a hacker can trick a user into revealing a password.

■ **Social engineering.** This refers to conning people into doing favors or revealing information that enables access to the system.

■ **Intercepting data.** A phone line can be tapped, or a telephone switch can be reprogrammed to forward calls or allow snooping.

In addition, there's now the prospect of higher-tech surveillance. Late in 1992 Don Delaney, senior investigator in a New York State squad specializing in computer crime, noticed an antenna on the balcony of a room on the nineteenth floor of the Helmsley Building in Manhattan. The antenna was like a small satellite TV dish, pointing down toward the street. It was aimed directly at the windows of a branch of Chemical Bank opposite.

Delaney thought it looked as if the antenna was being fine-tuned; but by the time he was able to get access to the Helmsley Building and locate the balcony, the equipment had been dismantled and its owner had fled.

A unit of this type would be capable of picking up radio-frequency (RF) emissions from a computer or its monitor. Computers create a lot of noise on the radio spectrum, and their circuits and external cabling are like miniature radio transmitters. FCC regulations minimize this noise to prevent it from interfering with radio or TV reception, but some leakage still occurs. You can test it yourself if you take a portable radio, tune it to a faint station on the AM band, then place it next to your computer and switch the computer on. The high-pitched whine that you hear is the sound of escaping data.

A computer can't be shielded perfectly—at least, not at a price that consumers will pay. Anytime text is scrolling up your screen, theoretically someone can pick up and reconstitute the data that you're seeing. It isn't easy, but it's possible.

This kind of exotic, high-tech snooping is more likely to be practiced by government agents than hackers. Still, there are some hackers who use their skills with premeditated criminal intent, as the Citibank case suggests. How can this be reconciled with the so-called hacker ethic? How can a crowd of good-natured, nerdy guys seem so trusting that they'll pay $25 apiece to a weirdo stuffing the money in a paper bag—yet they'll try to take millions out of Citibank?

The answer, of course, is that there are two very different kinds of hackers. There are the kids we've already met, who give themselves scary names, joust online, and break into systems just to prove it can be done. There's also a dangerous minority that isn't harmless at all; sometimes they're referred to as "darkside hackers."

Unfortunately, media hype has blurred the distinction between the majority who are basically harmless and the minority who aren't. Journalists are partly to blame for this—but so are the hackers themselves.

The Story and the Glory

The journalist-hacker relationship has always been an uneasy alliance in which each side tries to exploit the other. The writer wants the story; the hacker wants the glory. In the words of Dark Fiber: "Most hackers understand that the media are very easily spooked, and some of them take advantage of this. It's what I would call testosterone-influenced braggadocio. They enjoy it."

In everyday reporting work, the average journalist can often outsmart the average news source he deals with. He can nudge or tempt the source into speaking too freely, and he can use a dozen different methods to figure out whether someone has told him the truth.

But this no longer applies when the journalist deals with a smart, cynical, anarchic hacker. The hacker has the intellectual edge, and the journalist has no way of telling truth from fantasy. If we factor in the social engineering skills that any hacker is likely to have developed as a survival tool, it's not surprising that journalists can be conned and news stories can be wildly exaggerated or even totally untrue.

John Markoff of the *New York Times* is considered by many people to be a leading authority on hackers, yet according to some sources, even Markoff has been spoofed. "We told him all kinds of bullshit, just to see if he would print it," says a former member of the Legion of Doom. "This was back in the days when he was writing for the *San Francisco Examiner*. He made his initial reputation with those stories. But we were just playing games with him."

Seth, who wrote the history of the New York hacking scene in the 1980s, tells a similar story. "I called Markoff with a friend of mine, after he'd put the word out that he wanted stories about hackers. We talked to him for, like, an hour. My friend called himself Axe Handle, but I just used my regular name, Seth. We told him a whole litany of acts, computers that we had hacked, and he published it in the magazine section. None of what we said was true."

Was there any special reason why Seth chose to do this? "Well, it's just another form of hacking, telling a journalist a bunch of lies and seeing them get into print. The way I look at it, we hacked John Markoff."

In the online journal *Phrack*, one more hacker was accused of fabricating stories for Markoff—in this case, to make himself look good. "Another individual who wanted to publicize himself is Oryan QUEST. . . . QUEST has been 'pumping' information to John Markoff. . . . Almost everything Oryan QUEST has told John Markoff are utter and complete lies and false boasts about the powerful things OQ liked to think he could do with a computer. This in itself is harmless, but when it gets printed in newspapers like the *New York Times*, the general public get a misleading look at the hacker community which can only do us harm. John Markoff has gone on to receive great fame as a news reporter and is now considered a hacker expert—utterly ridiculous."

Katie Hafner immortalized Kevin Mitnick in her book Cyberpunk, *which she co-wrote with John Markoff.*

According to Markoff, Oryan QUEST was subsequently jailed for drug dealing. Markoff now admits that QUEST was not a reliable source but claims that some facts in his reporting were confirmed by a Stanford University system administrator—though he's not specific on the details.

Markoff's former wife and collaborator, Katie Hafner, also seems to have been spoofed by hackers while she was gathering material for *Cyberpunk*, a book that she coauthored with Markoff. Hacker Kevin Mitnick was graphically profiled in this account, and so was Roscoe (not his real name), a friend of Mitnick's who now claims that he conspired to deceive Hafner and never did tell her the whole truth.

"What she wrote only covered maybe ten percent of what had actually gone on and was interesting," he says. "I spoke to Kevin [Mitnick] and his ex-wife, and we decided to collaborate on what we were going to tell Katie, so that our stories would coincide. We gave her the impression that none of us were on speaking terms with each other, but in fact we collaborated on our roles, deciding who would play the victim, who would be the afraid person, and so on. We put it all together and had a blast. She wrote what we told her, and she only heard what we wanted her to hear. Some of it was not true, some of it was. She had no idea we had prepared it all together in advance."

Katie Hafner naturally objects to being characterized as a gullible victim of con artists and points out that she also relied on police reports and court documents for her information. "I spent months and months reporting that section of the book," she says, "and was as responsible as I could possibly be. So please don't just take Roscoe's word for this."

Still, Hafner and Markoff were never able to interview Kevin Mitnick himself, because he claimed that he deserved to be paid for his time. Eric Corley, editor and publisher of *2600* magazine, believes that Mitnick's attitude created a grudge. "It seemed to me that *Cyberpunk* was unfairly slanted against Kevin because he wouldn't talk without being compensated. They seemed bitter and unfair in the way they treated him."

In a letter to *2600* magazine, Mitnick said much the same thing: "It seems that the authors acted with malice to cause me harm after my refusal to cooperate."

In an interview for *Newsbytes,* an online newsletter, Katie Hafner denied this. "Mitnick's lack of cooperation certainly did not lead to any malice or bias directed toward him," she said. But she added that because Mitnick refused to talk to her, he forfeited his chance to respond to other people's statements about him.

"I have been interviewed on many occasions," writes Patrick Kroupa, "and I know roughly twenty people who have done the interviews that comprise the basis of about 90% of all media that exists in relation to the underground. . . . The reporter profits first by stroking the hacker's ego and giving him the spotlight that he thinks he wants so badly, and then continues to profit as the hacker rides a bigger and bigger wave of publicity that in every case leads to a very unhappy ending if the hacker in question doesn't have the foresight to get off the ride before it derails. In any case, whatever happens, the reporter always wins. When the hacker's ride reaches its date with fate, the journalist in question can now write the closing chapter in the hacker's saga and tell the public how this nefarious evildoer is being punished by the long arm of justice. This is followed up by the journalist taking on the 'official' mantle of 'hacker expert,' doing the lecture circuit, perhaps writing a book, and then going out and finding a new horse to beat to death."

Here again the classic example of this syndrome is John Markoff, who has literally made a fortune by writing about Kevin Mitnick. Markoff wrote his first Mitnick piece in the early 1980s. *Cyberpunk* profiled Mitnick largely in Katie Hafner's words (she confirms that her divorce settlement with Markoff gives her all future royalties from the book). But Markoff then went on to build a grandiose mix of fact and exaggeration on this relatively small foundation. Ultimately, in collaboration with security expert Tsutomu Shimomura, he personally reaped at least half a million dollars from Mitnick's story.

Eric Corley still doesn't understand how this was possible. "Markoff never even met Mitnick," he says. "But he *took ownership* somehow. A lot of the other media outlets don't seem to realize this depiction of Kevin is just one person's conception. Since Markoff benefits so much personally, you have to wonder how accurate he can possibly be when he has such a vested interest in the outcome."

One way or another, the Markoff-Mitnick case history is the most powerful illustration of the journalist-hacker dynamic—and the most surprising example of teenage pranks becoming a hugely bankable commodity.

From Jules Verne to John Markoff

Every age has its bogeymen. A hundred years ago, popular novelists cashed in on people's fear of science and scientists by creating fictional antiheroes such as Dr. Jekyll, Dr. Moreau, Captain Nemo, or Dr. Frankenstein.

Today computer criminals are the new antiheroes. Instead of Jules Verne we have John Markoff, and instead of Captain Nemo we have Kevin Mitnick.

Mitnick, of course, is not a fictional character. Yet in *Cyberpunk* he became larger than life, a "darkside hacker," omnipotent, obsessive-compulsive, egotistical, vindictive, using his computer to take revenge on the world that had spurned him.

Mitnick later claimed that this was "twenty percent fabricated and libelous." Maybe so, but the moody, petulant fat boy punishing his enemies via a computer keyboard was such a potent image, it was more believable than Kevin himself. In fact, it displaced reality.

Reality itself was not very exciting. Mitnick held down a succession of low-paying jobs, took a few computer courses, and spent huge amounts of time breaking into other people's computers and snooping around. He was arrested four times, spent some time in jail, was released, but was then accused of a probation violation, at which point he disappeared for a couple of years.

In February 1995 he was arrested for the fifth time and accused of copying thousands of credit card numbers from Netcom, an Internet service provider based in San Jose. His big mistake, though, was that he broke into a system owned by Tsutomu Shimomura at the San Diego Supercomputer Center. Shimomura was so annoyed, he gave up a two-week skiing vacation to help police find Mitnick and make the arrest.

Writing in the *New York Times*, John Markoff said that Mitnick had been on a "long crime spree" during which he had managed to "vandalize government, corporate and university computer systems." Markoff didn't actually name any systems or say what he meant by the word vandalize. He went on to quote Assistant U.S. Attorney Kent Walker, who had helped to run the investigation and naturally had an interest in making the arrest seem as important as possible. Walker claimed (again, without any proof) that Mitnick "had access to corporate trade secrets worth millions of dollars. He was a very big threat."

In fact, Mitnick hadn't physically damaged any of the computers that he had supposedly "vandalized," and he hadn't used any of the credit card numbers purloined from Netcom. Markoff tried to make up for this with another titillating tidbit: some of the credit card numbers belonged to "the best-known millionaires in Silicon Valley."

Other journalists swooped down onto the body of the story like carrion-eaters seeing a carcass that was so big and juicy, there had to be enough to share. Writing for *Time* magazine, Joshua Quittner artfully reworked the leftovers to create a whole new feature. "Kevin Mitnick, 31, stood in the federal courtroom," Quittner wrote, "his hands cuffed—unable, for the first time in more than two years, to feel the silky click of computer keys." Quittner confidently compared Mitnick with Billy the Kid, talked about his "hideout," and praised his "husky, spaghetti-western cool." No one would have guessed that Quittner's account was derived from wire stories and from John Markoff—who had never exchanged more than a dozen words with Kevin Mitnick.

Surely the carcass was now picked clean—but no, there were just a few more shreds of meat, not enough for a real meal, but maybe sufficient for some soup. In another article for *Time*, Quittner spiced this thin gruel with an authoritative psychological profile of Mitnick as cybercriminal. He spoke eloquently about the tragedy of Mitnick's absent father and typed him as "yet another Lost Boy in cyberspace, hoping, perhaps, to be found." In fact, according to Quittner, Mitnick broke into Shimomura's computer because he was "unconsciously asking to get caught."

This was truly a landmark in clinical diagnosis, bearing in mind that it was still based on information from another journalist who had never conducted an interview with his source.

After Mitnick was jailed, Katie Hafner managed to meet him face-to-face for less than a minute in a public hallway, where she exchanged a couple of words with him. Around this fleeting encounter she concocted still another Mitnick article. It appeared in the August 1995 issue of *Esquire* beside a full-page painting of Kevin Mitnick glowering into a computer screen, his brooding face lit by a sinister yellow-green glow, like a malevolent troll.

The Markoff Story

The summary of Kevin Mitnick's criminal record reads like the career of a small-town peeping Tom. He's an electronic voyeur who can't seem to stop himself from peeking into other people's computers. True, he's a repeat offender, but he doesn't steal anything, he doesn't do any damage, and he certainly doesn't make any money out of it. In a world where genuine computer criminals reap hundreds of thousands of dollars from banks or telephone companies, why has Kevin Mitnick been singled out as a menace to society?

Well, John Markoff certainly had a strong financial incentive to make Kevin Mitnick seem as frightening as possible. Markoff's first big success developing the "Mitnick threat" occurred after Mitnick had gone into hiding following a minor parole violation. "It was weird," says Eric Corley, "because Kevin hadn't actually *done* anything. I mean, how often do you see a front-page story in the *New York*

Times, with a picture, about someone who happens to be on the run for really minor crimes such as making free phone calls or accessing computers without damaging them? If he was a serial killer, it might make sense."

The story appeared in the *New York Times* on July 4, 1994. Headlined "Cyberspace's Most Wanted: Hacker Eludes FBI Pursuit," it described Mitnick as "one of the nation's most wanted computer criminals" who was "always fascinated by spying." Strangely, there wasn't much real news in the article; after noting that Mitnick had been on the loose for eighteen months, it mainly contained material reworked from *Cyberpunk*, the book that Markoff had coauthored with Katie Hafner. Markoff later claimed that "the news was that [Mitnick] was being pursued by the FBI (three agents full time), the California DMV, U.S. marshals, telco security, local police, etc." This sounded impressive, but *pursued* hardly seemed an appropriate word, bearing in mind that the case had gone nowhere for a year or more and many agencies seemed to have lost interest in it. According to journalist John Littman, a bounty hunter named Todd Young had actually tracked Kevin Mitnick down in Seattle months previously and had kept him under surveillance for two weeks. "But the Secret Service didn't think the crimes were significant. The U.S. Attorney's office wouldn't prosecute the case. Even the local cops didn't really care."

Still, the headline said "Cyberspace's Most Wanted," and the implication was clear enough: A weirdo who could paralyze vast computer networks was on the loose, and law enforcement had been too stupid to catch him.

When security expert Tsutomu Shimomura realized that it was Mitnick who had broken into his system, he called Markoff, initiating a collaboration that continued to the moment when Mitnick was finally captured. Law enforcement also asked for Markoff's help, and he told them what he knew, although it may not have been worth much. He said, for instance, that Kevin could probably be found at the nearest Fatburger (a fast-food chain in California) when in fact Mitnick now worked out frequently, was no longer overweight, and had become a vegetarian.

Still, the usefulness of Markoff's advice was a secondary issue. The real point was that he had crossed a line; he was no longer just a journalist reporting a story but was now helping to *create* the story. As he put it himself, with characteristic hyperbole: "I too became enmeshed in the digital manhunt for the nation's most wanted computer outlaw."

When Mitnick was finally placed under arrest, Markoff and Shimomura were ready to cash in. Just four days after Markoff's final story appeared in the *New York Times*, their book deal was negotiated with Hyperion. Shortly after that they had a movie deal with Miramax, and there were plans to get a CD-ROM out of it as well. Markoff and Shimomura retreated to a cabin in the beautiful country near Lake Tahoe to crank out the book. Mitnick, of course, was now behind bars.

According to John Littman's fairly sympathetic account of the saga, Mitnick was shunted through a worsening series of county jails, finally ending up in a cell with seven other men. He was allowed one piece of paper per day and a pencil that was shared among all the cellmates and taken away in the afternoons. Meanwhile, in the outside world, advance advertising for the Shimomura-Markoff book claimed that "he could have crippled the world."

Embarrassingly enough, the twenty-three-count indictment against Mitnick—which the Associated Press had suggested could put him behind bars for 460 years—was plea-bargained down to one count of possessing a list of fifteen phone numbers for purposes of accessing computer systems. He was also charged with violating probation. Suddenly it seemed that Mitnick might serve no more than a year or two of jail time, although the report of his successful plea bargain was buried on a back page of the *New York Times*. As of May, 1996, his final sentence had not yet been handed down.

Having spent a rumored $750,000 on the book deal, Hyperion obviously had a strong incentive not to back away from their own hype. Consequently they simply ignored the prosaic facts of Kevin Mitnick's situation and referred to him, in their dust jacket blurb, as "the most wanted hacker in history" who had enjoyed "one of the most dramatic and bizarre crime sprees in recent times." Actually, during most of the so-called manhunt, Kevin Mitnick had lived reclusively in a small apartment in North Carolina, spending most of his time with a small computer and a bottle of stomach medicine. No matter; the machinery of hype continued to run.

The online community was not impressed. "There is a factor here," a Net user named Ronald Austin wrote in an online newsgroup, "which did not manage to make the front page of the *New York Times*, and that is Mr. Markoff's sequel to his book *Cyberpunk* [i.e. *Takedown*]. He has created the story for that sequel by abusing his position and perpetrating a hoax on the public."

Austin was scathing about Shimomura also. "I want to see *exactly* what happened when, rather than using traditional signal strength meters and cellular service testing equipment, our hero pieced together his own OKI900 cellular phone with his HP palmtop to make a device (along with some neat software he helped develop) which is capable of following the audio of cellular phone calls from cell to cell. Why, I'd bet the software even lets him put in the numbers of the cellular phones he wants to overhear. How such a piece of equipment would not be considered 'primarily useful' for the surreptitious interception of oral communications, thus its mere possession a crime under 18 USCS Section 2512, will of course be thoroughly explained in the book."

In fact, Shimomura claims that since he was accompanied by an employee of the cellular telephone company and was working on the company's behalf, he had the right to listen in on phone calls. But once again, this isn't the real issue. Shimomura had helped to catch Mitnick basically by out-hacking him. Didn't that mean that Shimomura was himself a hacker? Were he and Mitnick brothers under the skin?

Supposedly Mitnick had broken into Shimomura's computer in search of software for hacking cellular phones. Early in 1996, however, a very different theory was proposed. John Gilmore, one of the founders of the hugely successful computer manufacturer Sun Microsystems, claimed that Tsutomu Shimomura had been working on some highly specialized software for the National Security Agency that was the real magnet for Mitnick's interest. Supposedly the code was designed to patch itself invisibly into the kernel (the most fundamental section) of a Sun computer's operating system, where it would hide and monitor all the data passing through. An enhancement would automatically forward interesting material to some other location on the Internet.

This would have been the ultimate surveillance system. "Think of it as digital telephony wiretap technology for the Internet," Gilmore wrote in a memo for the "cypherpunks" newsgroup, an online discussion forum for programmers who advocate the private use of secure encryption. "It's a tool customized for crackers. . . . Tsutomu has lots of glib rhetoric about how he just builds tools and they can be used for good or evil. This tool is custom-designed for evil."

True, Gilmore had a grudge against Shimomura, who had walked off with his girlfriend. On the other hand, Gilmore seemed to have a very clear understanding of the work that Shimomura had been doing, and he also claimed that Shimomura had threatened to release his invention freely to Net users.

Wasn't this just the kind of wild behavior that made people nervous about hackers? Didn't it imply that Shimomura was almost as unpredictable as Kevin Mitnick?

The idea was unthinkable—mainly because Markoff had already gone out of his way to typecast Shimomura as a gentle scientist with a strong moral code. As Robert Wright noted sardonically in a piece for the *New Yorker* titled "Hackwork," Markoff spared no adjectives in newspaper reports describing Shimomura:

> Shimomura went from being "a well-known computer security expert" to being "one of the country's most skilled computer security experts" and then to being (on the day of the arrest [of Kevin Mitnick]) a "brilliant cybersleuth." And that was just the beginning. Four days later, in a piece on the front page of the Sunday "Week in Review" section, Shimomura became a "master at manipulating computers."... Shimomura also had "a

deeply felt sense of right and wrong"—in contrast
to his nemesis, Kevin Mitnick, a "chameleon-like
grifter," a "darkside" hacker.

It was clear that if Shimomura really did have something in common with Mitnick, this was one story that John Markoff was not going to write. For the sake of the upcoming collaborative book project, Shimomura *had* to be a good guy.

This raised still more ethical questions. The *Nation* quoted *New York Times* assistant managing editor Allan Siegal, who admitted that his newspaper has "explicit rules about people writing about others with whom they have a commercial or business relationship. We don't allow it." Of course, Markoff contracted with Shimomura just a few days *after* he wrote his story for the *Times* about capturing Kevin Mitnick. But Markoff and Shimomura had worked together on the case for months before that. Had they really never talked about a book or movie deal? Had Markoff been "just a journalist" and Shimomura "just a source" until the precise moment at which Mitnick was caught, at which point—within a few days—they suddenly decided to get rich from their unexpected good fortune?

Other critics were more concerned with the crime itself. Kevin Mitnick had broken into some computers; so what? He had copied 20,000 credit card numbers; but even Netcom's CEO, Bob Rieger, had to admit in a public statement that "we have absolutely no indication that any of our Unix shell customers' credit card numbers have been used illicitly."

Some people suggested that the real crime was negligence by Netcom. Eric Corley claimed that he had published a news item about Netcom's lax security six months previously, revealing how easy it would be to access the credit card numbers via the Net. At that time, Netcom had said it was impossible.

According to Mitnick's friend Roscoe, "Netcom's credit card numbers were being *handed out* over IRC [the Internet Relay Chat network] *last year*, and we didn't hear anything about it from Netcom then." Roscoe added, "When talking of incompetence, don't forget to mention Tsutomu's gross negligence and incompetence at computer security, where he left himself open to penetration by a 'quirk' [in Unix] that was known for ten years! The bug that was used to get into his machine was written up in a paper by Robert Morris. You can look it up." In fact, Shimomura's blunder caused Roscoe to label him a "computer *insecurity* expert."

Risks

Even Hafner and Markoff have admitted (in *Cyberpunk*) that Mitnick "seldom if ever tried to sell the information" he obtained. Nor did he damage data, with the possible exception of one case in which some information may have been erased by accident. He just liked snooping around.

The real risk, as always, was in what Mitnick *hadn't* done. "It would not have been difficult," wrote Hafner and Markoff, "for Kevin and Lenny to take down the telephone service for the entire [Los Angeles] metropolitan area."

Yes, he *could have*, couldn't he? And maybe he could have ruined large corporations, sold secrets to Communists, or launched a nuclear attack. This was the kind of stuff that gave Mitnick his bogeyman aura and generated a deliciously marketable mixture of curiosity and fear.

But all of us, hackers or nonhackers, have a huge untapped potential for causing mayhem in the modern world. As Patrick Kroupa puts it: "Any idiot can get a gun, take a stroll down to the local mall, and start blowing away shoppers. Yet this just doesn't happen all that often. Just because someone has power, it doesn't mean that he is going to use it to inflict harm on others."

Most human beings simply choose not to be vandals or murderers. Society works on a cooperative basis of self-restraint that we take for granted.

But where hackers are involved, we lose this faith in human nature. We tend to assume that they *don't* know the meaning of self-restraint and will use their skills in the worst possible way. Why? Because they're not like us. They have the bogeyman aura, the mad-scientist image. They're alien and inscrutable. They set themselves apart from society. Their skills seem like black magic. In the words of John Markoff: "Federal officials say Mr. Mitnick's motives have always been murky." Translation: "We don't understand this guy. Therefore we don't trust him. So we'd better lock him up."

In *Cyberpunk*, Mitnick's obesity and his eating habits were mentioned more than a dozen times, presumably because this was the one simple, everyday, visible feature that the authors could relate to, while Mitnick's mental processes remained a total mystery. One reason Hafner and Markoff were baffled may have been their own relative naïveté about computers. Hafner claims that her mother is a computer programmer, but according to Roscoe, Hafner had to bring along a technical consultant to some interviews while she was writing *Cyberpunk* so that she could understand what the hackers were talking about.

Oddly enough, most other writers who have become "authorities" on computer crime lack any formal knowledge of computers. Joshua Quittner was a history major in college and has a master's degree in journalism. He became a regular journalist at the Long Island, New York, newspaper *Newsday* and freely admits, "I had no background in computers, and what little I know about them now I learned on the job." Even Bruce Sterling, whose *Hacker Crackdown* predates most books on the subject, was trained in the biological sciences, not computer science. It should be no surprise, then, that journalists such as Quittner and Markoff have an aptitude for echoing and amplifying the public's fear of the unknown.

Unfortunately, once a media figure has been created and given frightening powers, another syndrome kicks in: the witch hunt. Jim Thomas, the professor of sociology and criminal justice at Northern Illinois University who also edits *Computer Underground Digest*, wrote a paper with his colleague Gordon Meyer in which he compared antihacker hysteria in the 1990s with anti-Communist hysteria in the 1950s:

> Witch hunts are about images and social control. They have typically occured during times of social upheaval as a way of re-affirming normative boundaries or providing social unity in the face of a perceived threat. Similarly, in the 1950s, the imagery of good against evil was played out in media portrayals, political rhetoric, public ideology, and legislation. In both, the public was whipped into a paranoid frenzy by the creation of mysterious alien demons, in which the ends justified the means in removing the scourge from the public midst.

Thomas and Meyer continued by stating that a witch hunt is a form of scapegoating in which public troubles are traced to and blamed on others.

> Although sometimes the others are guilty of some anti-social act, the response exceeds the harm of the act, and the targets are pursued not only for what they may have done, but also for the stigmatizing signs they bear.

In other words, if he looks like a hacker and smells like a hacker, it makes no difference whether he stole a couple of million from Citibank or merely trespassed into someone's computer. The reaction is the same in both cases—and this is exactly the attitude we see toward Kevin Mitnick.

To people who actually know Mitnick and have some knowledge of computers, he's neither scary nor weird. Eric Corley met him twice in 1990 and talked to him on the phone many times, right up to the day in 1995 when Mitnick was captured by the FBI. According to Corley, "Kevin wasn't compulsive when I hung out with him. He didn't seem to be addicted to anything. A lot of people who use computers are portrayed as strange or compulsive by journalists, but to me, they just seem like regular people who just happen to be interested in computers."

Roscoe feels that Mitnick did have compulsive work habits, but not to a pathological degree. "It's true," he says, "that Kevin would stay up all night if he got started on something. He had to finish it; he

Jim Thomas is editor-publisher of Computer Underground Digest, *reaching an estimated 300,000 readers.*

couldn't pace himself. But in any other area, we'd call that kind of person a workaholic or an overachiever. When it's someone who's breaking into a computer, all of a sudden he has a psychiatric label attached to him."

Was there a vindictive streak? Corley doesn't think so. "I never saw a malicious side of Kevin. I've seen him frustrated and wondering why all this publicity is of interest to so many people, but he never wanted revenge; he just wanted not to be put back in jail. It seems to me they wanted to put him back no matter what. He had tried to get legitimate jobs, he was trying to fit in somehow, but he was never given the chance."

Roscoe is a little less sanguine. "FBI agents have already complained that while Kevin was on the run, they were getting strange things happening to them," he comments. What kinds of things? Mindful that anything he says might be used as evidence in some future trial, Roscoe is careful to answer only in general terms. "Hypothetically," he says, "a person might find all his credit cards reported stolen. Or he might be buying a car or trying to buy a home and find that the escrow is held up because of negative entries in the credit profile that don't belong there. He may have a quit-claim deed filed to the state on his property, which causes massive confusion with the title company. His kids can get pulled out of school for emergencies that don't exist—there are all kinds of possibilities."

Was Mitnick in any sense a "darkside hacker"?

"If 'darkside hacker' means Kevin was trying to steal national defense secrets to give them to a foreign country," says Roscoe, "that certainly isn't Kevin. He had no interest in military secrets, U.S. government items, anything like that. Here's what I told Katie Hafner for her piece in *Esquire*, where she quoted me out of context: There are many serious criminals plying their trade across the United States. But Kevin Mitnick was not in business making money from other people's computers. He only obtained information to show that he could do it. At worst he was a pain in the neck whose punishment should be that he has to walk around for six months with his pants off."

A Bankable Commodity

John Markoff adamantly maintains that he has presented an accurate picture of Kevin Mitnick at all times, with no undue exaggeration. "I didn't create the character, Kevin did," Markoff wrote in response to one critic. "He has now been arrested six times in fifteen years. Each time, except for this last time, he was given a second chance to get his act together. He chose not to. . . . He chose to keep breaking into computers. He knew what the penalty was. So what's the problem?"

Katie Hafner isn't so sure. She now admits that she characterized Mitnick unfairly in *Cyberpunk*. "It might have been a mistake to call him a darkside hacker," she says. "Still, that's how you learn."

Today, having benefited from her "learning experience" of erro-neously labeling Mitnick a threat to society and disseminating this distortion to a potential audience of millions, Hafner seems to have a kinder, gentler attitude. Speaking on the phone from her office at *Newsweek* magazine, she sounds sympathetic—almost motherly. "I really think he is not darkside in the sense of being an electronic terrorist," she says. "He's not out to cripple the world. He isn't, he isn't! Saddam Hussein, or Hitler, they were out to cripple the world. There are malicious characters out there, but Kevin is not one of them. But it was hard for me," she adds plaintively, "since I hadn't spoken to him personally till after I wrote the book, to know what his motives were."

Hafner is now divorced from John Markoff. She seems to be on friendly terms with her ex-husband and is reluctant to say anything negative about him, but she does agree that the exploitation of Kevin Mitnick has gotten out of hand. "He has been turned into this bankable commodity," she says. "Leave the guy alone! He's had a really tragic life."

The Roscoe Story

Roscoe is bitter about the way that he and Mitnick were treated by Hafner. "She would interview us with her nice smiling face," he says, "but once she got out of there, she labeled us cybercriminals."

He maintains a prickly relationship with journalists in general. While Mitnick was hiding from the authorities, reporters called Roscoe repeatedly, begging him to set up an interview for them with Mitnick. When they annoyed him enough, Roscoe made sure that they weren't disappointed. "I enjoy playing performance art on the media," he says. "There was a prime thing that happened to KCOP-TV, Channel Thirteen news. They got their interview with Kevin—or so they thought. The same thing happened with the *Los Angeles Times*. A reporter from the *Times* kept calling and calling, wanting an interview—so she got an interview. According to the Sunday valley edition, a source close to Kevin revealed he learned how to play classical piano at an early age in order to control his blood pressure. He had a secret penchant for opera, and he was devoted to a pet poodle." Roscoe chuckles happily. "Needless to say, nothing could be further from the truth."

Roscoe knew Kevin Mitnick better than almost anyone and had hoped to sell a book of his own that would tell the true story once and for all. Ironically, Roscoe had trouble finding a publisher for his book—presumably because truth is less salable than fiction.

I happened to catch Roscoe in a mellow mood one evening and spoke at length with him on the phone. Since he has admitted playing pranks on journalists, there was obviously a possibility that he wasn't being straight with me, and I asked him to document some of his claims—which he was ready to do. His story creates a valuable picture, not just of Kevin Mitnick but of Roscoe himself, who was just as much a hacker during his teenage years.

Roscoe freely admits that Mitnick was a master of online deception. "To give you just one example," he says, "Neill Clift, in England, specializes in documenting Vax bugs [defects in the Vax computer operating system]. He was using PGP encryption to send bug reports to Digital [DEC]. Eventually he learned that he was not really sending them to DEC, he was sending them to an intermediate site where Kevin was decoding the messages."

Of course, this is supposed to be impossible. Messages encrypted with Pretty Good Privacy (PGP) software are impregnable. So how did Mitnick break the code? Like any good hacker, he set things up so that he didn't have to.

According to Roscoe, Mitnick was already intercepting Clift's messages to and from DEC *before* Clift started using encryption. When Clift and Digital agreed on the code key that they would use for future messages, Mitnick intercepted this information along with everything else. "After that," says Roscoe, "it was simple for Kevin to decrypt the messages from Neill, copy them, reencrypt them with the proper key, and send them on their merry way. And this went on for *eight months*. Neill only found out in the end because some of the bugs were too good to waste, so Kevin kept them instead of passing them along. Neill finally talked to the folks at Digital on the phone, and he found that things didn't quite jibe."

Roscoe chuckles over the story. He obviously enjoys the Mitnick touch—spoofing that is so arrogant, so outrageous, it goes one step beyond what anyone assumes is possible.

Roscoe believes, though, that Mitnick will never serve any more time in jail. "They will never catch Kevin again. Every time, he has learned not to repeat his mistakes. In this case he learned the ultimate lesson: don't trust strangers. Do it alone, by yourself."

The stranger who betrayed Mitnick in 1995 was Justin Petersen, a former hacker who used the handle Agent Steal after he was recruited to work on behalf of the FBI. "Petersen was sitting in a Texas jail when they approached him," says Roscoe. "Later, while he was out there introducing himself to Kevin, he was also committing credit card fraud, using FBI-supplied ID, as well as wiretapping bank transfers. My attorney, Richard Sherman, now has an action sitting in Federal court accusing the FBI of complicity, and part of that is due to Justin Petersen, because he was acting as their straw man and setting up wiretaps without a warrant. He was also committing fraud with credit card numbers, so he's now at the Metropolitan Detention Center in Los Angeles, awaiting sentencing. So there you have it," he says, moving into sarcastic mode. "The FBI's trusted information source." (Petersen was sentenced to forty-one months in federal prison shortly after Roscoe made these comments.)

Some people might assume from this that Roscoe has a knee-jerk antiauthoritarian attitude, but that label doesn't quite fit. For several years he has been manager of information services for a large California corporation, and part of his job is maintaining system security. He also says that he does unpaid work for local law enforcement. "While these idiots at the FBI are themselves breaking the law in order to get a conviction, here I am doing volunteer work for the LAPD. They're understaffed, so I put together donated equipment from various vendors, and I write the code to do automatic call processing, so people calling the front desk can be transferred to the proper department. I also have a sheriff's department that wanted me to participate in the design of a data base to track narcotics crimes. That one was actually a joint project with the FBI! So I'm helping law enforcement in areas where they can use help. You see, I don't have any problem with authority figures unless they try to be authoritative. When they try to be pompous, then I enjoy playing with them."

That was what happened when his own apartment was raided a while ago. The FBI seized his equipment, then demanded the password that they needed to unlock his files. Roscoe refused; he said he would use the password himself while the FBI were present and would open up his system for them, but he would not reveal the password. The FBI refused to accept this, and so, Roscoe says, his attorney filed a court order ordering them to return his property. "The same agent who'd taken it out had to bring it right back," he says happily. "I told him, 'You can set that right there, Ken. Is there anything else missing that we might have to go to court on?'"

Behind the humor, though, Roscoe seems righteously angry about this kind of routine seizure. Like most hackers, he has a deep-rooted "don't tread on me" reflex; and he's also capable of being inhumanly persistent. As a result, he says, suing the authorities has become a full-time hobby: "I'm now pursuing the Department of Justice simply because it has to be done. For some time now, these guys have been finding any excuse they can to get a search warrant so they can break into someone's home whenever they suspect something about hackers. Most of their victims can't afford an attorney, and they have to settle out of court or reach a plea bargain arrangement—or go into debt for the rest of their lives. I want to put a stop to that. I can afford to hire a good attorney, and I can oppose them all the way through to the Court of Appeals." This, says Roscoe, is where his own case is currently pending.

"The Department of Justice said I had features on my phone line that I wasn't paying for, and therefore there was a crime being committed, and therefore there was justification for a search warrant. Well, we obtained a statement from the president of the department that does audits for Pacific Bell, and out of eleven million accounts, between one and four percent were getting features they didn't pay for. That's more than 100,000 people, minimum. I want a one hundred percent ruling in my favor. I want the search warrant declared void and invalid. Once I have that, I can file a civil suit against them."

How far does he pursue this hobby, and how much does it cost?

"Let's just say that even with the ungodly prices that real estate fetches in this area of the country, I could have paid for a good part of a house with what I've spent. But I already do own a three-bedroom home. I also have a vacation home, and I own land. So I'm able to spend money on my hobby."

And the ultimate objective?

"Hopefully, if all this goes through properly, when the FBI's abuses get to Congress with a court seal, it might set the FBI back to the 1960s."

Pirates of the Caribbean

Genuine darkside hackers are like international drug smugglers or white-collar criminals: They don't cooperate with the press. Why should they? Their motive is money, not fame. The last thing they want is public exposure.

Once in a while you'll see brief news items reporting their crimes. In October 1994, for instance, Ivey James Lay, who used the handle Knightshadow, was charged with stealing more than 100,000 telephone calling-card numbers and disposing of them through a network of dealers in Los Angeles, Chicago, Spain, and Germany, according to the Secret Service. Allegedly the numbers were used to make $50 million in calls. Lay, aged twenty-nine, was sentenced in March, 1996, to three years and two months in prison.

Lay was a switch engineer who worked for MCI in Charlotte, North Carolina. According to MCI, his thefts were the largest ever recorded. Yet he didn't get his picture on the front page of the *New York Times*, and most newspapers gave his story just a few inches of space on an inside page—because Lay wasn't talking to the press, nor were any of his friends. Even though this was the biggest theft of phone service in history, *Time* magazine didn't even bother to mention it.

Journalists who are commissioned by their editors to write about computer crime face a very real problem: The best sources are unavailable. Consequently, they turn to their second-best sources. I've felt this kind of pressure myself and have been tempted to exaggerate facts and enhance a story, knowing that if I tell the boring truth, the text may not be accepted for publication.

Only once have I met a genuine darkside hacker who wanted publicity. By "darkside" I mean that he wasn't following the hacker ethic, pursuing information as an end in itself; he was making money out of it. Still, he didn't think of himself as a criminal. He seemed to feel he was playing a highly ethical role, undercutting an entrenched monopoly by offering the same service to the public on an illegal basis at a discount price. American law enforcement didn't share his point of view, and as a result, he was operating out of the Bahamas.

His name is Fred Martin, and he worked in collaboration with a pirate/businessman who called himself Ron MacDonald. Together they were the most notorious and possibly the wealthiest figures in satellite video piracy, which was a wildly lucrative field in the late 1980s and early 1990s and is enjoying a renaissance today. The racket that Fred and Ron participated in was turning over about half a billion dollars per year, supplying illegally decoded TV programs to satellite dish owners in middle America, Canada, Mexico, and the Caribbean.

When I reported this for *Wired* magazine, it was the first time the story had been covered by any nationally distributed publication. Satellite video piracy, like CB radio, was almost exclusively a rural phenomenon. People took it for granted in the American heartland, but in media capitals such as New York and Los Angeles, no one had even heard of it.

This was a fascinating example of huge corporations trying to control information and hackers successfully stealing it, despite desperate attempts to protect it via encryption. Moreover, the story is now repeating itself. Direct broadcast satellites (DBS) are bringing a new wave of digitally encoded signals to people who can't get cable TV or want cheaper programming, and there are reliable reports that this new system has been cracked. Soon, it seems, the pirates will be running their DBS discount operation side by side with their previous satellite TV service. Bearing this in mind, Ron and Fred's story is as topical now as when I first covered it.

Two Million Criminals

Alone in a Holiday Inn, I sit watching the ocean, listening to the air conditioning, waiting for the phone to ring. I'm here to make a connection, to meet a figure from the information underground.

This man who calls himself Ron MacDonald (the misspelling is deliberate) has been described by a law-enforcement expert as "one of the kingpins" in video piracy. For eight years he's been supplying black-market hardware to hundreds of thousands of families scattered across America who use satellite dishes as their primary means of viewing TV. Ron's illicit hardware has one simple purpose: to decode transmissions so that dish owners can watch superstations and sports events without paying the usual fees.

Understand, they don't get the programming for free. They pay a reduced price—and the money goes to the pirates.

Usually a TV dealer serves as middleman on the local level, buying parts and software from a man such as Ron to modify a dish owner's decoder so that it will unscramble satellite signals. The federal penalties for this back-room electronics handiwork are mind-boggling: up to a $500,000 fine, five years in jail, or both. Only a few dealers have been imprisoned. My sources indicate that at least 1,000 have operated outside the law.

In the United States, legitimate decoders that unscramble satellite signals are made and sold by only one company: General Instrument Corporation, referred to by everyone in the business as GI. Initially GI sold 1.9 million VC2 units, capable of decoding the satellite signal encryption standard. Subsequently GI offered a new system— the VC2 Plus—absolutely free in exchange for the old decoders, which they warned users were about to become obsolete.

Strangely, only 300,000 people took advantage of this generous offer. Why didn't the other 1.6 million send in their hardware? Because, according to GI, their units had been illegally modified. That's 1.6 million dish owners who chose to become video criminals.

Meanwhile, in Canada, the government tries to protect local culture from American decadence by limiting the amount of U.S. program- ming that local cable networks can carry. As a result, consumers buy dishes so that they can receive American TV. This, however, creates a problem: Most American programmers don't own the right to sell their entertainment outside the United States. Consequently, they can't accept subscriptions from Canadian viewers, which means that almost all the 500,000 dish owners in Canada are violating U.S. copyright law, quite apart from regulations prohibiting the export of decoder equipment. One way or another, it's almost certain that these people have been paying pirates for television. The score so far: 2.1 million illegal users.

In Mexico and in the Bahamas, the situation is the same: You can't legally subscribe to U.S. programming, which means that every single satellite viewer, by definition, has been violating U.S. law.

The capital of the Bahamas is Nassau, located just the other side of a bridge from my hotel on Paradise Island. The town is an uneasy mix of ultra-rich and ultra-poor and has been scarred by two waves of imperialism. The British installed a government, laws, some funky

*Fred Martin and Ron MacDonald adopt a suitable
disguise at their Bahamaian hideout.
[Photo by the author.]*

little roads, and the metric system. The Americans added an airport,
dollar-denominated currency, and a bunch of modern tourist resorts.

Colonel Sanders and Tony Roma are now doing business
overlooking the marina—but that's just a facade, a clumsy imitation
of Mall Town USA catering to visitors for whom familiarity breeds
contentment. Two blocks back from the water, Mall Town gives
way to Shantytown, where local families live in colorfully painted
tumbledown huts, dogs lie around in the dirt, and sad-eyed, skinny

kids haul water from a communal faucet. Still, even here, among thickets of date palms and cypresses, you find eight-foot dishes aimed at the sky—because the only local channel is a graveyard of old movies and threadbare sitcoms, and the craving for ESPN, CNN, and HBO is universal. Even the humblest homes on the island have dishes outside.

The total score: about 2.5 million TV viewers who chose to break the law, located in and around the North American continent.

But let's be conservative. Perhaps some people became bored with satellite TV, while others stopped using their illegal decoders because the gadgets developed faults and couldn't be fixed. Let's suppose two million families ended up using illegal hardware and illicit authorization codes on a regular basis. Typically, a user would pay $15 a month for code updates and maybe $100 a year for hardware upgrades necessitated by ECMs (electronic countermeasures) employed by GI in its ongoing war against piracy.

This means that the average illegal user would be paying $300 annually for television access. Multiply that by two million, and we see how satellite video piracy turned into a business worth at least half a billion dollars annually. In fact, satellite video piracy became a multinational, information-age version of organized crime—although the participants don't quite see it that way. As one dealer in Arkansas told me, "The airwaves should belong to the people. If a TV signal comes trespassing onto my property, I should be free to do any darn thing I want with it, and it's none of the government's business."

Some folks with this kind of attitude have found themselves confronted with the stark reality of men in windbreakers with *FBI* stenciled on the back, swarming in, brandishing guns, seizing equipment, and serving arrest warrants. The video pirates who've managed to stay in business almost all opted to leave America. Some are located in Canada, while Ron MacDonald retreated to Nassau. His activities seem to be legal here, but he's still extremely cautious. Bounty hunters have occasionally seized video pirates and dragged them forcibly onto U.S. soil, where they can be turned in for reward money. Mindful of this, Ron never tells outsiders where he plans to be at any particular time, and he has communicated with me via a private computer bulletin board that he maintains in Nassau to serve his network of dealerships.

He offered me a simple deal: If I was willing to fly to Nassau, rent a car, drive to the hotel on Paradise Island, and wait in my room, he would call me at 5:00 P.M. with further instructions.

I was willing. So now I wait.

Marooned in Pirates' Cove

The phone rings at 5:02. He sounds relaxed, amiable, and matter-of-fact, like the owner of an appliance store—a straight-shooting businessman in his forties, offering the customer a fair deal. "I'll see you at Tony Roma's at eight," he tells me.

Tony Roma's? This doesn't sound like the glitzy subculture of data theft romanticized by writers such as William Gibson. I guess that's the difference between fact and fiction: I'm stuck here in a middle-American tourist trap.

When I venture down to the hotel lobby I see a van in the parking lot with "Cruising and Boozing" hand-lettered on its side, releasing a mob of lobster-red ocean enthusiasts. They've had a heavy afternoon of drinking-and-swimming and fishing-and-drinking and will soon be ready for a night of serious action at the local casino. Here they come, stumbling up the steps, dizzy from rum and sunstroke.

This Holiday Inn happens to be located on a bay named Pirates Cove, so the doorman wears a full pirate costume, including eye patch and tricorner hat. He ushers the sun worshipers into the lobby, where a Caribbean steel band is playing loudly enough to drown the screaming of caged parakeets, and teenagers in swimsuits are wandering around looking hot, wet, and horny.

Even humble homes in the Bahamas are served by pirated satellite TV programs. [Photo by the author.]

A communal faucet coexists with TV dishes in the background. [photo by the author.]

Video pirates Ron MacDonald and Fred Martin
arranged a clandestine meeting at this Tony Roma's.
[Photo by the author.]

Meanwhile, out back, free plastic cups of nonalcoholic Caribbean punch are being served beside the swimming pool, and a calypso band has set up on a life-size fake galleon on the beach. The pirate motif is everywhere: Teenagers are wearing skull-and-crossbones T-shirts, and little kids brandish cardboard pirate masks.

To the vacationers, piracy is a Disneyland concept, a laugh from the past. They'd be surprised to learn that it still flourishes here in the Bahamas and is now lucrative beyond Captain Hook's wildest fantasies.

Ribs, with a Modem on the Side

When I get to Tony Roma's shortly after eight I see them right away: two guys sitting side by side at a table where they can watch the door.

One of them has graying hair brushed straight back, a neat mustache, and a rounded, sunburned, prosperous-looking face. He's a large man resting his arms calmly on the table. His companion is younger, taller, thinner, paler, with a few days of beard. He's wearing glasses, and he looks nervous. He has hacker written all over him.

I go over to them, and we shake hands. The big man is Ron; the skinny guy is Fred Martin (he refuses to say whether this is his real name), and he's the one who writes the computer code that makes Ron's enterprise possible. The mood is very uptight, and neither of them makes much eye contact. Vacationers close by are talking about moisturizer and sunblock. Reggae Muzak is playing in the background. The waitress wants to know what we want to eat. Ron orders ribs; I go for marinated chicken.

I figure the best way to get acquainted with a hacker is to show some hardware, so I pull out my laptop computer, which uses a 14.4 kbps PCMCIA modem the size of a credit card. Yes, this breaks the ice. Fred eyes the modem covetously. "Have you opened it up yet?" he asks me in a soft, shy Canadian accent.

"He always opens things up," says Ron. He chuckles. "And sometimes he even puts them back together again."

Ron sounds like somebody's uncle, indulgent, fond of the slightly younger fellow sitting next to him. I imagine them doing a comedy routine, with Fred the Hacker saying something like, "Hey, Ron! I just got a great new idea for disassembling the code in a U–11 chip. It'll make us ten million bucks. Can I use the electron microscope? Can I?"

And Ron the Businessman says, "Not till you eat your greens, Fred."

The three of us make small talk, since this obviously isn't the place for an interview. After we finish eating, Ron pulls out his Motorola cellular phone. He murmurs something into it, then nods. "All right," he says to me, "I think you should see an actual setup. A dealer who fixes boards. Are you ready?"

The Code Distribution Network

They tell me to leave my car and travel with them. We follow a maze of back streets, through the shantytown and out the other side, into a middle-class suburban neighborhood. The lush landscape reminds me of canyons in Los Angeles, except that the tropical vegetation here is wilder and denser, and I see satellite dishes instead of swimming pools.

We pull into a concrete driveway where an open garage door spills light into the night. A fellow is waiting for us outside. He looks around thirty, short-haired, fit, clean-cut, with clear, penetrating eyes. For the purposes of this article, he asks me to call him Conchy Joe (the conch shell being a folksy national symbol here in the Bahamas).

His garage has been taken over by electronic equipment. Two black vinyl bar stools stand in front of a workbench where there's a monochrome television monitor, a satellite TV decoder, a control unit for the dish outside, an old Kenwood stereo, an MS-DOS computer with flying toasters on the screen, a soldering iron, an EPROM burner, and some items that I don't recognize. A washer and dryer stand close by. Circuit boards have been heaped on the bare concrete floor. Crickets are singing outside, and the warm night air ruffles the fronds on a nearby palm tree.

Fred homes in on the circuit boards and pulls one out for my inspection. "This is the original, the first release of the VC2," he says.

VC stands for VideoCipher, the scrambling protocol that General Instrument devised early in the 1980s using the Digital Encryption

Standard (DES) controlled by the federal government. GI has the exclusive license to use VideoCipher technology, which means it has total control of both the hardware and the software. This is the kind of market dominance that even Microsoft would envy.

I inspect the board and see that a wire has been added and a chip has been desoldered, allowing a socket to be put in its place. In the socket sits an EPROM chip—Erasable, Programmable Read-Only Memory. This is where Fred stores his program code, which takes control of the board and overrides its usual instructions.

"How easy was it to hack?" I ask him.

"The security processor is a Texas Instruments TMS 7001, which is an eight-bit chip, the same vintage as a 6502, which was the CPU of an old Apple][. If you know assembly language, you could learn TMS 7000 in about a day. Anybody can pick up a book on it."

These circuit boards can be modified by pirates to steal satellite video signals—at a price.
[Photo by the author.]

He takes another board from the stack. "Now, this is a more recent one. See, they poured epoxy on top of the components to make things a little more difficult for us."

"At first we tried to get it off with aircraft paint remover," Ron recalls. "We let it sit on the board overnight, and the next morning, half of the board was missing. But then someone came up with the bright idea of using a Black and Decker heat gun."

"Such as this," says Joe, holding up an item that looks like a hair dryer.

"If you use it right," says Fred, "you make the epoxy pliable without frying the components underneath, and then you just carve it away with an X-Acto knife."

He sounds as if he wants to do a demo, but I'm more interested in the way the boards are used than in the exact techniques for modifying them.

Codes and Countermeasures

Before I came to the Bahamas, I gave myself a crash course in satellite TV by downloading 300 KB of files from Ron MacDonald's bulletin board, which calls itself The Caribbean Connection.

Membership in this BBS usually costs $75 a year and is strictly controlled. If you're not part of the hacker underground, you'll have a hard time getting full access, though anyone can log on to look around.

The board is like a toolbox for safe crackers. It maintains a complete list of current codes for decrypting TV transmissions and has a huge library of software to reprogram EPROMs on chipped boards. if you can't find exactly what you need, friendly neighbors with online names such as John Buster, Barney Rubble, and John Conman will be happy to help you out. The board's slogan is "The

Pirates of the Caribbean have returned!" and it's so laid-back, you can almost forget the penalties—the five years in jail and the $500,000 fine. When you log off, though, your screen displays a little reminder:

BANG.....BANG.....BANG.....
Did you hear that!
Was that a knock on your door?

By sifting data and asking a lot of questions, I was able to map the structure and history of satellite TV. It runs like this:

A programming company such as HBO uplinks its signal to a satellite so that the satellite can rebroadcast the signal across the entire North American continent. Originally this setup was purely intended to serve local cable TV companies, which would receive the signal, pay for it, and distribute it to their cable subscribers. But in the early 1980s home users realized they could tap into the programming free of charge. They started buying their own dishes, paying up to $10,000 for a complete installation.

Ever since the earliest days of television these heartlanders had been poorly served with a handful of channels and unreliable, snowy reception. Now they suddenly had access to literally hundreds of choices, from movies to international sports events, and the picture quality was actually better than cable TV.

The free ride was too good to last. In January 1986 HBO, a Time Inc. subsidiary, started scrambling its signal, and one by one the other satellite programmers followed suit, using technology provided by General Instrument.

At first cable TV companies were the only ones who could buy decoders. Home users weren't allowed to own them at any price. Some months later, after their howls of fury finally penetrated the executive suites at HBO and Cinemax, VC2 decoders were offered for up to $700 apiece.

If you opened up the box and did a chip count, you found fewer components than in a home computer such as a Commodore 64; yet the price was three times as high. There was worse to come, though.

The decoder would do nothing unless it was given a wake-up call—a special authorization code that the TV programmer could send along with its regular signal. The code could be addressed to an individual box, because each box had a unique identification number stored in one of its chips.

How could a user receive this vital code? Simple: by paying a monthly subscription fee to the TV programming company. If you stopped paying, the programmer wouldn't send next month's authorization, your decoder would stop descrambling that channel, and you wouldn't be able to watch it anymore.

The people of the American heartland felt as if they had just been held up for ransom by a bunch of city slickers in New York and Los Angeles. And to complete this picture, HBO wanted to charge them a subscription fee that was actually higher than cable subscribers were paying! This was like taxation without representation, and even the slowest student of American history should have been able to foresee the consequences.

Six months after the VC2 was marketed, the first video pirates started circulating the first fix. According to an industry commentator quoted in *The Transponder*, a respected industry journal, a four-month survey showed that 95 percent of satellite TV dealers were ready and willing to sell illegally modified decoder boards, and 98 percent of them believed that their customers were ready to buy.

The first hack did not actually crack the code that encrypted the TV transmission. Instead, the pirates cloned hundreds of boards so that they all shared the same code number and would all respond to the same wake-up call, or authorization signal. This "all for one, one for all" system was nicknamed a "Three Musketeers fix." The disadvantage was that all the boards could be turned off just as easily as they could be turned on. As GI retaliated with ECMs (electronic countermeasures) and hardware revisions, the hackers resorted to increasingly complicated workarounds.

After three years of this battle, GI basically admitted defeat and introduced a totally new encryption system: the VC2 Plus. This was when they invited consumers to send back their old boards for a free Plus replacement. According to GI, the old VC2 encryption system was going to be phased out completely, and illegally modified VC2 decoders would no longer function.

It looked as if there would be no way out when the old VC2 signal was discontinued. And yet, mysteriously, the VC2 signal *wasn't* discontinued—at least not on many channels, and not for several years. For reasons that still remain a mystery, GI continued broadcasting VC2 authorizations to cable companies that were hanging on to their old decoders.

Suppose an employee at one of these sites could be persuaded to copy the "seed keys" from one of the decoders. These special code numbers could then be inserted in a home VC2 decoder, if you knew how; and after that, the decoder could process the authorization signals and decrypt them, yielding a number known in the trade as a "wizard code."

What did all this mean? It meant that the wizard code could be manually punched into *any* modified home VC2 box, and this would serve as a *substitute* for the authorization that GI wouldn't send to private VC2 owners anymore.

The pirates sold new software to the dealers, who used it to create EPROMs that would upgrade the decoder boards. The dealers then obtained the necessary wizard codes from someone such as Ron MacDonald and passed them on to the customers, who started keying the numbers in each month. Everyone was back online, happy again, although still mad as hell that the programmers had tried to hold them up for ransom.

But the war wasn't over. GI started switching things around so that new wizard codes weren't just needed once a month, they were needed almost every day. And they introduced a separate forty-four-digit number for each channel. Imagine a little old lady in Des Moines, peering at the numeric keypad through her bifocals, punching forty-four digits to decode each of fifty channels, every two days, just to watch TV. Obviously this wasn't going to work.

The pirates were undaunted. In 1992 an enterprising pair of guys named Jeff Carr and Jeff Mayes came up with a radical concept that they named VMS. This was a subassembly that could be mounted on an old VC2 board and would work like a modem, receiving wizard codes from a local dealership, by phone, automatically, as often as necessary. In this way the code numbers that people needed to decode TV transmissions could be distributed over regular telephone lines, and no one would have to do anything manually.

Jeff and Jeff (as they were known in the trade) supposedly used their VMS modification to set up an automated code-distribution system that would pass the "magic numbers" through a chain of dealers all linked by modems, spanning the entire continent. This was such a big hit that Ron MacDonald commissioned Fred Martin to reverse-engineer the product so that they could market their own version. Subsequently a lot of Ron's business came from wizard codes distributed via this system.

In 1993 Jeff and Jeff were raided by U.S. Customs agents, who hauled away many VMS business records. In response, the two Jeffs published a disclaimer in a trade magazine calmly stating that it was all an unfortunate mistake. Their VMS system had never been intended for signal theft (although they now realized, with great surprise, it could be used that way). VMS, they claimed, was not an acronym for Video Modem Service, as many people believed; it meant Video *Marketing* Service, and its purpose had been to distribute advertising messages to TV screens.

As a cover story, this was a bit hard to swallow. Ultimately Jeff Carr was convicted, fined $30,000, and imprisoned for forty months. From his jail cell in Ashland, Kentucky, he still claims that he never intended his system to be used illegally.

We're Only in It for the Money

In his garage, Conchy Joe turns to his TV monitor. "Let's suppose you want to watch a particular channel, and your authorization has run out. Here's all you have to do." He presses a single button, and I hear a cascade of tones. "The modem in my decoder is now dialing the local dealership."

There's a pause. From somewhere inside Joe's house, we hear a phone ringing. "Seems like the dealership is very close by," I say.

"Very, very close by," Joe agrees blandly. "But suppose you were a customer outside, calling in. You wouldn't know what number the modem had dialed, and so long as it's a local call, it wouldn't show up on your phone bill."

"This keeps the dealer secure," says Ron.

There's the hiss of a connection being made, and the monitor screen lights up with text. *Connected to Deep Thought*, it reads. *System operational.*

"Now the dealer's computer starts sending the updated wizard codes to the decoder here," says Joe.

Numbers on the screen begin counting bytes and packets.

"But where does your dealership get the codes?" I ask.

"From Ron's bulletin board," says Joe. He turns back to the screen. "See, this system also does billing."

I look at the message. *Send $35 for the next three months*, it reads. *Make checks payable to Ron or Joe.*

I look at him in surprise. "People pay you by check?"

Joe smiles. "You're in the Bahamas now."

"And all boards in Nassau use this system?"

"Not all," says Joe. "You can buy a legal, unmodified VC2 Plus decoder through an American dealer, who will subscribe on your behalf to the channels that you want, using a fake American name and address. Naturally, you have to reimburse him for the subscription fees, plus his service fee. But this is a violation of U.S. law, and if General Instrument finds out, they stop sending your Plus board authorization codes, and it's permanently dead."

"Permanently?" I ask.

Until now, the mood in the garage has been upbeat. Suddenly there's a silence. Everyone is uncomfortably aware that the VC2 Plus has not yet been successfully hacked, while more and more TV channels are switching to its new encryption protocol.

As of May 1994 only fifty stations out of literally hundreds were still using the old VC2 standard, including superstations and sports networks. But the numbers were dwindling as dish owners started realizing that the party was finally over. Many now paid $400 or more for a VC2 Plus and also subscribed to a package of channels for an additional $300 or $400 per year.

Joe drags another board out of the stack. "This is a VC2 Plus," he says.

Fred points to the largest component. "They put together five separate chips in that VLSI chip."

"That's the bugger that nobody can crack," says Ron. There's another thoughtful pause. "Actually," he says, "I will tell you that I've seen electron micrographs of that chip. Inside it, and also in the code that we found in it, there are the words *Team Bonsai*. We think that's what the guys who designed it call themselves. You see—" He seems to be thinking carefully, deciding how much to reveal. "We happen to have a VC2 Plus board, an 029, which is an early version, which we bought for $5,000. It came out the back door of General Instrument in Puerto Rico, prior to its security bit being set in the U–11 processor. That, of course, makes it vulnerable. Eventually we'll turn that unit on and work on it."

I ask why he hasn't done it already.

He laughs. "I'm waiting for somebody else to spend the money. I figure we've already spent $60,000 to $70,000 on small projects related to the Plus so far. It would take another $150,000 to crack it."

"You have to understand, we don't believe in doing everything ourselves," says Fred. "Why reinvent the wheel? If someone else has something and it's good, we go with it."

Is that what happened with the VMS system? Do they regularly steal from their competitors?

Ron sighs. "Jeff Carr was a member of my BBS. Over a period of two or three months, he kept telling me about the software he was writing, to download wizard codes. Eventually Jeff showed up in Canada with a working sample. The original selling price was $100,000, but then he decided it wasn't for sale, and he wanted to market it through my BBS. I agreed to this. The first software disks we sold for $5,000 each, and each decoder required a VMS modem attachment, which sold to dealers for $100. I was buying the software from Jeff for $2,500 and the VMS modems for sixty-five dollars. That represented a reasonable, healthy profit."

So what went wrong?

"They agreed not to sell to anybody else in Canada. I had the exclusive rights, and all orders would go through me. Three months later I found they were selling to somebody in Ontario. I complained about this, so Jeff said he would give me a seven-dollar commission on each Canadian sale. When he owed me $20,000 in commissions, and I hadn't seen a nickel, we reverse-engineered the board inside of six weeks." He shrugs. "I did what you'd expect a pirate to do."

"Basically," says Fred, "there are three kinds of people in this business. There are people who do no R and D at all and rip other people off. Like there'll be a guy who pays $1,000 for a program disk from us, makes three copies, and sells them to three friends for $500 each, and each of his friends sells a copy to three of his friends for $250 each, and so on, with each person making a profit. Then you've got another type of guy who looks for stuff on BBSs, downloads it, packs it up with documentation, and resells it for $2,000 to $3,000, whatever he can get, even though it's already available free. There are maybe two or three people doing that full time, and we know who they are. And then finally there's people like us, who actually do original work."

"You have to understand," says Ron, "everybody is in it for the almighty buck. Go to the street market in downtown Nassau, and for ten dollars they'll sell you wizard codes that have been downloaded off our own bulletin board."

So even the pirates are being pirated. In that case, shouldn't they try to protect their information more carefully?

"No." Fred sounds very decisive. "As soon as you start trying to restrict what people do with the information they get, you become the enemy."

"We don't want to become a policing force," Ron agrees. "That's the worst side of this industry."

How to Eliminate Video Piracy

The next day I receive instructions to go to a pizza parlor in a mini-mall. When I get there, the decor looks like Burger King, all red and yellow Formica. Outside the big windows, palm trees and white hotels stand against a brilliant blue sky.

Fred Martin comes wandering in, even less shaven than the day before, with his computer in a case hanging from his shoulder. He dons a dowdy black cotton jacket to ward off the air-conditioning.

He orders tea; I get myself an individual pizza. A large, deeply tanned, disapproving couple is sitting at the next table, wearing sunglasses. They stare in our direction as we drag out our two computers. I start typing notes on mine; Fred doesn't use his, but he seems to feel better having it open beside him.

I ask him how he got into the piracy business.

"I've known Ron for about ten years. He called me in to take a look at the very first VC2. Somebody had already done a lot of work on it. I did some debugging on a chip, fixed it up." He shrugs.

I ask him how the VC2 was cracked so quickly.

"It's no secret that information has been leaked from General Instrument. I have some myself, papers that say, *General Instrument,*

Sensitive Materials, Do Not Release. Now, how they came out of a high-security factory, I don't know."

It sounds as if he does know.

"Well," he says, "it would have been in the interests of GI to see that the VC2 was hacked as quickly as possible. They sold a lot more units once people could use them to get free programming."

Is he saying that the corporation knowingly released its own secrets after taking development money from broadcasters and promising them that the system couldn't be compromised?

He nods.

I ask if he personally resents the way that programmers market their product.

"Sure, it makes me mad. You pay thirty bucks a month, and what do you get? You're being overcharged and not getting enough in return."

If it cost less to buy programming, would his outlook really change?

"GI has said from day one that people pirate the signal because they don't want to pay for it. But everyone who's using a pirate modem in their VC2 board is now paying for it! The fact is, people *are* willing to pay, but only so much. If you want to eliminate video piracy, all you have to do is bring down the prices and let dealers sell the programming."

The New Orleans Sting Operation

Fred is thirty years old and has lived most of his life in his native Canada. He's happy to be in the Bahamas now, because he loves hot weather. I get the impression that although he seems shy and soft-spoken, he has a tough, unyielding personality. Often in a conversation he refuses to let go of a topic until it's been thoroughly examined to his satisfaction. And when he digresses and mentions his love of bicycle riding, it quickly becomes clear that he's the sort of militant rider who kicks cars if they cut in on him.

I ask if, as a lawbreaker, he ever gets scared. He starts telling me about the big bust of 1993, in which General Instrument set up a sting operation through U.S. Customs, luring a number of hackers (including Jeff Carr) to New Orleans, where they thought they were going to purchase the elusive fix for the VC2 Plus. The customs agent, who called himself Richard Collins (his real name was Richard Coleman), almost persuaded Fred to join the party.

"Originally," Fred recalls, "he got in touch with us by ordering our products, as if he was a dealer. Then one day he left a message on the BBS saying he had a friend in Arkansas who had developed a Plus fix and would only sell it through Collins.

"It seemed odd to me that he'd been an amateur, and suddenly he was a kingpin. There's a lot of scams that go around, and I've seen people who take a board, solder some wires, and say, 'Look at my fix. For only $100,000 you can have this.' So I figured this guy was bullshit. But I try to keep my mind open, so I went and met him in a shopping mall in Buffalo, New York.

"He wore cowboy boots, blue jeans, a white shirt. He was in his mid-thirties, clean-shaven, average weight. What sticks in my mind, though, is that he was really paranoid. He kept asking where we were going and exactly what would happen. Well, we went and talked in a restaurant in the shopping mall. I seem to recall I had a fruit cup. They didn't sell fruit cups, but I got them to make me one.

"Anyway, Richard said he had the modules in a briefcase in his car trunk, so we went and visited a dealer I knew nearby and borrowed his shop for a couple of minutes.

"The boards were regular Plus boards, except the big chip had soft brown epoxy all over it. I was given a demonstration which convinced me that the codes in the original board had been cloned. So he asked me if I was interested in buying it. He said a few select people were being invited to New Orleans, and they should bring $50,000 each, and they'd each walk away with the Plus fix."

And was Fred really tempted to go?

"The guy was convincing. He got me hyped up. Sure, I wanted to go! But then we started getting calls from little guys, out in the boondocks, who knew nothing or less, and they had been approached with the same kind of line. Ron said something smelled fishy about it, so we stayed home."

Others weren't so cautious, and in September 1993 they fell into the trap. The headline in *Satellite Business News* announced, "Customs Sting Nabs Hackers." According to the article, "Satellite signal pirates took a major blow this month with the arrest of at least six key underground players. . . . The project culminated Sept. 7 during meetings in Kenner, LA, near New Orleans, where agents demonstrated 'modified' VideoCipher II Plus decoders prepared by General Instrument Corp.'s (GI) VideoCipher Division. Customs is believed to have videotaped the meeting. As a result of the investigation and subsequent raids, federal agents seized key computers feeding wizard codes to chipped VideoCipher modules, leaving thousands of owners of modified units unable to steal programming. The operation sent shock waves through the hacker underground."

But according to Fred, this wasn't the most interesting aspect of the story. Two of the people arrested were Jeff Carr and Jeff Mayes, originators of the VMS modem system. While reverse-engineering the VMS system to develop his own version of it for Ron, Fred had found a "back door" in its program code. In other words, if someone knew a secret password, that person could dial into any dealer's VMS code-distribution system without being detected. Moreover, because all the dealers' systems were linked together so that codes could be passed along automatically by modem, the intruder would be able to step through the entire dealer chain from top to bottom, gathering every dealer's name and every customer's phone number along the way.

To Fred it looked as if Jeff and Jeff had written themselves an insurance policy. If they were ever arrested, they could plea-bargain by offering to hand over the back-door password that would unlock their entire system.

But there was another implication that was even more mind-boggling. As Fred put it: "GI can now pull ECMs on modems." In other words, if Jeff Carr told the authorities how to get access to the VMS code distribution network, and this information was passed along to General Instrument, GI could hack into it themselves and sabotage the pirates' program code. So far as anyone knows, this never actually happened; but it was a fascinating concept. The programmers had built a network for TV distribution that was vulnerable to hackers. In response, the hackers had built their own network for illicit code distribution—which was now vulnerable to countermeasures by the TV programmers.

Meanwhile, somewhere in this war of hack and counterhack, bewildered consumers were getting tired of the whole game. They just wanted to watch TV.

Friends in High Places

After an hour or so, Ron MacDonald and Conchy Joe join us at the pizza parlor. Ron has his laptop with him, so now our red Formica table has three computers on it. "I want to show you something," says Ron. He goes into Norton Commander, which he uses to maintain a simple database. "See here, this list of names and addresses. This is, uh, the kind of list that a satellite TV dealership might have." He points at names scrolling up the screen.

The display stops, seemingly at random, at a man named Ford. His title is U.S. Ambassador to the Bahamas.

"It's fairly common knowledge where his house is," says Joe. "I can tell you how to find it. You might want to stop by and look at his dish. You see, everyone in Nassau is breaking U.S. law. I even know some DEA agents down here who have chipped boards. It's accepted. There's nothing to it."

Ron closes his computer. "Now," he says, "were there some other questions that you wanted to ask me?"

I tell him I want to know how he got started in the business.

"I was renting out videos back in the early 1980s when I realized that I could tape HBO from satellite broadcasts and rent copies of the tapes to my customers. My customers loved them, because the titles weren't available on video in Canada. Then I started selling satellite TV systems. But in 1986, when HBO started scrambling their signal, I was driven out of business. I had dozens of customers for whom I was in the process of doing site checks and dish installations, and I lost all of those sales because HBO was no longer available."

After that, Ron went on the road for a while as a salesman for auto parts. But he maintained his interest in satellite TV, and a year or so later, at an industry convention, he found someone who had the first VC2 fix. "I came back on the plane with it," Ron recalls. "It was a partnership investment that I made in collaboration with another Canadian. The only problem was, we couldn't get enough of the decoder modules to modify. The distributors were gouging the satellite retailer on pricing. So we went directly to the United States, bought 200 or 300 pieces at a time for $339 each, drove them back to Canada, cleared them through customs legally, chipped some, and sold the rest.

"Then a dealer who had the VC2 fix, who we were dealing with, screwed us out of $58,000 and ended up in trouble, closing down his business. I made an offer to his three employees and formed another organization called the Blues Brothers. Around that time, GI introduced the 018 board. No one had a fix for it, and nobody could pull seed keys and write software for it. Through the efforts of my new team, we extracted seed keys and started selling them through the United States and the Caribbean, and eventually sold seed key pullers. We accidentally released the first set of seed keys to one Canadian and one U.S. guy; within twenty-four hours, they were sold throughout North America and Canada and the Caribbean, and we lost $500,000 on that. That was the famous set of seed keys, 97FA, and after that we realized that pirates will pirate pirated software from other pirates, any time of the day or night. It's the nature of the industry."

Even government officials seem unable to resist the lure of gray-market CNN. A satellite dish (circled) lurks behind the home of the U.S. Ambassador to the Bahamas. [Photo by the author.]

But he seems to set himself apart from the worst type of dog-eat-dog mentality.

"It's ultimately self-defeating," says Fred. "People trust us today, more than anyone else in the business, because they know we don't bullshit."

Is there a truly positive aspect of video piracy?

"Absolutely," says Ron. "If it wasn't for piracy, the price of programming would not be as low. We have forced programmers to compete with the cost of chipping the VideoCipher."

"And when you consider that reasonable pricing was all we asked for at the start," says Fred, "we had to go through a lot of shit to get it."

"You also have to remember," Ron goes on, "other organizations are just as much involved in this. All along the border between the U.S. and Canada, small cable companies grab Canadian signals and put them on their systems, and vice versa. And then you have Can Com. Can Com was stealing Detroit TV, uplinking to a satellite, then sending it out to snowbound towns in northern Canada and charging them an arm and a leg."

I ask Ron if video piracy involves any weapons or threats of violence.

"I know of two suicides caused by the FBI raiding small satellite dealers who chipped boxes," he says. "But no other violent acts."

"I met one guy who claimed to be well connected with the Mafia," Fred puts in. "But I've never had anyone stick a gun in my face or threaten me."

I tell Ron and Fred that when I get back home, I'm planning to call General Instrument for their side of the story. Are there any questions I should ask?

Ron smiles. "I'd like to know about the rumor that GI paid John Grayson $3 million for his version of a Plus fix. You know, Grayson definitely owns the capability. He did all the necessary background work."

"I saw it," Fred agrees. "There was a strong indication he was planning to release it in March 1994—and then it just didn't happen."

Who is this Grayson?

"He built his own proprietary implementation of the VC2 decoder several years ago, to compete with GI. It was a completely different, legal board. He was in the midst of negotiating to set up his own authorization network and uplinks when GI organized a raid on his business. They went after him for copyright and patent infringements, although I'm not even sure the product is patented in Canada."

"After two years of trying to follow the case through the courts," says Ron, "I lost track. The point is, Grayson has marketed no product for the last two years—yet an engineer who works for him just bought a new helicopter."

(Subsequently, my attempts to verify this story with Grayson have been unsuccessful. He seems to have left the United States, and pirate sources claim to have no idea where he's gone. The story remains just another unconfirmed rumor in a field where rumors are common currency.)

I ask Ron whether, if he had a Plus fix himself, he would be tempted to sell it to GI, assuming GI was willing to negotiate.

He's quiet for a moment, and I imagine he's weighing up the money that would be involved. Then he shakes his head. "No," he says. "If I had a Plus fix, I'd have more fun and I'd make more money by marketing it than by selling it back to those pompous pigs at GI."

Chipping for Fun and Profit

If and when someone does market a Plus fix, TV dealers will find out about it easily enough. All they'll need to do is open up their monthly copy of *Satellite Watch News*.

SWN is a living tribute to unfettered capitalism. With unabashed pleasure it has informed dealers of every new opportunity for signal theft, and it has even lab-tested some of the illegal products that it advertises in its own back pages. These ads have been even more outrageous than the editorial content, offering VC2 fixes via mail order and instructional videos to take the neophyte step by step into the black art of chipping boxes in the privacy of his own basement workshop.

Ron MacDonald has advertised in *SWN*, and I made my initial contact with him simply by dialing the number listed in his ad. Other suppliers have been equally accessible, although they prefer not to talk about their products over the phone. As Ron said when I first called, "You already know what we sell, and you know what it does, so we don't need to go into that."

Getting the products into the United States is tricky, since importing them carries that same maximum penalty of $500,000 and/or a five-year jail term. In some cases products have been smuggled in via Indian reservations. For obvious reasons, no one wants to discuss the details.

The publisher of *SWN* is Dan Morgan, a former subscriber who purchased the magazine in January 1994. Unfortunately for Morgan, after the New Orleans sting advertisers backed off. He seems unconcerned, however. "The advertising has dropped," he says, "but I foresee, in the near future, a revolution in the pirate industry. You would be amazed if you could see the work that's going on in laboratories right now."

Morgan is a Vietnam veteran, a gun-owning, liberty-loving heartland American who is deeply disturbed by trends toward greater government control and regulation. He believes in free access to the airwaves and is outraged that in thirty states local laws make it a crime to own descrambling equipment even if you never actually use it. "I think you should be able to possess any damn thing you want, so long as you don't hurt people," he says.

He describes himself as an R and D engineer, and he says that his company, Morgan Engineering, designs electronic devices. Does that include VC2 modifications?

"I just report on the industry," he says carefully. "It would be foolish for me to get involved in any way. But I will say that it's people like them [video pirates] who make the world a great place."

Does this mean he endorses piracy?

"I'm in a position where I cannot say that piracy is okay. However, I believe in the Constitution of the United States very strongly, and I think that officials in the industry are losing contact with the Constitution. . . . They've come down harder on dealers than they have on cocaine addicts."

Psychological Warfare

The man who could take most of the credit for this crackdown is Jim Shelton, former vice president of consumer sales at General Instrument. Shelton, forty-two, is a deceptively mild-mannered, amiable, laconic Southerner who learned about cryptography when he worked on top-secret communications in the U.S. Air Force.

When Shelton took his job at GI, he felt that the company was mishandling the piracy problem. They were dealing with it, he recalls, "as British soldiers dealt with the Indians. They were very staunch and proper, while they got slaughtered. Myself, I deal with them on their own level."

Shelton has now left GI, but while he was there he was an avid reader of pirate magazines such as *SWN* and sent undercover agents to infiltrate the pirate community. He practiced psychological warfare, timing his ECMs to have maximum effect. He released one during a trade show where pirates were known to gather, forcing them to abandon their meetings, rebook their air tickets, and go running back to Canada to cope with floods of phone calls from dealers whose chipped boards didn't work anymore. Another time, Shelton waited to kill TV reception till the coldest day of winter, figuring that consumers depend most heavily on their TV when they're snowed in. "Have you ever had cabin fever?" He chuckles happily. "You get to know your family *real* well."

He seems to enjoy reminiscing about his cat-and-mouse games, but when I suggest there's a humorous side to it, he quickly reverts to a corporate tone. "It's no more amusing," he says, "than people who don't pay their bills."

I ask if the name Ron MacDonald means anything to him.

"Oh, yes. He's a big-time pirate. He's made a lot of money. I met him at a trade show one time. When I started doing some back-ground checks, I found out he was one of the kingpins involved in piracy. . . . I was very disappointed he didn't come to Louisiana [for the New Orleans sting operation]."

Is Shelton aware of the rumor that General Instrument released its own encryption secrets to boost the demand for decoders?

"I can find no evidence of that activity," he says. "And once security was broken, aggressive countermeasures were taken, followed by the realization that a complete rework was needed, with the focus on the consumer market." He adds, "Our initial purpose for encryption was not for the home market, but to secure the cable market using commercial decoders." In other words, if GI had known that there would be such a huge consumer demand, they might have made the VC2 more secure.

Does Shelton have any sympathy for the concept that the airwaves are a public resource to which everyone should have free access?

"We grew up with broadcast signals that were advertiser-supported. Then cable came along, and people said, 'You mean, I got to pay for the programming? That's not right!' But people are now starting to understand that HBO will show better-quality movies, and in greater quantity, because part of the money goes back to the studios for production.

"You're always going to have theft," he goes on, "just as department stores have theft. But to what degree? At one point it was calculated that eighty percent [of satellite TV dealers] were involved. It was a matter of getting it under control. You know, Turner Classic Movies was launched thanks to the direct-to-home market, because there are now 1.7 million authorized decoders receiving satellite TV. So the market base is there, and we are going to have better-quality programming."

This sounds reasonable. Yet Shelton's smooth, amiable manner distracts from the darker implications of his work. GI has been accused by many satellite TV dealers of hiring ex-FBI agents who are paid on a commission basis to entrap dealers, subjecting them to penalties that seem cruelly severe compared with their crime. John Norris, whose title is manager of special projects at GI's

Access Control Center, has had a hands-on involvement in this legal process. While Shelton is there, Norris describes himself as "Jim Shelton's trigger man."

"I've testified recently at trials where guys got ten months in prison," he says calmly, unemotionally. "In Great Falls, Montana, a guy got thirty-seven months in prison. All these guys were thumbing their noses at the system, and now the system is coming back and whacking them."

He's helped to achieve more than 100 convictions. Does this give him any mixed feelings?

"I don't feel good or bad about it," he says. "It's up to the justice system to decide what they deserve. I merely provide help gathering and presenting evidence. And I will sit down and drink with any people who have been arrested through my testimony, and they'll say I acted like a gentleman. Many of them respect what I've done, because I didn't take it personally; I dealt with them in a proper way."

Norris sees piracy in very simple terms: "It's not so different from a movie theater. Some kid opens a side door and lets people come in—and as a result, the theater may go out of business."

So Norris protects the business by rounding up the kids and putting them behind bars.

It's Only Television, Right?

A few weeks later I make contact with one of John Norris's victims. He currently participates on Ron MacDonald's bulletin board under a fake identity, but he's so nervous, he refuses to use even this name during our telephone conversation. He refers to himself simply as Dave.

"There was a knock on my door," he recalls, "and I looked out and saw all these guys with bright orange letters on their dark blue windbreakers. FBI, Customs, police. There were guys at the front door, the back door, the sides of the house. They were in the carport—it was like I was Charlie Manson. They scared the shit out of my wife and kids. They searched every room, and they took photographs when they came in and when they left, so I couldn't claim they tore the place up. They took everything, all my guns, my cash, my records, my UPS shipping book. It was unbelievable."

Dave is certain that he was caught because another pirate betrayed him. "There's no honor among thieves in this business. Under the federal system of determinate sentencing, if you've done a crime over a certain amount of money, you get a lot of points against you, but you can work those points off by pleading guilty or by cooperating. Somebody cooperated and gave the Man my name, and I got hit, and I'm not proud to say it, but I ended up cooperating, too, so I wouldn't have to go to prison. I gave them my customer list. I don't know what happened. They never called me to testify against the people I named."

Dave lost just about everything he owned. "My house is up for sale, they took all the cash I had, and my new pickup truck—it's called civil seizure. Anything they figure that I bought with money from the pirate business, they can take away."

Like many people in the business of chipping boards, Dave served in the armed forces and is largely self-educated in electronics. "I didn't graduate from high school. I went through the military, I was overseas, I got some training in cryptography and some radio stuff, and in 1986 I realized, Hell, *this is not that hard to do*. And I wasn't hurting anybody. And the money was good. I'd say I made close to a quarter of a million in the first three years. I've been to Okinawa, I've been to Le Havre, to London—we took trips you wouldn't believe, based on the money from this. It was big money, and it was easy money."

He's now partway through five years of probation. If he gets caught again during that period, he'll serve jail time not just for the new charges but for the old ones as well.

Even so, he says, "I'm still involved with the business, because it's the only way I know how to make a living."

Like many others, Dave was invited to New Orleans. Fortunately for him, he didn't believe the Plus fix was real, so he chose not to go. "If I had," he says, "I'd be in prison right now."

Dave was personally acquainted with the man in Montana whom John Norris helped to put in jail. "He's an Indian, he was operating out of a reservation, so he figured he was safe. But he had the FBI there, and Customs, and the Bureau of Indian Affairs, and now he's doing thirty-seven months in prison. I mean, *prison*, for over three years! It's only television, right? I don't think it should be such a serious crime. We've got drug dealers out there, gangs, but for some reason the government thinks this is more important than going after the Crips and Bloods and Black Muslims and everybody else. Seems to me GI must have undue influence over the government."

For Dave, it's partly an issue of freedom. "I feel there's constitutional issues. I think the airwaves are free, and I have a right to see what's out there. I should have the right to own guns, too. I had a collection, from muskets to old Winchesters, I had a Mauser, a Walther PPK, and they took everything. One of the agents went in there when they were doing their search, and he said, 'What are you, trying to start an uprising?' It's none of his business. If I like guns, the Constitution says I have the right to own them, and it doesn't say I can only have just one. I'm not a vigilante, I'm not crazy. I'm not an off-the-wall guy, but I feel I have certain rights. And if I want to watch television and I figure out a way to watch it, I don't think I should be a felon."

Does he think that satellite TV piracy still has a future?

"Among the end users, there's maybe ten percent who are diehards and won't go legal no matter what. The rest are waffling. Some of them have bought the VC2 Plus from me, because I can sell that legally. I pick up maybe forty dollars a board profit, not very much. They'll use that for their Playboy channel or HBO, and then they'll still use their old modified VC2 board for the other channels it can get, so they don't have to pay $200 a year for that programming."

And so, cautiously, Dave continues to eke out a living, aided by Ron MacDonald's code distribution system.

"Ron has promised me that he's got my name, and all the subscribers to his bulletin board, locked in a bank vault in the Bahamas. I've got a lot of faith in this guy, but if he ever sells off that list, you can probably say goodbye to piracy—unless somebody comes up with a crack on the Plus."

Would that really make a difference?

"Oh, yeah. If you pop the Plus, it'll start all over again. I would be willing to move anywhere and start a new business under a different name, change my fingerprints, whatever it takes. I would make a million dollars in thirty days, then relocate to Australia or somewhere."

Surely it wouldn't be that easy.

"Yes, it would. Here's how it goes. I walk into a customer's house and I've got me a busted Plus. I plug it in and tell them, you watch it for a week, and I'll come back, and if it's still working, you buy it from me for $700. Believe me, they'll buy. I could drive across this country with a van full of boards, and I could stop at every satellite dish, and every place I stop, I could make a sale. I guarantee it."

But General Instrument claims there are ECMs inside the Plus just waiting to be set off.

"I don't know that I believe that. See, they can't change the access keys so often, because there are so damned many boards out there. Only 200,000 VC2 boards were ever authorized, so they can change the code every three days. But they got damn near two million Plus boards, and they can't change it every three days, because they can't process the keys fast enough."

If Dave is correct, the Plus is a disaster waiting to happen, and as the installed base keeps growing, the temptation to exploit it becomes greater. It seems inevitable that sooner or later, someone somewhere will hack this board.

The only thing that might prevent it is if General Instrument can introduce yet another new encryption technology.

And this is exactly what the company plans to do.

Not-So-Smart Cards

MPEG is a system for digitizing a video signal and removing redundant data. When a video picture is stored or transmitted, MPEG can squeeze it by a ratio of 10:1. Theoretically, this means that ten times as many channels can be broadcast from the same number of satellites.

Some programmers are already considering digitized uplinks, although this would potentially exclude the home dish owner, who has no way to process an MPEG-coded signal in order to view it.

To address this imminent situation, GI has proposed DigiCipher, an MPEG-compatible system that could be used to scramble the digitally compressed TV signal at every point in the distribution system— not only in satellite TV, but inside cable networks as well. Since GI would retain exclusive control over DigiCipher technology, the corporation would acquire the sole right to build or license the manufacture of DigiCipher decoders for sale to every satellite TV subscriber *and* every cable TV viewer in every city in America. More than thirty million consumers would be forced to buy the GI product, which would have no competitors, ever.

Even legitimate businesses in the industry seem to feel uneasy about this expansion of the GI monopoly. In fact, out of all the people I spoke to while researching this book, no one had a kind word to say about General Instrument Corporation—not even the TV programmers. When I asked the publisher of a conservative trade journal if he thought it was conceivable that GI could have paid John Grayson

$3 million not to release his fix for the VC2 Plus, the publisher wasn't sure whether Grayson would have accepted such a deal, but he didn't doubt that GI could have made the offer. Rightly or wrongly, GI is perceived as a company that has cut more than a few corners in order to achieve a position of total market dominance.

In the meantime, while DigiCipher is nothing more than a promise or a threat, GI is test-marketing a decoder that provides additional security using the existing VC2 Plus format. Named the VC2 Plus R/S, it allows "renewable security" via a permanent telephone line connection and a "smart card" that is inserted by the user. If the card isn't valid, the unit won't work; and the unit can be tested over the phone at any time.

This may seem like antihacker overkill—yet even so, the pirates are unimpressed. Smart cards have already been used in European satellite TV decoders, and hackers over there have already defeated them. According to John McCormack, a veteran observer of the European scene who was interviewed in an underground publication titled *Scrambling News*, one way the card has been beaten is by making counterfeit copies with the addressing and turn-off routines removed. McCormack says this is known as the Ho Lee Fook hack— not because it's Asian, but because its name "conveys the sense of dismay" that TV executives feel when they first learn about it.

Another strategy (which McCormack modestly lists as The McCormack Hack) involves "lifting a live data stream from inside a decoder and using it to activate other decoders in the area." In other words, the validation code is taken off the circuit board and broadcast via a small radio transmitter to other decoders that have been fitted with miniature receivers. The signal will be virtually impossible to detect, since it will last for only a few milliseconds.

As for DigiCipher, if it is ever introduced, even this may be vulnerable, since it too resembles schemes that have been hacked in Europe. Moreover, if GI's dream comes true and DigiCipher is used in every cable network in America, video pirates will be motivated to spend almost any amount of time and money to crack it. Thirty million viewers feeling mad as hell about being overcharged and exploited, and all of them using the same system . . . it's a lure that no pirate could resist.

In the same way that a monoculture is more vulnerable to pests than a diverse ecology, a single encryption standard would be far more vulnerable to piracy than the mosaic of different schemes being used in cable networks today. "In a way, we're hoping that GI goes with DigiCipher," Ron MacDonald says cheerfully. "It will renew the pirate underground."

Legalized Signal Theft

In Europe, most countries have no laws against descrambling TV signals that originate outside national borders. Consequently there's no way for law enforcement to crack down on piracy. In the United States, video piracy is illegal—or is it?

Pirates like to quote the 1934 Communications Act, which banned the use of jamming or scrambling equipment and guaranteed the right of all Americans to receive any form of radio transmission. There was an important underlying principle behind this legislation: The radio spectrum is a limited resource, like air or sunlight, and everyone should have equal access to it.

In 1984, however, the Cable Communications Policy Act changed all that. Nudged by lobbyists from programmers such as HBO, Congress decided to make satellite TV transmissions a special case, exempt from public access.

The act begins, "No person receiving, assisting in receiving, transmitting, or assisting in transmitting, any interstate or foreign communication by wire or radio shall divulge or publish the existence, contents, substance, purport, effect, or meaning thereof."

This reads like an attempt to protect the privacy of communications that are addressed to specific individuals. How can it apply to TV broadcasts? Well, the next section of the act suggests that "satellite cable programming" isn't really broadcasting. It's a private communication, and if the signal is encrypted, the act protects it from interference.

But that's an odd phrase, "satellite cable programming." Why has the word *cable* been put there?

The phrase is defined a little further on as "video programming which is transmitted via satellite and which is primarily intended for the direct receipt by cable operators for their retransmission to cable subscribers."

So the intent is now clear. Satellite TV is considered a private communication because it is "primarily intended" for cable companies, not for broadcast to the general public.

Unfortunately, in the years since this act became law, the situation has changed radically. Can HBO still claim that their signal is a form of private communication (please, don't call it broadcasting!) when there are hundreds of thousands of individual dish owners now paying to receive it? Can Turner Classic Movies be considered "satellite cable programming" when it is being sent *only* to home dish owners and not to cable networks at all?

The Will of the People

Satellite TV sounds like a dull little backwater, far from the cutting edge of personal communications; yet its quirky history offers lessons that are painfully relevant to our immediate future.

Lesson #1: Grass-roots opposition becomes a formidable force when it uses computer technology.

Backlash against scrambled satellite TV astonished companies such as GI and HBO, who thought they had everything under control after some help from friendly congressional lawmakers. They grossly misjudged the resourcefulness of everyday people in the American heartland who were hypersensitive about their liberties, unimpressed by laws serving special interests, and well equipped to fight back using consumer electronics.

Lesson #2: There ain't no such thing as secure data.

The DES algorithm is mathematically impregnable and has never been broken, even now, by any of the pirates. That doesn't mean that if you use it to scramble a signal, the signal is safe. Sooner or later, if anyone is going to be able to use the signal, it has to be decoded. At that precise moment it becomes vulnerable. The decoding device can be cloned, or its decryption keys can be copied, or the signal can be tapped and retransmitted.

Lesson #3: Encryption protects little guys better than big guys.

When a scrambled TV signal is sent to millions of decoder modules, it becomes a tempting target, and dozens or even hundreds of people can collaborate on ways to steal it. By contrast, when two individuals exchange a brief encrypted message, it attracts virtually no attention. Video pirates have started test-running PGP (Pretty Good Privacy, the "people's encryption software") to protect private messages they exchange via their bulletin boards. This doesn't just put the pirates on equal terms with the programmers; it gives them an edge.

Lesson #4: Computers really do empower the individual.

We've heard this so many times, but now we're starting to see the results. For ten years a handful of video hackers battled some huge, cash-rich corporations—and the corporations still haven't won. In an information economy, a powerful institution can be thwarted and maybe even ruined by a few smart, ornery people owning microcomputers.

Lesson #5: Protecting your data may cost more than letting people steal it.

Encrypting satellite TV required a huge capital investment, while millions more went into unsuccessful attempts to defeat piracy. Public money has been wasted on elaborate police operations to trap hackers, and more money is now being spent to keep some of them behind bars. Lives have been ruined, lasting resentment has been created in rural communities, and respect for government and the law has been eroded—all because HBO didn't want freeloaders tapping into its data stream. Remember, dish owners were never the primary market. The TV programmers could have ignored them and still made a good profit from cable redistribution.

There's an analogy here with copy protection of floppy disks. For years software publishers wasted countless man-hours devising byzantine protection schemes while hackers wasted an equal amount of time cracking them. Bit-nibbler software was marketed for anyone who wanted a bootleg copy of dBASE or Lotus 1-2-3. Meanwhile, legitimate consumers were maddened by disks that couldn't be backed up and programs that didn't run properly on hard drives.

In the end, the software publishers gave in and abandoned copy protection. None of them went out of business as a result. As Fred Martin points out, many consumers are willing to pay for the legitimate product when the price is reasonable, especially if they reap extra benefits such as proper documentation and technical support.

But this compliance *cannot* be achieved by threats. For most people, theft of data is in no way a moral issue; it doesn't create even a twinge of guilt. Consumers today are unimpressed by the legalities of copyright or the potential penalties involved.

Bearing this in mind, which is the better policy? To make concessions to consumers, or to clamp down and try to force them to obey?

The history of copy protection proves that concessions can be workable. The history of satellite video piracy indicates that clamping down leads to draconian law enforcement, huge unforeseen expenditures, and a flourishing black market patronized by everyday, law-abiding Americans.

Signal Theft: The Second Wave

By the end of 1995, the video piracy business was in the doldrums. Some diehards were still punching in code numbers or downloading them from their local dealers, but more and more stations were switching over to VC2 Plus encryption—and despite dozens of hopeful rumors in *Satellite Watch News*, the Plus never was cracked. As a result, hundreds of thousands of consumers gave up waiting, paid their money, and purchased legal VC2 Plus decoders.

Meanwhile, RCA's Direct Broadcast System (DBS) has been introduced, sending digitized signals to a small dish that is easier to install, since it is not steerable and remains pointed at just one satellite. In Mexico, Canada, and the Caribbean, DBS seemed a great new way to get American programming—except that copyright restrictions still made this illegal. Worse still, every DBS decoder had to be wired into the phone system so that it could autodial an 800 number and receive automatic updates for its decryption system. Since 800 numbers aren't accessible from outside America, this created a problem.

Naturally, pirates moved quickly to find a solution. Ron MacDonald now offers a gadget that sits between the decoder and the phone jack. When the decoder starts autodialing its 800 number, the pirate equipment quickly intercepts it and keeps the line open while it dials a different number located in the United States. There, a computer receives the call and redials the original 800 number, to link the DBS decoder outside America with its U.S. source for code updates.

Naturally there's a charge for this service, but it does enable people outside the United States to receive DBS. Of course, they still have to pay for the programming via dummy addresses on the mainland.

That need to pay may not last much longer, though. Ron MacDonald now claims that the DBS system has been cracked. "We estimate that the new fix could generate millions for the pirates," he says. "A consumer may pay between $500 and $700 to modify his RCA decoder. There'll be a time stamp in the modification, because it will receive all the regularly scheduled programs plus all the pay-per-view movies, which are worth two dollars and ninety-nine cents each. So the fix will be worth a lot of money, and the consumer will need to make additional payments to renew it periodically, maybe every year or two."

John McCormack, editor of *Hack Watch News,* has posted additional details on his Web page, noting that a key component of the American DBS system is a "smart card" that's very similar to cards used in Europe. Through some bizarre error, the precise function of this card is on public record at the Patent Office. "You have got to wonder," says McCormack, "at the kind of mind that would put a patent number on a smart card. It is just like telling a burglar what kind of lock your door uses."

The European cards were quickly hacked, and in fact the source code for this hack was distributed over the Internet—much to the disgust of pirates, who were deprived of a chance to control it and charge money for it. Consequently, according to McCormack, the slightly different U.S. system is being cracked in a way that is more difficult and therefore less easy to imitate. Also, the fix will include its own protection routines to prevent the pirate program from being pirated. So it now looks as if video piracy is ready to renew itself. And this time, technically at least, it could be legal.

DBS is transmitted directly to consumers, not to cable networks, which means that it cannot be covered by the Cable Communications Policy Act. And broadcast signals, by definition, cannot be owned.

Of course, there's a big gap between the law in theory and the law in practice. Several events must occur before the legality of DBS piracy can be challenged. First, a pirate must be arrested and charged. Second, a judge must permit testimony about the 1934 Communications Act—which has been disallowed in some previous cases. Third, a jury must be willing to believe that a huge corporation such as HBO is actually unprotected by the law, while signal theft by pirates such as Ron MacDonald is perfectly legitimate.

Obviously, no video pirate is going to go looking for that kind of test case. Video pirates will probably continue on the same basis as before, operating furtively from outside the United States and hiding from the authorities, even though, technically speaking, they are now legitimate businessmen.

The Limits of the Law

Whole books have been written on federal laws relating to computer crime. (*Netlaw* by Lance Rose and *Cyberspace and the Law* by Edward Cavazos and Gavino Morin are two good examples.) It's a complex area that's still evolving, creating confusion along the way.

When the Secret Service seized Steve Jackson's computers during Operation Sundevil, they seemed genuinely unaware that they were violating the Electronic Communications Privacy Act, which protects e-mail on hard drives. This was a major blunder that caused severe embarrassment when the agency was forced to pay substantial damages. No branch of federal law enforcement wanted to fall into that kind of trap again, especially in such a highly publicized operation.

Clearly the government needed a computer expert who could establish safe guidelines and give advice to federal prosecutors before they tackled technical cases involving computer crime. Ideally, this expert would also serve as a legal consultant whenever congress started drafting new computer legislation.

The Department of Justice eventually found a man who could perform all these functions. His name is Scott Charney, and he's the government's leading authority on computer crime.

The first time I saw Charney, he was on a panel debating Net freedoms at the 1994 Computers, Freedom, and Privacy conference in San Francisco. He looked diffident and nerdy, a slim, bearded man with thinning hair, slouching in his chair at one end of the table, literally keeping a low profile. He didn't say much, and when he did speak he was an amiable diplomat, stressing topics that the audience wanted to hear, such as the importance of protecting our constitutional freedoms. Yes, he worked for the Department of Justice—but he made it sound as benign as Mr. Rogers' neighborhood.

Scott Charney of the Department of Justice plays a vital role in the evolution of net laws and advises federal prosecutors on strategies to combat computer crime. [Photo courtesy of the Department of Justice.]

Just before the panel ended, something happened that modified that image. A flamboyant character in motorcycle leathers and shoulder-length red hair stepped up to the microphone in the audience. His name was Dan Farmer, and he had just lost his job at Silicon Graphics for releasing and promoting SATAN, a cracking program that was designed to break into Unix systems in order to test their security.

Dan Farmer named his cracking software SATAN and gave it away online. Security experts were outraged.

Farmer had designed the program with the best of intentions, but there was no doubt it could also be used as a tool by criminals.

He gave Scott Charney a wicked grin and asked a playful question. Suppose someone just happened to start giving away a program of this kind, and suppose people started using it to crack systems across the nation. Would the author of the program be an accessory to the crimes?

Charney leaned forward, looking suddenly serious. "Unauthorized intrusion," he said, "is not a laughing matter. It's illegal and should be prosecuted to the full extent of the law."

He paused, seeming to realize he had stepped out of character. He relaxed back in his chair. "I'm not going to give you free legal advice," he added with a thin, detached smile. "I only do that for the President of the United States."

For just a second there, Mr. Rogers had seemed more like J. Edgar Hoover. Or had my paranoid imagination gotten the better of me? I stared at Charney, but all I saw was the same mild-mannered, nerdy guy as before. The inner man, if there was one, was back under wraps.

A Free Trip to Fedworld

Precisely what does Scott Charney do at the Department of Justice? Something like this:

■ **When a U.S. District Attorney out in Ohio wants to know how to seize a computer that has electronic mail on it, and he wants to avoid violating the Electronic Communications Privacy Act, he picks up the phone and checks his strategy with Mr. Charney.**

■ **When a high-profile hacker is caught by the FBI and placed under arrest, the Department of Justice may monitor and direct the case every step of the way— drawing on Scott Charney's technical expertise.**

■ **When a right-minded senator wants to draft legislation to control online porn without violating the First Amendment, his staffers are more than likely to run the legalese past Mr. Charney.**

But does Charney give instructions or just advice? How far do his powers extend? What exactly is the relationship between the Department of Justice, the government, and law-enforcement agencies?

To begin answering these questions, let's make a field trip to *fedworld*. Yes, that's the name of the Web site:

http://www.fedworld.gov

Associatively linking our way through the archives, we find that the Department of Justice is run by the attorney general. It devoured slightly more than $10 billion of federal funds during 1994.

The Department of Justice serves the government in the same way that a private attorney would serve you. That means if the government gets sued, it has a $10 billion law firm to help it defend itself. This same defense is available for government employees and legislators.

The Department of Justice is also "responsible for planning, developing, and coordinating the implementation of major criminal and civil justice policy initiatives of the Attorney General and the Administration." This means that if the President dreams up a vote-getter such as the war on drugs, the Department of Justice manages the show from top to bottom. It develops strategies, allocates resources, and monitors the results.

The only thing it doesn't do is the actual legwork of investigation. The Federal Bureau of Investigation, the Drug Enforcement Agency (DEA), or the Bureau of Alcohol, Tobacco, and Firearms (ATF) takes care of that. But they are controlled by, and they report to, the Department of Justice.

With the exception of some work handled by the Secret Service, almost *all* federal crime is prosecuted under the supervision of the Department of Justice. Illegal aliens, child exploitation, fraud, racketeering, money laundering, drug use, terrorism—the Department of Justice has an interest in any criminal activity that affects interstate commerce.

Wait a minute—what does interstate commerce have to do with it? Here lies an interesting digression.

Under the U.S. Constitution, the federal government has only a limited ability to make laws, and those laws are the only ones that it has the authority to enforce. This is because our Founding Fathers intended law enforcement to be handled by sheriffs—local officials elected by their own communities.

As crime became national in scope, legislators wanted to control it nationally. How could they acquire the constitutional power to do so? Like all good lawyers, they looked for a loophole. In Article II, Section 8 of the Constitution they found it: The U.S. Government has the right to regulate "commerce between the several states."

Fine! With a little creative interpretation, this could mean that Congress could also regulate anything that *interferes* with interstate commerce—such as crime. And to regulate crime, the government would naturally need its own law-enforcement personnel, prosecutors, courts, and jails.

Thank goodness for the interstate commerce clause! Without it, the entire federal justice system might never have been created, and the Department of Justice would not exist.

These days, the Department of Justice is so well established that hardly anyone considers its constitutionality. This has allowed the federal/state dividing line to become extremely blurred.

The Department of Justice now funds and trains task forces that contain a mixture of state and federal employees working side by side; and some of these task forces focus on computer crime. Also, in 1994 the Department of Justice paid for 100,000 new police at the local level, which means that federally funded cops will now enforce state statutes. Maybe this seems unacceptable, since interstate commerce is not even remotely involved; but no, it's still sort of constitutional, because the federal money gets laundered through state government before it's turned into paychecks.

The bottom line: Federal law enforcement has grown steadily larger and more powerful, and the Department of Justice's supervisory activities have grown with it. As a result, when federal agents decide to raid a residence (that of a religious group in Waco, Texas, for instance), the local sheriff may have a hard time telling them that they have no jurisdiction.

From our point of view as computer users, the Department of Justice is now potentially interested in all levels of computer crime, from massive online bank fraud to hacker acts performed on a $500 computer by a kid in his parents' home.

The Criminal Division of the Department of Justice has a General Litigation and Legal Advice section, which is where Scott Charney works. He is now *the* computer-policy expert advising the most powerful government and the richest law-enforcement organization in the history of the world.

The Meeting

The lobby is like a giant jewel box fabricated from tall, glittering panels of glass and black marble. There are trees in tubs. Fountains are spraying.

When I get out of the elevator on an upper floor, I find art deco light sconces, mahogany paneling around the elevator doors, modern art on the walls, and marble tiling around the edges of the floor. This is a federal building?

No, the Department of Justice has merely rented overflow space here. As I walk into their offices I cross the line from plush post-modernism to public-sector austerity. A receptionist with the demeanor of a post office clerk is sitting behind a chest-high wall painted latex white, marred by countless black scuff marks. The thin carpet of the hallway is worn and shabby, spotted with small stains and cigarette burns. Utilitarian gray doors are identified with numbers, no names.

Scott Charney comes to meet me, and he guides me into a conference room where a wood-grain Formica table is flanked by overstuffed brown vinyl chairs. The furniture looks as if it was picked up cheap from Wal-Mart. "It'll be easier for us to talk in here," says Charney.

Easier? Easier than where? Easier than in his office, of course. The conference room is for civilians. The offices are private.

Charney reclines in his chair in the same laid-back style I saw when he was on the panel at the conference. But his eyes are alert, and I don't relish my role here. I sense he's likely to be as cautious and unrevealing as possible.

So I decide to start with some simple background. Does Scott Charney have a press release or handout describing his career?

"No," he says, looking mildly surprised that I would want to know anything about his personal past. "Although I was profiled in *Federal Crime Week*."

Is that periodical at my local library? Probably not. Can Mr. Charney spare me a copy? "Sorry," he says with his amiable smile.

All right, I'll begin at the beginning. What he did he do before he came to the Department of Justice?

"I was assistant district attorney in Bronx County, in New York State. For seven years I tried a lot of violent criminals, such as rapists and armed robbers. After that I was an Organized Crime Strike Force attorney, and then I was converted to a U.S. attorney in Honolulu. Finally I came to Washington, D.C., and was here for about two or three months before I got into the computer area, really by a fluke."

A fluke? He seems so calm, precise, and organized. It's hard to believe his career would advance by chance.

"When I started here," he explains, "they put me down at a workstation, so I set it up the way I wanted it. My boss walked in and saw the DOS prompt, and he asked what I was doing. When I told him I was creating subdirectories, he seemed to feel this branded me as a computer expert. So three months later, when they moved computer crime from the Fraud Section to General Litigation, he told them I was the best-qualified person to run it."

It's a charming story, because it undercuts any notion of Scott Charney being a smart, competitive, powerful figure. It portrays him as a regular guy who just got lucky. It's an anecdote that says, in effect, "Trust me. I'm just a computer nerd, not so different from you."

How much computer knowledge does he really have?

"I was programming in COBOL when I was eight. Back in the vacuum-tube days, my father worked for a mutual fund company on Wall Street. I used to spend some time with him, and we'd process the punched cards with a Honeywell computer in its special air-conditioned room. So I had a long informal history with computers, and I owned a PC relatively early on. Even now I still write programs as a hobby, for the department here—mostly in FoxPro, dBASE IV. I've toyed with C, but I don't have the time."

One reason he doesn't have the time is that shortly after he acquired his current position, he launched what he called the Computer Crime Initiative. The goals were:

1. **Ascertain the scope of the computer crime problem**
2. **Provide computer crime training to agents and prosecutors**
3. **Insure that multi-district investigations and prosecutions are coordinated**
4. **Develop an international response to the threat posed by international hackers**
5. **Work for legislative changes necessitated by advances in technology**
6. **Formulate uniform policies for conducting computer crime investigations and prosecutions**

Was this a bureaucratic move to enlarge the scope and importance of his department? It certainly seems to have had that effect. The Department of Justice has designated computer crime a "special emphasis area," and Charney now seems to have amassed considerable influence.

So I decide to talk with Charney about computer crime. What are the investigative techniques? Do agents routinely stake out bulletin boards or Internet service providers?

"If you're in a public place," Charney tells me, "the U.S. Constitution allows law enforcement to watch you and even follow you. But there's a policy against following you without any cause, because of the chilling effect it might have. Similarly, in networks, the FBI might want to go onto a BBS just to see what's there. There's no constitu-

Charles Platt

126

tional reason why we shouldn't allow that approach if the BBS is open to the public. But if you're a board user, it would chill the use of the board and people would get nervous about exercising their freedom of speech. So we don't hang out on boards. We need some reason to believe there's criminal activity before we go looking."

That's nice, but I find it hard to believe that law-enforcement officers simply never hang out online.

"Well, suppose we have an agent who says he's a computer nerd and he wants to surf the Net at home, on his own time, not as a police officer. Do we tell him he can't do that? If so, we're saying that law-enforcement officers are not part of American society. Surely they have the same rights as everyone else. And there's another point: If we want agents to investigate high-technology crimes, they have to have some practice using the technology. So an agent must be allowed to have an account on Prodigy or AOL. But he shouldn't be running from board to board looking for criminal activity."

Okay, let's suppose the person I've just run into in an AOL chat room is a cop. Under Department of Justice policy, does he have to admit this?

The answer, says Charney, is no. "I'll make a comparison," he says. "Suppose you go into a bar, and you're thinking about robbing the bar. You get up and ask if anyone at the bar happens to be employed by law enforcement. Well, an agent at the bar is not obligated to volunteer that information. So why should it be any different on the Net?"

Maybe because the online world is not like the real world. In the real world, there are a dozen different ways to identify an off-duty cop. Online, he can present himself as a ten-year-old boy, and no one's going to know the difference. Police seem to have much more of an advantage online—and may be more tempted to go outside the precise limits that Charney is describing.

This brings up the whole issue of selective enforcement. How does Scott Charney decide which cases to go after and which to skip?

"We learned our lesson the hard way, from *The Cuckoo's Egg.* We turned down that case because the financial loss was only seventy-five cents. This taught us very quickly that the dollar amount does not affect the seriousness of the case, and the FBI changed its classification for computer crime as a result. There's no dollar amount required anymore. What we're really trying to protect is confidentiality, integrity of data, and availability of systems. When a case comes to us, I hate to sound unscientific about it, but we just make judgments based on our experience.

"I'll give you an example. We've gone after phone phreaks very seriously because of our concern about the phone system. If you get control of the system and shut down 911, what's going to happen to a person having a heart attack?"

I point out that even when the Legion of Doom penetrated computers used by Bellsouth in conjunction with the 911 service, they never interfered with it.

"Hackers have not shut down 911," Charney concedes, "but they have interfered with phone service."

For him, it seems to be a short leap. For any hacker I've ever met, it would be inconceivable. But the nature of law enforcement is to fear the worst and guard against it, and one way of doing this is by imposing severe penalties.

What's the worst that Charney can foresee on the Internet? Are there really any possibilities for serious crime?

"Well, there was a big case out of Phoenix, with people advertising products over the Net and taking credit card numbers—and there was no product. I think we're going to see more cases of fraud of this kind. But a lot of the Net stuff we do is not fraud in the usual sense, but theft of information, including economic espionage, theft of proprietary economic information, trade secrets. Theft via computer isn't like old-fashioned theft. You can only burglarize so many homes—but when you have a fast modem, you can carry tons of stuff away. Also, no one necessarily notices. The information has only been copied, it hasn't been physically removed, so nothing is missing."

The situation is very different, though, if law enforcement decides to move in. Usually data isn't merely copied; the computer itself, along with the monitor, the printer, and anything else that plugs into it is hauled away. By the time the equipment is returned, it may have depreciated to half its value. Isn't this overkill when you're just dealing with a kid suspected of making free phone calls?

Charney gives me his thin, detached smile. "It's very hard to do this in a way that makes everyone go away happy," he says, as if he's talking about supervising games at a children's birthday party. "It's fine in theory to go into a house and find the files you need without removing the hardware. But how are you going to find hidden files or information stored under filenames that are intentionally misleading? And what are you going to do if the owner of the system starts erasing evidence? I understand your concern. This is why, in July 1994, we issued federal guidelines for searching and seizing computers."

The guidelines that he's talking about contain more than 40,000 words. But when Charney says this document was "issued," he doesn't mean to the general public. It was sent to U.S. attorneys' offices for internal use only. The Electronic Privacy Information Center (EPIC) had to file a Freedom of Information Act request to get a copy.

The guidelines evolved from an informal group whose members came from many agencies, including the FBI, IRS, ATF, U.S. Air Force, Secret Service, and U.S. attorneys' offices. They reported, ultimately, to Charney. Among the highlights of the guidelines are:

■ **If a computer is on a local area network that allows file sharing, and the owner of that computer gives police permission to search his system, everyone else's computer on the network can be searched, too.**

■ **If you store text on a large system or commercial provider, it may be searched without a warrant, since you should be aware that a system operator already has access to your data, and therefore you should have less expectation of privacy. (Apparently this guideline was applied when the FBI went looking for child pornography on America Online.)**

■ **If your data is protected by passwords or encryption, you may cite the Fifth Amendment and refuse to divulge the password or the encryption key on grounds of self-incrimination.**

Generally speaking, Charney feels that seizure is not just the safest option but also a moral imperative. "Here's the dilemma: Suppose you're a hacker with a PC at home and you're stealing data, and we just come in and copy the stolen files but let you keep the machine. And the following day you use the computer to attack someone again. What would people say about law enforcement and its role in this affair? We went in, searched, and left you with the weapon. It's like catching someone with a knife and giving it back, and the next day he stabs someone."

Well, sort of. But we have to remember that this situation involves a suspect who has not yet been proven guilty of any crime. The police could be making a mistake.

"Yes, the hacker says he's not guilty and is entitled to be treated like an innocent person. But if we have probable cause that you've done something criminal, and the judge has authorized seizure, how can we just give your system back?"

Charney also feels that if you're convicted of computer crime, there should be a law allowing authorities to keep *and sell* your computer. Back in April 1993 he was quoted in *Computerworld* advocating this kind of forfeiture legislation (which already exists for racketeering crimes and has enriched police departments across the nation).

Scott Charney is not what you'd call hacker-friendly. Interviewed in *Computerworld* in May 1995, he said, "For a long time, hackers felt they were off-limits. They thought, 'Law enforcement doesn't understand this, and our chances of getting caught are nil.' Now they are going to jail. The Legion of Doom went to jail; Masters of Deception went to jail; Kevin Mitnick is sitting in a prison."

Charney is in complete agreement with the federal law that says if you access a computer without proper authorization, even if you do nothing at all, you're still committing a crime. He comments, "Forget this notion of victimless hacking. We had a hacker who penetrated the Seattle district courthouse. He got there through a Boeing avionics computer. We had no reason to believe he altered any data at Boeing, but Boeing decided to check the entire system. It cost them $75,000. They didn't find anything, but as a frequent flier on Boeing jets, I think it was money well spent. And if Boeing had said, 'There's this thing called the hacker ethic, and this guy is a good hacker, so we're not going to bother to check the system,' people would be so shocked they would be laughing in disbelief."

I ask if these are his personal views or just the policy of his department. "These are very much my personal views," he says. "But they're also the views of the department."

In fact, the department seems like a seamless extension of Scott Charney, and vice versa. Every time I address him using the word *you* he assumes that I'm referring not just to him but to his segment of the bureaucracy. I wonder if he's willing to talk on a more personal basis. Does he mind telling me how old he is?

He hesitates for just a second. "Thirty-nine," he says, looking slightly uncomfortable.

What month is his birthday? I need to know this so that I can be sure his age will still be valid when this interview is published.

"My birthday's in December," he says, still trying to sound amiable, but looking irritated.

Married? Children?

"I'm married with no children." He hesitates. "You know, when I was profiled in *Federal Computer Week*, they didn't ask my date of birth. So that must mean you're nosier than we are." He gives a forced laugh. He's not entirely amused.

I ask if he has any press releases at all. Surely there must be something about the work that he's done?

"Wait here," he says. He walks out and comes back with a manila folder containing old photocopies of news clippings. "We're far too busy most of the time to write press releases. But I think we may have something. . . ." He finally finds two short, badly photocopied releases, pries the staples out with his fingernails, and goes and copies the copies for me. When he comes back, he doesn't offer anything else from the file. He's in the business of gathering information, not releasing it. In fact, divulging data almost seems to be against his principles.

"If you really want to know more about me," he says, "you should just do a Nexis search." (Nexis is the most widely used and comprehensive database of publications in America.) "In fact, that might be a quick way to build a dossier on me." Once again he looks uncomfortable. "When you consider that someone can run my name and find everything I've said and done—it's a scary thought, isn't it?"

Well, it might be scary if Scott Charney had ever said or done anything remotely controversial. In fact, in a subsequent search for material mentioning his name, I find nothing but the safest, most neutral public statements imaginable. Here's a typical sample from an interview in *Investor's Business Daily* on April 18, 1995: "As computers become more ubiquitous and more and more people become computer-literate, then the computer crime problem is going to grow."

I ask him what he enjoys most about his job. He gives a loud, slightly forced laugh. "The money! It must be the money!"

This sounds like a standard quip from the federal bureaucrat joke book. "Seriously," I ask, "why do you do what you do?"

He tries to oblige me with a sober answer. "What makes this job so exciting is that the issues are so complicated, and changing so constantly, you cannot get bored. You run the gamut from privacy and civil liberties, to search and seizure issues, export control, international issues, economic espionage—you name it, it's here. The greatest reward of this job is the intellectual challenge."

Maybe this sounds like another carefully neutral statement, but he delivers it sincerely. With his quiet, methodical manner and his precise knowledge of the law, I sense he has a genuine love for the

technicalities of justice: drawing boundaries, establishing precedents, and weighing appropriate penalties to discourage people from
violating each other's rights.

"But there's another great reward," he goes on, "which is that we're
part of a technological revolution. It's fun to have some small impact
on what the future's going to look like and whether we're going to
like living in it."

Now this is an interesting perspective. In effect, Charney is saying
that it's fun to have some power over the world of computers. Of
course, in his case this power is legally sanctioned and applied, and
from his point of view, he's trying to build a safe and equitable
environment for computer users in the future.

But isn't the fun he has just a little bit similar to the fun that a hacker
has, wielding a slightly different power over the world of computers?
And when all is said and done, who will have more of an impact
on our hopes and fears as computer users: teenage hackers, or the
Department of Justice?

Feedback from the Opposition

After I spoke to Charney, I checked with a couple
of people who know him—or at least know *of* him. Mike Godwin,
counsel to the Electronic Frontier Foundation, sounded cautiously
friendly. "I agree with Scott Charney," he said, "that computer
intrusion by nonmalicious hackers is wrong and should be discouraged and punished. I disagree about the intensity of the punishment.
It doesn't make sense to send the hacker to a federal prison. For
someone who's a first offender, it seems crazy to turn these people
into felons."

In general, according to Godwin, Charney is the best we could hope
for at the Department of Justice. "I've been watching him for four
years. He tells the truth as he sees it, and if he can't say more, he
shuts up. When I first knew Scott, he pushed people's buttons with

scare stories. I don't think he did that in a Machiavellian way; he wanted to bring home to people the significance of criminal law problems. What he does now, which I admire as a matter of both principle and rhetoric, is he balances his presentation and acknowledges the arguments on the other side. He puts the case, in his view, squarely, and lets his audience make their decision. If I were in his position, that's exactly the way I would operate."

David Bannisar of the Electronic Privacy Information Center has a more uncompromisingly radical point of view. Bannisar spends a lot of time worrying about the ways in which agencies such as the Department of Justice are liable to intrude on our lives in future, especially if they expand their ability to snoop on online communications. "Can you trust the Department of Justice not to abuse your information?" Bannisar asks. "Experience shows you cannot. If they have the information, they will abuse it no matter what the act says. Bear in mind that before the 1968 [wiretapping] act, there was massive illegal wiretapping, even though the Supreme Court had banned it in 1934. There were taps of members of Congress and of the Supreme Court itself."

Of course, Bannisar is not an objective observer. He distrusts just about anyone in government. "Something happens when someone goes into a bureaucracy," he says. "They adopt the hard line of the bureaucracy. Formerly reasonable people become zealots; they're basically forced to, or they quit."

The Maverick Out of the CIA

One man who chose the quit option is Robert Steele, the burly maverick who told hackers at the H.O.P.E. conference that he sees them as "law-abiding citizens who have immense potential to contribute to society."

Steele spent most of his working life in various sections of the government bureaucracy until, at the age of forty-two, he finally decided to go it alone. "I was deputy director at the Marine Corps Intelligence Center," he says, relaxing on the couch in the comfortable, traditionally furnished living room of his home, which is nestled in wooded country in Oakton, Virginia. With nicely bound books, a couple of antique clocks, and elegant furniture, it's a peaceful refuge within easy reach of his former employers at the CIA, and no more than an hour's drive from the center of Washington, D.C. But there is nothing peaceful or genteel about Steele himself.

"I had spent eighteen years as a professional intelligence officer," he says, "and discovered that a whole lot of classified data wasn't really there. We just had a whole bunch of facts about Soviet missile silos. Nothing on the Third World, for instance. At the Marine Corps Intelligence Center we were spending $2 million a year on a system for accessing classified data from the CIA, NSA [National Security

Robert Steele has been lobbying loudly for a national information policy to deter online crime.

Agency], and DIA [Defense Intelligence Agency]—and I found that for $25,000 a year I could get better data from open sources."

By "open sources" he means academic studies, published papers, books, and databases accessible by private citizens via the Internet, with no security clearance necessary.

"In 1992," Steele continues in an abrasive, rapid-fire style, "I had made open sources a policy issue at congressional level by working with Hill staffers who then forced Bob Gates, director of Central Intelligence [DCI], to set up an open-sources task force to review how he did things and come up with recommendations for improving them.

"Remember, Gates is the person whose nomination as DCI was strongly opposed by many of the senior analysts at CIA, who seemed to think of him as a man who represented everything that is evil or corrupt about politicized intelligence. Someone in fact called him 'the pandering pimp of political pap.' Gates really does seem to epitomize the ultimate oxymoron, the politically correct intelligence analyst.

"Anyway, had Gates fulfilled this task properly, I would still be a civilian in the Marine Corps. But he didn't. Gates turned the project over to the deputy director for science and technology, Jim Hersh. Hersh turned it over to the director of the Foreign Broadcast Information Service, Bob Shriner. Shriner turned it over to the director of his East Asia division, Ken Hughes. Hughes found a GS–14 with nothing to do and gave it to him. This guy knew nothing about open sources. He wrote a rotten report that said open sources was nothing more than the Foreign Broadcast Information Service, which merely samples the media, and only major capital city media at that."

Steele shakes his head, still disgusted by the bureaucratic myopia that triggered his resignation three years ago. "So I wrote, over the course of a three-day weekend, on a virus-infected computer that lost pages of my work at a time, a fifty-five-page report that trashed their report line by line. And I spread it all over town. Then I went to my general and asked permission as a civilian to run a conference on open-sources intelligence. I got permission to do this after hours, with my own money, on my own time. I spent six months working till midnight every night, seeing my family half an hour a day. We expected 300 people, and 629 showed up."

Among the speakers were the chief of staff of the Defense Intelligence Agency, a former science advisor to the President, and the deputy director of the CIA. Attendees included people from the intelligence community, John Perry Barlow (cofounder of the Electronic Frontier Foundation), and an assortment of hackers. The event gave Steele instant notoriety. "I became a public figure," he says. "I was named as one of the industry leaders and unsung heroes in the industry in *Micro Times*. At this point the lawyers said I had to choose between my job and running a second conference. I resigned from the Marine Corps, ran the second conference, and 808 people showed up. You have to understand, any conference that attracts over 200 people in this town is considered serious."

Steele was profiled in Alvin and Heidi Toffler's book *War and Anti-War*. He authored dozens of articles and papers with titles such as "A Critical Evaluation of U.S. National Intelligence Capabilities." In testimony and comments for the Presidential Inter-Agency Task Force on National Security Information in 1993, Steele opened with the claim that "eliminating excessive security will save millions if not billions of dollars."

Encouraged by his successes, he became more ambitious. "My vision expanded," he says. "I wanted to help the American economy make better use of open sources. I became concerned with information security. Finally it seemed to me that the only answer was to devise and implement a national information strategy. I'm hoping that Gingrich or Gore is going to use that phrase—"national information strategy"—in a speech within the next two months, because I'm working with various staffers on the Hill and in the administration whom I really respect. My ideas are bipartisan."

Even though Steele became personally disillusioned with his area of government, he still sees government policy as the only way of taming anarchy online and safeguarding systems from intruders.

"The role of government is to inform the citizenry about security problems that exist," he says. "Then it can establish standards to which the computer industry can rise."

But why is a government policy needed? Why can't this problem be tackled by private industry?

"The communications and computing industries have been criminally negligent, have not been held to any standards of adequate engineering. If we don't have a national information strategy that provides standards and due diligence law, we will never be able to protect ourselves. The first fundamental step is that our nation as a whole must be committed to communications security."

I'm beginning to feel stuck in government-speak. What exactly does he mean by *due diligence*?

"Due diligence is defined by regulation. Right now there is no due diligence requirement for communications and computing security. Stockholders are being screwed. They don't realize it, but they're paying a price for corporate management not protecting proprietary information properly. There's no law, no regulations, and no public perception." He pauses for emphasis. "This, I think, is the most fundamental single weakness in this nation."

There's not a hint of doubt in Steele, and not a lot of false modesty, either. In 1994 he wrote a bill that was introduced in the Senate to establish his national information strategy, which would be managed by a chief information officer to be appointed by the Vice President. Steele would have liked Paul Strassman to hold that position. For himself he thought that a suitable title might be director of national intelligence, with a subordinate director of classified intelligence and a subordinate coordinator for public information who would also be director of a national information foundation that would encourage the free flow and accessibility of data through the nation. The whole package was supposed to cost half a billion dollars in the first year, rising to two billion in the fourth year and maintaining that level thereafter.

The bill, of course, was never signed into law, and Steele admits that it had "zero impact." I suggest to him that the cost of it alone made it impractical, but he waves aside that objection. "If you're not talking in billions, no one takes you seriously. When you have trillion-dollar federal budgets, a program worth less than a billion is not significant because it's not going to have an impact on the nation as a whole."

And having an impact seems to be Steele's primary objective. He's a genial man with a wicked sense of humor and a charming smile, but he also seems totally driven, talking in hyperactive sound bites, monitoring his daily schedule to the nearest minute, and measuring his achievements in inches of press coverage, numbers of conference attendees, dollar revenues, and names of people in power who have been persuaded—maybe—to take him seriously.

His offices are in the basement of his home. He itemizes their contents with characteristic precision—"three rooms, five desks, seven telephone lines, with ten in reserve"—but they have a cramped, unpretentious, improvised look beneath low rafters packed with glass-fiber insulation. To Steele, however, this is merely the launch pad for his ultimate ambitions. He has no regrets about leaving the Marine Corps; he says he was too unconventional for them, they didn't trust him, and he could see he was never going to make supergrade. He now sees one possible future in which he succeeds in his mission to enlighten legislators and enact some version of his information strategy—and another possible future in which he abandons his campaign, retires to Bermuda, and spends his time writing books.

If nothing else, though, he has carved a niche for himself as an expert on making information available while maintaining system security. And his warnings—once again, expressed in hyperbolic sound bites—are salutary.

"The typical computer network," he says, "isn't like a house with windows, doors, and locks. It's more like a gauze tent encircled by a band of drunk teenagers with lit matches."

At the same time, though, he still insists that hackers are not a cause for concern. "It is clear that eighty percent of bad things happening to computers are being done by authorized users doing unauthorized things. This was the conclusion reached by the Department of Defense during a one-year study. Hackers are just our warning signal, the sneeze that tells you you have a cold. Hackers are not a threat. Ignorance is the greatest threat. The individual, the organization, the nation that doesn't understand its electronic vulnerabilities is essentially placing itself at risk."

Once again he stresses the need for a national policy to establish security standards. In the meantime, while we're waiting for government to implement his vision, he's scathing about institutions that don't take proper steps to protect themselves. "At the Computers, Freedom, and Privacy conference, the system administrator from the University of Wisconsin wanted law enforcement to protect him from his own incompetence. That's unacceptable. It used to be that system administrators built their own systems and were very bright, but now they are administrators, not technicians, and they are clueless." He gropes for an analogy and goes back to his image of a leaky gauze tent. "It's as if they expect law enforcement to protect them from *rain*." He caps it with another sound bite: "Bad law is not a substitute for bad engineering."

Will we ever see his idea of "good law"? Do we even want the government to legislate computer security? Wouldn't we be safer to stick with the current system of anarchy and benign neglect, which seems to work reasonably well despite all its imperfections? Steele doesn't believe this last option exists anymore; he's sure that *something* has to happen. "The threshold of pain in the banking industry has finally been crossed," he claims. "There've been unacceptable extortions and losses. The Citibank case was the wake-up call. Now Wall Street is going to come to the White House—which it owns—and will *insist* on communications and security measures."

Maybe so. But right now the Internet is full of computers storing personal data and corporate records, and, as Steele says, many of these systems are no more secure than a leaky tent.

In 1995 a nonconformist security expert sounded his own unique wake-up call to focus attention on the situation.

SATAN

Dan Farmer, who lost his job at Silicon Graphics when he released his cracking program SATAN to test security at Unix sites, makes no secret of his strangeness. With a pierced right eyebrow, leather pants, Marine dog tags, and shoulder-length red hair, he's as far from the computer nerd stereotype as he can get. He talks freely about his interest in death and his taste for sadomasochism and bisexuality. "Why should I hide?" he said to a journalist from the *San Jose Mercury News*.

When it comes to computer security, Farmer is just as adamant about not keeping secrets. "Trying to restrict access to 'dangerous' security information has never seemed to be a very effective method for increasing security," he wrote in a paper titled "Improving the Security of Your Site by Breaking into It," coauthored by Dutch programmer Wietse Venema of Eindhoven University of Technology.

According to Farmer, malevolent or playful hackers often pool their knowledge about security loopholes and how to exploit them, just as phone phreaks once published the *Tap* newsletter to share tips and tricks for making free long-distance calls. Therefore, if people in charge of maintaining security don't share what they know, they're operating at a disadvantage. In fact, according to Farmer, many sites are insecure "simply because the system administrators don't know any better—they aren't stupid or slow, they simply are unable to spend the very little free time that they have to explore all of the security issues that pertain to their systems."

From this, Farmer reached the conclusions that alienated him from many security experts and ultimately lost him his job.

First, he devised a program that administrators could use inside their own systems to test security. It simulated tactics used by hackers that Farmer had observed during his job at Sun

Microsystems, where he says that the corporate network of 25,000 computers was frequently broken into.

Second, Farmer wrote SATAN, a suite of programs that didn't just test the system where they resided but were designed to be used outside the system to find ways of breaking in. The idea was that system administrators could simulate attacks by unauthorized outsiders, and according to Farmer, SATAN "succeeded with ominous regularity in finding serious holes in the security of Internet sites."

He made SATAN freely available to anyone who wanted a copy. Anyone at all. And this, of course, was what caused the trouble, since hackers could download the software and start using it as a cracking tool on any system they chose.

Going back to Steele's analogy, Farmer was distributing matches and gasoline to the teenagers around the tent, to dramatize the risk of fire and force people to take preventive measures. This seemed an extreme, risky tactic—yet Farmer pointed out that he had already tried the orthodox approach without success. When he circulated advisories to system operators, they mostly ignored him. His paper lists dozens of Unix problems that are often left unfixed, and it's an amazing list of disasters waiting to happen. In fact, reading the list creates a gathering sense of disbelief: that an ancient operating system that allows or actually invites this kind of abuse should have become the de facto standard on most large systems in the Net and still isn't being properly patched to prevent intrusion.

Maybe Congress will eventually establish minimum standards for security, along the lines of Robert Steele's grand plan. Or maybe a new, properly secure operating system will eventually displace Unix. In the meantime, as Steele likes to say, "Unix security is an oxymoron."

Is the situation just as bad on individual computers in an office network? Probably not; most local-area networks now have firewalls to protect individual PCs.

And yet there is one threat that does frequently penetrate to single-user computers. This, of course, is the computer virus.

Michelangelo Pays a Visit

My wife, Susan, called me from her office in a state of panic. "I switched on my computer," she said, "but nothing's happening. It just sits there."

Computers always seem most likely to fail when you have the most urgent need to use them. Susan was up against a deadline; she had a heap of work waiting to be done, and she couldn't do it without the text that she'd saved on her hard drive. I grabbed a copy of Norton Utilities and an emergency start-up disk with MS-DOS on it, and I went over to her workplace.

When I got there and turned on the power, the computer went through its usual self-test sequence, then beeped twice. A message appeared on the screen: Non-System Disk or Disk Error. Normally a computer starts itself by loading its operating system from the hard drive, but in this case, the computer seemed unable to read its own disk.

I inserted my emergency disk and tried again. This time there was no problem. The system was fully functional within less than a minute. So now it was just a matter of finding out why the hard drive had become unreadable. I ran the main program of Norton Utilities and told it to check the file structure.

There were no files.

I stared at the screen with a sinking feeling, wondering how I would break the news that all the data had suddenly disappeared. Well, there was no point in causing panic till I was sure of the situation. I told Norton to start showing me the contents of each sector on the disk, right from the beginning.

The screen filled with zeroes. Every sector was the same. The entire disk had been wiped, and nulls had been inserted where all the data had been.

Today, I said to myself, *must be Michelangelo's birthday.* I switched to another disk and ran Norton Anti-Virus. The computer started whooping. A message appeared, telling me, as I'd expected, that the computer was infected with the Michelangelo virus, which erases the hard drive completely and permanently if anyone happens to start the computer on Michelangelo's purported date of birth.

When I told Susan what had happened, she was furious. She felt as if her system had been violated. It was the same feeling she would have if her apartment had been robbed.

"But you've been making backups, haven't you?" I asked hopefully. When I'd set up the system I'd installed a Syquest drive so that backups would be quick and simple. It's a commonly observed fact that if backups are *not* quick and simple, people don't make them.

"I backed it up just last night," she said.

"So you have no problem. The Syquest data is on a removable cartridge, so it escaped being erased when the main hard drive was wiped. All we have to do now is get Norton Anti-Virus to kill Michelangelo on any of your floppy disks that are infected. Then we reformat the hard drive, and then we copy everything back onto it from the Syquest."

She wasn't entirely happy. "I just don't like this," she said. "I don't like the feeling that someone created this thing, and it got into my computer and did this to me."

Well, of course not; but there's not much we can do about this. Computer viruses invade electronic hardware in just the same way that biological viruses invade the human body. They're a menace. But there's no way to be totally safe from them.

We figured out that Susan's computer became infected when she loaned to a friend a floppy disk containing an old version of a DOS word-processing program. The friend ran the program on her computer, then returned the disk. Unfortunately, the friend's computer was infected with Michelangelo, which attached a copy of itself to the word-processing program on Susan's disk. The next time Susan ran that program in her computer, Michelangelo made another copy of itself and added it to the file containing the computer's operating system on the hard drive. After that, each time Susan started her computer, Michelangelo briefly came to life, looked around, and copied itself onto any floppy disk that happened to be inserted at the time. Susan ultimately found that Michelangelo had spread onto half a dozen floppies in her collection.

We cleaned and restored her computer easily enough—but the story didn't end there. She had been working with a group of writers who frequently swapped text on disks. Also, since different people in the group used different word-processing programs, the programs were often loaned along with the data. Susan now had to call everyone and warn them that she might have unwittingly infected *their* systems with Michelangelo. "It was very embarrassing," she said later. "I felt as if I had picked up some bad social disease. And sure enough, I *had* passed it on to some of them."

It could have been worse. Susan was able to reach her friends and warn them not to switch on their computers. Some of them weren't as conscientious as she had been about doing backups. They could have lost weeks or even months of irreplaceable work. Michelangelo is easily eradicated by any modern antivirus program, but if it's allowed to run wild, it can be devastating. The effects are irreversible for anyone who hasn't taken precautions.

The Doom Merchants

Who creates viruses, and why do they do it?

Patrick Kroupa has some insight into the mentality. "When someone writes a virus," he says, "he isn't sitting there thinking about how many people this will hurt. He isn't necessarily some guy who tortures small animals and will grow up to be a child molester. He is usually just this angry kid who happens to be very clever, and what's going through his head when he codes this thing is how fuckin' cool it'll be when it starts blowing holes through the infra-structure of some industrial monolith like IBM, where a bunch of drones will start going bugfuck when everything stops working."

Kroupa himself is not a virus writer, but he did go through a period during which his hacking had a malicious edge. "At the time," he says, "I was very angry at what I perceived to be an unjust and corrupt system. One of the first things that happens to you when you begin to really educate yourself and become aware of the reality of the global socioeconomic structure as opposed to the fantasies that the mass media sells you, is you realize just how utterly and totally insane all of it is. It really is just one big game that is totally fucked up beyond belief and has little relation to any kind of romantic notions of right and wrong, or justice. And I was about thirteen years old when all of this was first set in motion, and I was pretty fuckin' pissed off."

When angry kids—or adults—take revenge on society by writing viruses, there are several simple steps that the rest of us can take to protect ourselves. First, buy antivirus software. You may resent paying $50 or more as "protection money," plus another $30 or so each year for updates, but it's liable to be cheaper than dealing with virus damage.

Second, make frequent backups—ideally, at the end of each day's work. Catastrophic viruses often run amok when you first switch on your computer. If you made a backup the previous night, you're covered.

Third, avoid swapping programs with friends. A computer virus has no life of its own; it can only function when it attaches itself to an executable file—in other words, a program or "application." Plain text is safe; you don't have to worry about sending and receiving e-mail or reading a floppy disk that has only text on it.

This is a fundamental fact of viruses—and yet in December 1994 naive Net users were horrified by news of a deadly "text virus." According to one Usenet message, "Other, more well-known viruses such as Stoned, Airwolf, and Michelangelo pale in comparison to the prospects of this newest creation by a warped mentality. What makes this virus so terrifying is the fact that no program needs to be exchanged for a new computer to be infected. It can be spread through the existing e-mail systems of the Internet. Luckily, there is one sure means of detecting what is now known as the 'Good Times' virus. It always travels to new computers the same way—in a text e-mail message with the subject line reading simply 'Good Times.' Avoiding infection is easy once the file has been received—not reading it."

Was "killer e-mail" really running rampant? A lot of people seemed to believe it. The warning wasn't just copied around the Net; it was circulated through institutions such as AT&T, Citibank, NBC, Hughes Aircraft, Texas Instruments, the Department of Defense, the Federal Communications Commission, NASA, and even the U.S. Census Bureau. Even as late as January 1996, people online were warning each other about the deadly threat.

But Good Times was never anything more than a hoax. There was no virus. There was no file named "Good Times." An official document was circulated reassuring everyone that it was technically impossible to damage your computer merely by reading e-mail.

And yet, toward the end of 1995, it turned out that a certain type of text document *could* function as a virus if it was created and subsequently opened by one particular program: Microsoft Word. It's important to understand how this is possible.

When you use a word-processing program, you may find yourself doing repetitive tasks. For instance, you may need to search for an old address and update it with a new address on many different documents.

Long ago, programmers invented the macro, a gimmick to make this kind of task more bearable. A macro is just a series of keystrokes that you would normally type while doing your word processing. The keystroke sequence is saved onto your hard drive (usually by giving it a name). When you want to run it, you call it up by name, and it replays the keystrokes so that you don't have to type them again.

What's happening here is that the macro tells the word-processing program what to do, and the word-processing program tells the computer what to do in order to edit your document.

The first macros were saved separately from documents. This meant that a macro would be available regardless of the piece of text you happened to be editing. But some people wanted a different set of macros to match each document. To please them, Microsoft Word allowed the option of saving the macros along with the text, so that when you retrieved the text, you automatically retrieved the macros at the same time.

The next and final step was to allow a macro that would run *automatically* whenever the document containing it was opened. This was a useful idea, because often you want to set things up a certain way when you start editing a particular chunk of text. For example, you might want to turn on automatic hyphenation and select a particular typeface.

In this way, macros developed to the point where they became a kind of computer language in their own right. They could tell the computer to do large, complicated tasks. They could even erase files.

This was a recipe for disaster. It didn't take long for some mischievous person to write a file-erasing macro, save it as an attachment to a document with an attractive-sounding name, and then spread the document around the Internet. Anyone who downloaded the text and opened it using Microsoft Word would suddenly find a bunch of files wiped from his hard drive.

Just to make things worse, the macro also included an instruction to attach itself to *other* documents that were created in future using Microsoft Word. In this way, the macro would replicate—which meant that it truly was a computer virus.

The Word macro couldn't do anything on its own; it had to be attached to a Word document, and it needed Microsoft Word to obey its commands. Bearing this in mind, there were four options for dealing with the potential threat:

1. **Avoid using software such as Microsoft Word with fancy features such as automatic macros. Stick with something simpler.**
2. **Don't download any text, ever.**
3. **Wait for a fix to be released by Microsoft.**
4. **Learn how to fix it yourself.**

Most users went for option three, and Microsoft was soon circulating a new, safe macro to kill the dangerous macro.

But the fourth option bears some consideration. Really, the Word virus was very easy to deal with: You just had to write a new macro of your own containing the command "DisableAutoMacros." As one online commentator put it: "Control is in your hands. Don't panic. Take the opportunity to learn more about features of the software you use, to test and verify any security features you plan to utilize, and then to configure accordingly. Don't treat this new Word virus as a nightmare; use it as an opportunity to take stock, and to learn."

Most Word users probably didn't appreciate this kind of advice. Why should they have to learn arcane commands to stop rogue macros from trashing their hard drives? They'd bought Word because they thought it would make their lives easier, not more complicated.

Well, they were wrong! As each new release of a program adds powerful new features, there's always a risk that the power can backfire in some way.

Moreover, this risk is liable to get worse as time goes by. In the same way that air travel has made it easier for biological viruses to spread around the world, the Internet has become an ideal distribution medium for computer viruses. This is a special cause of concern now that applets are coming online.

An applet is a small application, or program, that is automatically downloaded into your computer when you access a Web site. If you're using a Web browser such as Netscape, which has some general capabilities, a Web site can transmit an applet that will run in conjunction with Netscape to add some extra specific functions, such as sound or graphics. Moreover, since Netscape interprets the instructions from the applet before passing them on to your computer, the applet will work regardless of which brand of computer you happen to own.

For the time being, at least, all applets will be written in a new computer language named Java. It opens up a new world in which computer software is scattered at Web sites all over the world, and you can download and run a program simply by going to a particular site. But this also opens up wonderful opportunities for virus writers. A virus needs a host program in order to do its dirty work—and at first sight a Java applet seems ideal for the job, since it will be transmitted and activated automatically.

Bill Joy was actively involved in the development of Java since its beginning, in 1992. He participated in designing the language and wrote a lot of the final documentation. He believes that the virus threat has been minimized—although it can never be totally eliminated.

Joy has already played a vital role in the evolution of the Internet. In 1982 he cofounded Sun Microsystems, which quickly became the number-one supplier of computers for Internet service providers and now employs more than 14,000 people. Joy wrote a new version of Unix to simplify the problem of networking computers together, and this Unix was given away free with every Sun. "The reason the Net grew so fast," says Joy, "is there was one implementation of the protocols that everyone could get, and they got it from us." His operating system created a uniform communications standard, eliminating the hassle of incompatibilities.

Joy has avoided taking a managerial role at Sun and still spends much of his time designing hardware and writing software. Speaking in a soft, gentle voice from his office in Colorado, he explains why Java can serve as the next unifying standard for the Net—and why viruses require us to develop a new concept of trust.

First it's important to understand that Java allows you to limit the power of any applet that comes into your computer. "The language can allow you to prevent a program from doing much of anything," says Joy. "By default, it doesn't get to do very much, maybe just play with your screen."

On the other hand, if the person sending you an applet is someone you know—a coworker on an office network, for instance—you may feel trusting enough to allow the applet to do more interesting things. "It's like deciding whether to open the door and let someone in," says Joy.

He insists that this decision has to be made by the individual consumer on a case-by-case basis. But how can you make a properly informed decision if an applet comes from someone you know only slightly, or by reputation? Well, a personal referral may help. Joy refers to this as "the concept of introducers." He explains, "If I know you, and I give you some level of trust, and you introduce me to someone else, that gives me a basis for trusting that new person without any centralized authority being involved. *National Geographic* magazine works that way; a member has to nominate you before you can become a member."

Joy feels we could achieve complete security against viruses—but this would be possible only by limiting the capability of applets to the point where they aren't very interesting. "For things to be useful," he says, "we have to have some trust. This was all worked out a long time ago as a social process . . . now we have to work it out again on the Net."

Java is probably the first language that has been written with an adjustable "trust level" built in, placing responsibility entirely on the end user. The writers of Java assumed that viruses will continue to exist no matter how many laws are passed; therefore, we have to learn to assess the risk and live with it, just as we live with the risk of catching the flu. Some people prefer not to visit a friend who has the flu; others will take the chance of catching it. Only an extremist would spend every winter completely isolated in a sterile environment.

Likewise, we could isolate a computer from the Net and never use any software loaned to us by friends—although even this may not provide total security. According to Robert Steele, you can still get infected even if you only use brand-name software straight out of the box. "There's a private report that was published by a large government agency," he says. "I won't say which agency; I'll just say they are highly literate in computers and foreign languages. They

Bill Joy of Sun Microsystems helped to create Java, a new language that Joy insists can be safe even though it seems an ideal virus-distribution vehicle.

intercepted all software and hardware reaching their loading dock during one year. All the packages were brand-new and shrink-wrapped. And when the agency scanned this software, they found 500 distinct viruses."

The underlying message is the same for individuals as it is for the operator of a Unix site: Take precautions, assume you'll have to waste some time and money protecting your system, and don't imagine that law enforcement is the answer.

Perspective on the Threat

If this sounds grim, consider the upside. Electronic networks are far safer than networks in the physical world. The highway system, for instance, is the primary link between most Americans, and it's horrifyingly hazardous compared with the Internet, taking thousands of lives annually. Even the railroads are not secure; multiple derailments in late 1995 and early 1996 were proof of that. In fact, it's far easier to hurt passengers on a train than it is to threaten people's lives online.

From this perspective, the dangers of the "hacker threat" have been vastly overplayed. Hackers are a minor irritant compared with sociopaths in real space.

Of course, we'd be foolish to pretend that hackers aren't a problem at all. Despite Scott Charney's claim that they've largely been put in jail, there are more hackers today than ever before. Heavy federal penalties destroyed the modem world of the 1980s but haven't worked as a long-term disincentive, probably because there's always a new generation of kids who feel tempted to fool around online and assume that they're too smart to get caught.

In fact, according to Roscoe, this is a particularly good time for hackers. "There's so much you can exploit in the anarchy online," he says. "The Internet is the perfect arena to beat some federal agencies, to make them look like the dunces they are, and make the public mad at them. The authorities think they know it all, but they're the most ill-equipped to handle it technically. Ninety percent of their catching people is acting on tips. They have the hardest problem with someone who doesn't rely on others and keeps the information to himself."

Bruce Fancher agrees. "In my experience," he says, "the way the Secret Service finds a hacker is not by tracing him after he intrudes in a system. Clifford Stoll did it, but he spent six months on the case. The usual way hackers are caught is through other hackers. You monitor someone's phone line to find who he's talking to."

Intruders in a Net site are hard to trace because hackers typically work via several intermediate systems located in far-flung parts of the world. "It's actually easier to get access to a system through the Net than through the local operating system," says Fancher. "And Unix services are still full of holes. Large universities and businesses are installing firewall software, but many more new sites are coming online without proper security. And it's very easy to develop attack strategies when you're sixteen years old, because you have nothing else to do—unlike security specialists who have to go home to a wife and kids."

Chris Goggans, former member of the Legion of Doom, puts it this way: "I've said this before: You can't stop burglars from robbing you when you leave the doors unlocked and merely bash them in the head with baseball bats when they walk in. You need to lock the door."

In other words, we need to take elementary precautions against Net hazards in the same way that urban dwellers avoid carrying large sums of cash in dangerous areas at night or country folk protect themselves from predators, insects, and other pests.

Once we recognize the hazards, they may turn out to be tolerable. "I think hacking is still as harmless today as when I was using my Apple][," says Bruce Fancher. "There are still very few hackers who maliciously delete things. Their attitude has shifted—they used to like to project that they were wizards, while now they like to project that they're gang leaders. But that's just a pose."

The Internet site that Fancher co-owns is a tempting target for playful teenagers because many of them know that Fancher used to be one of them. Still, he seems unworried. Most of the attacks fail, and when one succeeds, he says he wouldn't even think of calling the police. "The point is to fix the security hole, get the system back in shape, and serve the customers. It's no big deal."

Jim Thomas recalls that when he first went online in the 1980s, he was virulently antihacker. "Then I started learning the facts," he says. "I was forced to realize that I had unwittingly bought the media myth, and it didn't match reality. I also realized that I could not accept some of the legal definitions that prosecutors were trying to enforce. Hacking equates with breaking and entering? No, I don't think so. Software piracy by the end user is equivalent to felony theft? No. We have to be very careful, especially when listening to people who don't really understand the issues, because they can be very adept at manipulating symbols and language. They can demonize a group of people or a type of criminal behavior, and if we aren't properly aware of what is happening, we may risk losing our freedoms."

Thomas helpfully supplied me with a videotape showing an actual hacker bust. In fact, it's the bust that I described right at the beginning of this section of this book. There's a story behind that incident: The "hacker" turned out not to be a hacker in the usual sense at all. He was a journalist who had been fired from a TV news program and was using an illicit password to get into the computer at his old job, where useful tips and sources were stored. He had no special knowledge of computers and was just a disgruntled ex-employee who wanted something that he felt belonged to him.

The news media were aware of this background, but they still labeled him "the Hollywood Hacker," as if he'd been a member of the Legion of Doom. It made a better story that way.

The fact is, real cybercriminals are hard to find—even at an event such as the H.O.P.E. conference. That teenager wearing a black jumpsuit with flames hand-painted across his shoulders, soldering components onto a piece of perf board—he looked vaguely sinister, which is why the camera crews clustered around, but what *was* he really doing? *Was* it illegal? *Was* it scary? *Could* it paralyze vast computer networks with a single pulse?

Well, no. In fact, he was building a very simple switched oscillator known in the trade as a red box, which has one function only: It imitates the tones that an operator hears when someone puts a coin in a pay phone. Its sole purpose is to cheat the phone company out of twenty-five cents.

Of course, he might have been able to build something much more interesting. He could have come up with a gadget that would have crippled the AT&T long-distance network, or paralyzed the 911 emergency response service, or cut off all communications in and out of the White House.

But even if such things were possible, and even if he knew how to make them happen . . . he chose not to.

ANARCHY ONLINE

1996

ANARCHY ONLINE
by Charles Platt

HarperPrism
An Imprint of HarperPaperbacks

Contents

Part 2: Net Sex

Senator Exon somehow manages to discover netporn————3

The Carnegie-Mellon crackdown on Usenet groups————8

Martin Rimm's survey of BBS erotica————11

Deceptive aspects of Rimm's study of Internet porn————16

The misleading statistic on netporn————18

Net users uncover Martin Rimm's colorful past————19

Academics attack Rimm's study————30

Rimm attempts to reply to his critics————35

Rimm's motives and alleged links with rightwing groups————37

Net vigilantes may never forgive and forget————41

The netporn problem: access, content, and distribution————43

Comparing the Net with an urban environment————45

How Usenet evolved————46

Samples of extreme speech on Usenet————48

Two people who manage and monitor Usenet————53

Unintentional absurdities of net censorship————59

Who cares about hate speech online————63

"Community standards" online————66

Pedophilia online————71

FBI busts AOL users for kiddieporn, with meager results————89

Why pedophilia is uncontrollable on Usenet————90

Looking for little girls on Internet Relay Chat————96

Intractable problems filtering online content————103

The Guardian Angels troll for porn————107

How state laws have curtailed Net liberties————111

Lorne Shantz's BBS is busted by a state prosecutor————113

Contents ■ *continued*

Local busts intimidate legal BBS owners————115

Bob Emerson's Cincinnati BBS is shut down—temporarily————117

Background history on smut-busting sheriff Simon Leis————120

A Cincinnati law suit targets the sheriff————122

Chilling effects on the Cincinnati BBS scene————125

Ann Beeson crusades for net liberties at the ACLU————129

Cornell students are punished for sending offensive e-mail————133

Jake Baker's sadistic online stories————141

Baker is baffled by outaged response————144

Baker is held without bail—then released————148

Legalities of threats vs. obscenity online————150

Judge Avern Cohn finds Baker's stories unthreatening————151

General lessons from the Jake Baker case————156

How Phil Zimmermann gave encryption to the Net————159

Law enforcement vs. encryption————168

The promise of digital cash—and some dark implications————170

Louis Rossetto's quiet radicalism at Wired magazine————180

Imagining the consequences of a netspeech crackdown————184

Epilogue

The ultimate fate of Exon's amendment—and beyond————192

Appendices

Survey and tabulation of state laws on computer crime————199

List of useful web-site URLs————207

The Senate chaplain prays for a world without porn————211

Part 2

Net Sex

For many years there was porn in the net and no one cared. Then an unholy alliance of fundamentalists, legislators, prosecutors, and pundits discovered the horrors of netspeech and launched a lucrative crusade to criminalize it. A ragtag band of computer geeks, student activists, libertarians, and anarchists rose up in wrath to oppose the crackdown, claiming it would be as expensive and unenforceable as the War on Drugs. Result: an ongoing epic struggle to control the most exciting medium in communications history.

Shocking!

There was porn on the Net, and everyone was shocked. In the Senate, James Exon waved bestiality pictures at his fellow legislators and warned that children all over America could view this vileness with a click of a mouse button. But bestiality was just the tip of the erotic iceberg as far as Senator Exon was concerned. He wanted to outlaw everything from pictures of naked female breasts to common swear words if there was any risk of them being seen by minors accessing the Internet.

Exon was from Nebraska. Was he promoting a crackdown on smut just to win votes from conservatives in Heartland USA? Apparently not; he announced that this was his last term in the Senate, and he was ready to retire. He had a purely personal interest in cleaning up the Net—which he compared nostalgically with the ham radio network he'd enjoyed using as a kid. In those days there had been no indecency, and on commercial radio stations today, indecent language is outlawed during periods when children are likely to be listening. So why should we tolerate indecency in cyberspace?

Civil libertarians were outraged, and Net users were exasperated. Commercial radio, they pointed out, is totally different from the Net. A radio program emanates from one source to many listeners. The Net enables everyone to communicate with everyone else, like the telephone network or the postal system. Why should it be illegal for people to type the word *shit* on a keyboard when they can speak it freely on the phone?

Senator James Exon's "decency amendment"
threatened to turn bad language into a criminal act
if it was propagated via the Internet.

But Exon didn't just want to punish people sending and receiving indecent messages; he also wanted to go after Internet service providers (ISPs) that merely transmit the indecency. Lobbyists complained that this was unreasonable, like prosecuting postal workers if they happen to deliver indecent mail. In any case, ISPs would have a hard time monitoring the huge volume of text and images passing through their systems. In fact, under the Electronic Communications Privacy Act, they aren't *allowed* to snoop at random in personal communications.

Exon responded by adjusting his law so that it would punish only ISPs that failed to take reasonable precautions to protect children. What, exactly, was a "reasonable precaution"? Maybe at some point the FCC could figure that out. Meanwhile, on June 14, 1995, Exon's legislation was approved as an amendment to the telecommunications deregulation bill working its way through Congress. A large majority of senators voted in favor of it.

They were afraid of doing anything else. Netporn was a hot issue; all the national media were picking up on it, from *Newsweek* to CNN. Anytime you looked at a magazine cover or switched on your TV, you were liable to see some cute little kid who had been strategically posed in front of a computer where just about *anything* might materialize on the screen. Conservatives, liberals, Christians, atheists—everyone was shocked.

Well, not quite everyone. Writing in the *San Francisco Chronicle,* Jon Carroll scorned the whole idea of controlling netporn:

> Fifty out of fifty states have laws against prostitution. [This is true even in Nevada, although counties have the right to opt out.] In fifty out of fifty states, prostitution flourishes. . . . There will always be sex on the Net, on the phone lines, in the books, on the streets. There will always be sex in your heart and on your mind. The Exon amendment is a lie, a lie you want to believe because society is falling apart and the children you know are surrounded by panderers. Fear makes us all stupid.

Still, to be fair, an element of truth was buried in the netporn hysteria. Sexy pictures and stories do exist online, and any unsupervised child with full Net access can look at them.

On the other hand, this has been true for many years. Why did the issue suddenly start making headlines in 1995?

James Exon didn't even have an e-mail address; he seemed clueless about computers. No one believed he had found his dirty pictures all by himself. Who had helped him? Was a special-interest group secretly orchestrating this circus?

In fact, the key source of information about netporn turned out not to be affiliated with any religious or political organization. He was a thirty-year-old undergraduate student studying electrical engineering at Carnegie-Mellon University in Pittsburgh, Pennsylvania. His name was Martin Rimm.

Rimm had spent more than a year conducting secret research into pornography online, using grants provided by his college. In 1994 he circulated preliminary results. When the final version of his 21,000-word study was published in the June 1995 issue of the *Georgetown Law Journal*, he was asked if he'd be willing to testify before an upcoming Senate Judiciary Committee hearing on children and netporn. He found himself featured prominently in *Time* magazine, interviewed on network TV, and quoted in all the major newspapers.

Rimm's study was precisely the weapon that conservatives needed. It purported to prove that netporn was more prevalent and perverse than anyone had thought possible. Thanks to Martin Rimm, it looked as if the Exon amendment (or something like it) could be pushed through the remaining legislative stages and signed into law.

Yet this turned out to be not so simple. Within a few short weeks, Rimm's wild ride to notoriety was derailed. His study was swiftly and viciously discredited. He was no longer welcome to testify before the Senate Judiciary Committee, and the decency crusaders were forced to disown him.

Martin Rimm in his younger days, before he discovered online porn.

The story of how this happened is remarkable. It features a most unlikely mix of journalists and rank-and-file Net users, many of them college students, most of them with no experience in activism. Together they mounted a grassroots counterattack that demonstrated some amazing new powers of the Internet: to excite the public, agitate the media, confuse politicians, shock the nation—and ruin someone's reputation almost overnight.

A Quick Lesson on Netspeech

The first rumblings of controversy surrounding Martin Rimm were audible back in September 1994, when Rimm sent e-mail to Robert Mehrabian, president of Carnegie-Mellon University, notifying him that students all over the campus were accessing pornography via the university's internal computer network. Rimm noted that at least one of the images seemed to have been copied from Amateur Action, a California bulletin board system (BBS) whose owners had been convicted under federal obscenity laws. So here was the ominous implication: Carnegie-Mellon's students—some of them under eighteen—were viewing pictures that had been proven obscene, and the college itself was catering this tainted feast.

Carnegie-Mellon happens to be one of the most thoroughly wired universities in the world. It is situated on the backbone of the Internet, literally straddling the so-called information superhighway. Every single person on campus has an e-mail address. Each student's terminal is capable of siphoning data from the Net more than thirty-five times as fast as the best transfer rate available to modem users in the outside world. As a result, students can download erotica as swiftly as turning pages in a magazine, and according to Rimm, that was precisely what they were doing.

If some Carnegie-Mellon administrators had been aware of the situation and had chosen to ignore it—well, Rimm deprived them of that option. His warning put them in the position of *knowingly* transmitting obscene images into the dorm rooms of students all over campus.

You didn't have to be a rocket scientist, or even a computer scientist, to predict what would happen next. Orders were given to shut the electronic spigot, and the flow of porn abruptly ceased. All discussion groups with the word sex in their titles were henceforth banned. This was a rough-and-ready form of censorship; some serious plain-text forums for discussing child abuse and safe sex ended up getting axed along with the porn.

You didn't have to be a professor, or even a grad student, to predict how people would respond. Campus demonstrations were organized. The ACLU issued a statement, and angry articles appeared in the student newspaper. Declan McCullagh, president of the student body, called an emergency meeting of the student senate, which passed a resolution condemning the decision. On November 9 McCullagh staged a Freedom in Cyberspace rally that attracted notable free-speech advocates such as Mike Godwin, counsel to the Electronic Frontier Foundation.

Godwin told students that no charges had ever been filed against any university for allowing full access to the Usenet feed that supplied the sexually explicit material. He said the volume of messages made it impossible for the university to be accused of knowingly distributing obscenity. And he waxed eloquent on the educational value of sexually explicit text. "They [Carnegie-Mellon administrators] want you to remember the poetry of Dante and Shakespeare and Shelley," he said. "But they want you to forget that human sexuality, which often inspired these poets, is equally the inspiration of those who write stories and poems for rec.arts.erotica."

Did the link between Shakespeare and Usenet seem a little bit *thin?* Student Donna Riley, who had been asked to present the women's perspective at the rally, suggested a different rationale. "We've seen this stuff before," she said. "In fact, it permeates our culture. But the Internet is one of the few places where we can fight back on a more even footing, using the most powerful tools we have—our imaginations, our wits, and our keyboards. Carnegie-Mellon women don't need to be sheltered from a bunch of horny men's dirty pictures and stories on the Net."

This was a powerful argument because it did an end run around the whole issue of whether porn was good or bad. If it was good, everyone should be allowed to enjoy it. If it was bad, the Internet was the best place for it, because everyone had an equal voice and women could shout just as loudly as the pornographers.

According to Donna Riley, administrator Erwin Steinberg protested that the university had a moral obligation to protect students from

pictures of sex "with women, children, animals, and the like." This was a very unfortunate choice of words. First, it suggested that sex with women and sex with animals were pretty much the same thing. Second, like every censor throughout history, Steinberg was claiming the right to shield citizens from stuff that was bad for them, and naturally enough, the citizens felt they didn't need his help, thanks all the same. Donna Riley soon started circulating fliers with sarcastic messages such as, "Do good girls think porn is icky? Fuck, no!" and, "Oh, Erwin! Protect us again!"

Three weeks later she formed an action group "to explore erotica from a female perspective and fight the Carnegie-Mellon administration's patronizing decision to censor 'offensive' (read: sexually explicit) images from our bboard system because of their concern for our fragile sensibilities." With an unerring instinct for maximum shock value, she named her group the Clittoral [sic] Hoods.

Soon the "hoods" were organizing regular "erotic story hours" during which participants would get together and read to each other their favorite fiction and poetry. Meanwhile, the faculty senate had passed a resolution unanimously demanding that their own administration should restore access to all the newsgroups.

The backlash had now become just as embarrassing as the porn— and twice as visible. The story was soon in the national press. The November 21 issue of *Time* magazine contained an article by Philip Elmer-DeWitt that referred to Rimm and his at-that-time incomplete study of pornography under the headline "Censoring Cyberspace."

So here was a quick lesson on the nature of netspeech. If you didn't try to control it, Net users would gorge themselves on a smelly smorgasbord of obscenity, raising the specter of legal liability. If you did try to control it, anticensorship forces would rise up in wrath, cause just as much trouble, and threaten you with other kinds of legal action.

There was no room here for compromise. It was an irreconcilable dilemma—and the drama at Carnegie-Mellon was just a preview of what was about to happen on the national stage.

Researcher Rimm Meets Dirty Marty

Why, exactly, did undergraduate engineering student Martin Rimm decide to warn the president of Carnegie-Mellon about porn on the Net? Did he really imagine that no one knew about it? Did he think he was, in some sense, doing the right thing? These questions were especially hard to answer since, as Rimm later put it, "most people who speculated about my motives never knew me, and those who know me well . . . were rarely if ever quoted."

Rimm came from Atlantic City, New Jersey, where his well-connected family included a state tax court judge and a city commissioner. He was not politically naive, and even though he claimed to be inexperienced in the thorny issue of pornography, he must have had some idea of the furor his revelation would create.

Was he a decency crusader? He claimed not to be. In private correspondence with an anticensorship activist, Rimm stated, "I consider myself to be someone who is deeply concerned about civil liberties." In discussions with a fellow student named Christopher Reeve, he agonized over the possibility that conservative organizations could use the existence of netporn to advance their repressive agendas. He even criticized the Carnegie-Mellon administration for closing down the sexually oriented newsgroups.

After Donna Riley's speech at the rally, she recalls, Rimm came up to her and said he absolutely agreed with her because "porn is bad but so is censorship." He didn't seem to realize that this was a totally inaccurate rendering of her feminist arguments. Was he trying to create some sort of working relationship with her? In retrospect this seems possible, since he actually invited her to contribute to his study. Was he trying to placate her by telling her what he thought she wanted her to hear so that she wouldn't cause any trouble for him? This is also possible, though Riley had no sense of it at the time. "I had no suspicion that the work would end up a gift to anti-porn crusaders," she wrote later. "I figured he was a clueless undergrad who needed help."

According to Riley, Rimm "looked a lot less geeky than I expected. He had an urban, Greenwich Village look to him, pretty atypical for Carnegie-Mellon engineers." She said he wore faded jeans, a black motorcycle jacket, and heavy black shoes. He had very short blond hair, almost a crewcut. "I figured at the time that he was your garden-variety horny electrical-engineering undergrad and had chosen to study porn out of a desire to view thousands of pictures of naked women."

Actually, Rimm had high ambitions and a strong streak of self-importance. Riley remembers that he referred to himself as the "principal researcher" in his sociological study, which struck her as pretentious since the label is more often reserved for a faculty member or graduate student.

Rimm made some arrogant claims. He wrote that he had developed an "entirely new methodology for the study of pornography." Supposedly he had persuaded various computer bulletin boards to let him count how many times each image was downloaded, circumventing the usual problem of consumers lying about their buying habits. He presented this as a genuine breakthrough in sociological data gathering.

Here it's important to remember the difference between a BBS and the Internet. A bulletin board system is a privately owned business, and sexually oriented boards are open to adults only. You have to submit proof of age (such as a photocopy of a driver's license) to gain access, and you usually have to pay a monthly membership fee plus an additional charge for each download. In this sense an adult BBS is like a porno bookstore with a strict door policy.

By comparison, the Internet is global and open to people of all ages. You generally get access through an Internet service provider's local "point of presence," or your computer may be wired into a local network that is connected with the Net itself (as at Carnegie-Mellon). Either way, the Net is wide open and extremely cheap, like a huge library that charges a minimal hourly rate and lets you take a free copy of anything you want.

Maybe one-tenth of Internet capacity is consumed by Usenet, which feeds the Internet in much the same way that a TV station feeds programs into a cable network. Usenet messages are sorted by topic into discussion groups, to which anyone can contribute. It's a sprawling information exchange embracing millions of readers. But almost all the messages consist of text; only a handful consist of pictures. This is totally unlike an adult BBS, which contains mainly pictures and hardly any text at all.

At first Rimm's research included only adult bulletin boards. In fact, he narrowed his scope to a handful of boards that contained the biggest stocks of erotic images. Since these boards were not on the Internet, he had to dial them via long-distance phone lines using a 14,400 bps modem. This meant he couldn't possibly download and inspect every single picture, because receiving the huge amounts of graphics data would have taken weeks or months. So he took a shortcut: He downloaded just the *contents listings* written by BBS owners to advertise their wares.

Rimm claimed he accumulated more than 300,000 of these two-line contents listings. Some of the text was highly explicit, but he didn't flinch from including it in his study. In fact, he tackled the task with gusto. His academic prose was peppered with dozens of quotes such as "Piss orgy! 3 horny guys piss all over their girlfriends!"

Having acquired the text, he asked a programmer to write a routine to analyze it and compile a dictionary of recurring keywords so that the material could be sorted into categories. In other words, he wanted a Dirty-Word Detection Engine that would classify each piece of pornography according to its perversions.

This created some semantic problems. As Rimm put it, "if the word *fucks* was assumed to imply the vaginal category, the computer dictionary would have classified such descriptions as 'he fucks her in the ass' or 'he fucks her mouth' or 'she fucks herself with a dildo' as vaginal, when clearly they were not."

Therefore, he said, it was necessary to check for other words that might be used in conjunction with fucks. These "fuck phrases" could establish the dominant theme of each picture.

But what if a picture included *two* dominant themes? In his serious, academic study, Researcher Rimm picked a random example: "'She licks her girlfriend's asshole.' The image could be classified as {oral}, {anal}, or {lesbian}." He dealt with this by allowing one picture to be classified in multiple ways. Yes, it was a tricky business trying to deconstruct the vocabulary of porn, but the Dirty-Word Detection Engine was rewritten and upgraded, and soon it was ready for the job. It swiftly sorted the 300,000 listings using the criteria that Rimm had developed.

There was still one possible snag. Did the listings describe the pictures accurately, or had BBS owners pumped up the text to make the pictures sound more exciting? The only way to find out was by manually checking some sample images. Rimm downloaded 400 of them and commissioned some "judges" to decide whether each listing was accurate.

These judges turned out to be sticklers for detail. Confronted with a picture captioned "She finishes shitting! She has shit specs [*sic*] on her asshole!" Rimm noted, "One of the judges unable to perceive fecal matter." Examining another image titled "She chokes on thick dog cock! Dog sperm on her sexy lips!" Rimm commented, "Two of the judges unable to perceive the ejaculate."

All of these quotes come from the final version of Rimm's study as it appeared in the *Georgetown Law Journal*. Imagine the typical reader of this serious review, browsing through the pages of solid text, perhaps expecting some abstruse essay on recent precedents in patent law—and finding, instead, this head-bending exercise in scatological weirdness. The study was bizarre; it looked as if it had been written by someone with a split-personality disorder. Researcher Rimm maintained his dry academic style as he discussed methodology, tabulation, and analysis, but he seemed to have an evil twin named Dirty Marty pawing through the pornography and getting cheap thrills by picking out the most extreme examples he could find and filling whole pages with absurd procedural quibbles about fecal matter and dog semen. The study claimed to be academic, but this was just a shaky facade. It read like a wild romp into slavering voyeurism.

The voyeurism stopped, however, when readers finally struggled through to the end. Researcher Rimm regained control here, solemnly warning that online porn was available in huge quantities and was even kinkier and nastier than the stuff in magazines (which was hard to understand, since many pictures online are pirated from magazines). Worst of all, according to Rimm, computer users actually *prefer the sick stuff.* Supposedly his analysis proved that the more perverted it was, the more often people downloaded it. Pictures of plain old vaginal sex were b-o-o-o-ring. "The supply of vaginal sex imagery exceeds the demand," Rimm commented. "The market for computer pornography is driven by a strong demand for pedo/hebephilic and paraphilic imagery."

As a case study he singled out Amateur Action, the BBS whose owners had been imprisoned under federal obscenity laws. Amateur Action was notorious for its no-holds-barred policy, but Rimm claimed he picked it merely because it was the "market leader" (a term that his study never defined, although later he said it meant "the BBS which generated the most downloads").

He reported that Amateur Action employed sophisticated techniques for satisfying users' perverse tastes. In particular, the BBS slyly played up a "power imbalance" between the sexes, "including a disproportionate representation of women in acts which may be considered degrading."

For instance, women were shown being penetrated by animals. "The pie chart in Figure 10," wrote Researcher Rimm, "illustrates the variety of animals engaged in sexual acts with humans, the most popular of which was 'BRUNETTE SLUT TAKES A HUGE HORSE COCK IN HER TIGHT PUSSY!'"

Of course, Rimm maintained his objectivity. He didn't say he disapproved—but he didn't have to. The material spoke for itself. It was outrageous. It was—well, it was shocking.

There was just one little problem. Amateur Action wasn't accessible via the Internet. *All* of the pictures analyzed by Rimm's judges and sorted by the Dirty-Word Detection Engine were downloaded from limited-access, adults-only, XXX-rated bulletin boards.

Rimm was a sophisticated online user. He must have known the difference between a bulletin board and the Internet, just as any reader knows the difference between an adult bookstore and a library. But for reasons that he didn't explain, he blurred this sharp distinction. In three separate places his study referred to "Usenet boards" when he really meant Usenet newsgroups. In one of his footnotes he said that "Information Superhighway" and "Cyberspace" could mean "any of the following: Internet, Usenet, World Wide Web, BBS, other multimedia telephone, computer, and cable networks."

Why confuse the issue? Rimm later claimed that he never intended "to muddle or deceive." Perhaps he originally intended to study only bulletin boards—and then realized, during 1994, that the Internet was attracting huge amounts of hype. By accident or by design, he downplayed the difference between adult BBS services and the Internet, and he added a small amount of additional work that focused exclusively on the Net. This enabled him to reap far more publicity for his work as an "Internet study." And this was how he purported to prove—by a creative use of statistics—that the entire online environment was a pit of perversion.

Deceptive Data

Rimm's additional coverage of the Net was skimpy at best. There are more than 10,000 Usenet newsgroups available worldwide, and more than 99 percent of them have nonsexual themes. He was able to find only seventeen groups specializing in explicit sexual pictures, and in August 1994 he spent one week browsing through them.

He downloaded actual images from only five groups. This was still a considerable number; 3,254 pictures altogether. But he was on the Internet now, which meant he didn't have to use a slow modem through a long-distance telephone line. Thanks to Carnegie-Mellon's speedy Net feed, Researcher Rimm needed only a few seconds to capture each image.

Usenet pictures aren't consistently captioned, so there were no contents listings for the Dirty-Word Detection Engine to work on. The only way of categorizing the material was by evaluating the pictures one by one, and Rimm seemed unwilling to attempt this. Instead he divided the pictures into just three groups: those that seemed to have been copied from adult bulletin boards because they carried text advertising the board; those that seemed to have been placed by private users; and those that were so soft-core they weren't really pornographic by his definition.

So much for content. What about quantity? He quoted data circulated by Brian Reid, the world's most widely known and prestigious analyst of Usenet activity. Rimm concluded from Reid's tabulations that about *one fifth* of the Usenet flow consisted of data in newsgroups "containing pornographic imagery."

How could this be so, when Rimm had found only seventeen out of 10,000 news groups devoted to sexy pictures?

Imagine that you have a massive book containing millions of words of text and a handful of pornographic illustrations. First, using a magnifying glass, you count all the tiny colored dots in the printed pictures. Then you count the number of letters and spaces in the text. You find there are five times as many letters and spaces as there are dots in the pictures. From this, you reach the strange conclusion that the "information flow" of the book is one-fifth pornographic.

This is almost exactly how Rimm chose to measure the flow of data online. Text is sent in bytes of data. One byte can convey either a single alphanumeric character or a single dot in an image. A typical text message might require only 5,000 bytes, but a single image can easily require 100,000 bytes. This means that a small number of porno images can constitute one fifth of the Usenet flow while hundreds of thousands of text messages make up the remainder.

If Rimm had wanted to be fair and accurate, he should have measured the *number of messages,* not the number of bytes. But this would have meant counting every new message every day in every one of the thousands of newsgroups at Carnegie-Mellon and trying

to decide how many were pornographic. Either because the task was too laborious or because it would have yielded less sensational results, Rimm didn't bother.

Instead, he chose an additional option. He ranked newsgroups according to consumer demand. Instead of counting messages, he counted the number of people at the university who accessed them. It turned out that alt.sex.stories attracted the most users, followed by alt.binaries.pictures.erotica. After that came newsgroups specializing in football, baseball, local news, and humor.

This, of course, confirmed everyone's worst suspicions. Students weren't using the Net for serious research; they were reading dirty stories, viewing dirty pictures, trading off-color jokes, and frittering away their time in chitchat about sport.

Once again, though, Rimm's use of data was misleading. By concentrating on a few popular newsgroups, he distracted attention away from the thousands that have nothing to do with sex. In other words:

There are a few sexually-oriented newsgroups.

On average, each attracts a moderate number of readers.

If we multiply the moderate number of readers per group by the small number of groups, the total is relatively small.

There are thousands of non-sexually-oriented newsgroups.

On average, each attracts a small number of readers.

If we multiply the small number of readers per group by the huge number of groups, the total is relatively large— although no one would have reached this conclusion by reading Rimm's study.

The Traumatic Statistic

Rimm finished with a few choice conclusions. Most of them were general statements, such as "Computer networks represent a fundamentally new technology for pornography distribution and consumption." But one statistic stood out. Rimm wrote:

"83.5 percent of all images posted on the Usenet are pornographic."

Wait a minute! Where had that come from? It seemed totally damning. It was, in a word, shocking.

Remember, though, pictures on Usenet take up only a fraction of its message traffic. Many of the available pictures are in fact sexual— but most users of Usenet aren't interested in pictures.

Moreover, although Rimm later claimed that his figure of 83.5 percent was "rock solid," in fact it was not reliable.

He admitted that he wasn't able to view about 13 percent of his downloads because his software wouldn't display them; and so, even though he hadn't seen those images, he just assumed that 83.5 percent of them were erotic, exactly the same as the ones he did look at.

Another percentage, which he didn't disclose, turned out to be so soft-core that they weren't pornographic by the definition that he was using, but he included them in his total anyway.

He counted text messages in the "pornographic" Usenet groups as well as images.

These defects obviously made Rimm's conclusions vague at best, but in the summary there was that 83.5 percent figure sitting on the page, with its decimal point implying scrupulous scientific accuracy.

This turned out to be a big mistake—not just for Net users, but also for Martin Rimm.

Total Humiliation Through Total Exposure

Philip Elmer-DeWitt had made a name for himself writing about the Internet. He was one of a handful of journalists who were savvy about technology and trusted by Net users.

Now, however, he was contemplating a writing assignment that could be seen as sabotage of the Net. He knew that netporn was a

Philip Elmer-DeWitt broke the story about Martin Rimm's online sex study. He later wished he hadn't. [Photo by Mary Elmer-DeWitt.]

sensitive topic—but *Time* magazine wanted a story that could sell a lot of copies in its ongoing battle for market dominance with *Newsweek,* and Elmer-DeWitt found himself with an exclusive that he later described as "too good to pass up."

Elmer-DeWitt had learned about Rimm's study when it was still a work in progress, back in November 1994 during the Carnegie-Mellon censorship fracas. In June 1995 Rimm asked if *Time* would be interested in an exclusive look at the finished text. As Elmer-DeWitt later put it, "I knew the Rimm study would be big news and I figured better I cover it than someone else."

Martin Sirbu, Rimm's advisor at Carnegie-Mellon, assured Elmer-DeWitt that the study was a serious piece of work. After all, it had been accepted by the *Georgetown Law Journal.* "If they hadn't accepted it for publication," Elmer-DeWitt wrote later, "we wouldn't have done our story." He didn't realize that the journal is entirely edited by graduate students.

Donna Hoffman, an associate professor of management at the Owen School at Vanderbilt University, warned that Rimm's sex study might be sloppy or malicious. Time *magazine didn't listen.*

Elmer-DeWitt contacted his friend Mike Godwin for comments, and Godwin urged him to call Donna Hoffman, an associate professor of management at the Owen School at Vanderbilt University who had extensive experience researching Net issues. She had seen an abstract of the Rimm study and was concerned that it might be sloppy or even malicious. When Elmer-DeWitt assigned a *Time* bureau reporter to check with her, "I raised what I thought were several red flags," she wrote later. "Those concerns were apparently ignored."

Hoffman's anxieties may have been discounted partly because she had seen only an abstract, not the whole thing. In fact, she hadn't been *allowed* to see all of it. Back in March 1995, Rimm had submitted it to the *Georgetown Law Journal* under conditions of total secrecy. Only the editorial staff had been permitted to read the text. David G. Post was a visiting associate professor of law at Georgetown University Law Center; when he was asked for advice on questions arising from the study, even he wasn't allowed to read it all.

Why was Rimm being so secretive? Well, he might have feared that a premature leak would lessen the ultimate impact. Or he might have wanted to protect his study from advance criticism. Certainly

none of his data could be challenged and none of his conclusions could be debunked so long as people weren't allowed to read them.

Philip Elmer-DeWitt started writing his story on Tuesday, June 20. Meanwhile, *Time*'s PR people consulted with Rimm. There was a sense at the magazine that this was a hot item. They were going to push it with a sensational cover showing the blue-tinted face of a horrified child. They even thought they could get some exposure on TV.

Rimm had no problem with that; and so, just a few days later, before the magazine was actually on sale, he found himself reciting his shocking conclusions on ABC's Nightline. He appeared as a self-conscious, shifty-looking, repressed individual. "On the World Wide Web," he said, finding pornography was "as easy as the click of a button. Within the next year or so it will become child's play." (In fact, Rimm's own study had found virtually no porn on Web sites.)

Later in the same show, Ralph Reed of the Christian Coalition claimed that one quarter of all images online showed "the torture of women." This statement was total fantasy; it wasn't supported by Rimm's study.

Then the *Time* article appeared. In 24-point type across all three columns, a headline claimed: "Porn is immensely popular: in an 18-month study, the Carnegie-Mellon researchers found 917,410 sexually explicit pictures, short stories, and film clips online."

Wait a minute. What was this "online"? Did that mean the Internet? It certainly sounded like it. But most of those explicit pictures had *not* been on the Internet. They were stored on private bulletin boards that were inaccessible to kids. Rimm's confusion of bulletin boards with Usenet was now producing its predictable results: a misleading statistical mess with maximum shock value.

That wasn't the worst problem. On the first page of the *Time* article, under a subhead that read "There's an awful lot of porn online," Rimm's Traumatic Statistic appeared in the text, soberly claiming that 83.5 percent of all images on the Net were pornographic.

Mike Godwin of the Electronic Frontier Foundation was horrified. Despite his friendship with Philip Elmer-DeWitt, Godwin publicly denounced the article, calling it "an utter disaster." He went on: "I think this survey will be used again and again and again to characterize the Internet as a place of wild and lawless behavior that cultivates extreme taste and degrading sexual imagery that goes beyond adult bookstores."

His reaction was just the beginning, a pistol shot that marked the start of a nuclear attack. The denizens of the Net saw that their freedoms were endangered, and they rose up in wrath.

They seemed an unimpressive army, just a bunch of nerdy guys and couch potatoes scattered around the country with keyboards as their only weapons. But the Net has powerful capabilities as an information retrieval tool. Within a matter of hours, highly motivated Net-heads were digging for facts about Martin Rimm . . . and uncovering a mother lode of bizarre revelations that had them gaping in amazement.

It turned out that Rimm's study of online porn wasn't his first attempt to draw controversial conclusions from questionable data. Ray Robinson of the Atlantic City *Press* revealed that in 1981, when Rimm had been a sixteen-year-old student journalist at Atlantic City High School, he had conducted another "scientific survey" purporting to prove that sixty-four percent of his fellow students had illicitly gambled in local casinos. To dramatize his point, young Marty dressed up as an Arab sheik and conned his way into the Playboy Hotel and Casino. Later he claimed he had never intended the stunt as a means to seek notoriety, but news of it spread as far as the *Wall Street Journal*, and Rimm ended up testifying before New Jersey's gambling commission. Legislators later raised the legal gambling age from eighteen to twenty-one. Rimm claimed the action was actually taken "because the Division of Gaming Enforcement commissioned its own yearlong monitoring program." His report, though, was the one that grabbed headlines.

There was more. Ray Robinson revealed that in 1990 Rimm had self-published a 208-page novel titled *An American Playground*. The book

was unavailable in stores, but Carnegie-Mellon student Declan McCullagh, who had organized the Freedom in Cyberspace rally, checked the catalog of the Library of Congress, which is accessible via the Net. He found that Rimm had submitted his novel to the nation's number-one literary archive—and there it was, shelved in the Jefferson Building.

McCullagh happened to be in Washington during the summer, so he went and read Rimm's novel, which turned out to be peppered with wildly salacious prose. McCullagh photocopied the "good bits," then spent a happy evening feeding them into the Net. Some of the dialogue was especially memorable:

> "I'm gonna go pump Nadah with my R.R. tonight."
> "Your R.R.? What's that, Rich?"
> "Don't you know? Come on, get with it Donny! That's my <u>rectum rocket</u>!"

Or:

> "After I knock you out, I could inject your ventricle vein with sodium cloroxide, thereby inducing a bioculminary collapse in the lower cavity of your central nervous system, followed by an epileptic seizure from your spinal cord through your intestinal cords, all the way up to your brain, through your stomach, down your dick, and out your ass." (Page 72)

Researcher Rimm had evidently been out on his coffee break when these words were written; they sounded like Dirty Marty totally out of control, and they shed a whole new light on Rimm's pious warnings about the degradation of women online.

But this was still only a mild jolt to the system compared with the next revelation. Another Net user checked *Books in Print* and found that in March 1995 there had been a sixty-seven-page nonfiction work by Martin Rimm titled *The Pornographer's Handbook: How to Exploit Women, Dupe Men, and Make Lots of Money*. The book had been published under the so-called Carnegie imprint—which, by an odd coincidence, happened to be based at the same street address as a Martin Rimm in Pittsburgh, Pennsylvania.

Declan McCullagh unearthed Rimm's naughty novel at the Library of Congress and disseminated excerpts via the Internet. Rimm claimed it was all a joke; netizens were unconvinced. (Photo by the author.)

Rimm claimed that the book was a "satire on the pornography industry which was never printed, published, distributed, or sold to anyone."

This was hard to believe, especially when a man calling himself John Russel Davis (whom Rimm claimed he had never heard of) uploaded some excerpts from the supposedly nonexistent book, which he obtained from an unspecified source. Satire? Apparently not. The book turned out to be exactly what the title said it was: a guide for owners of adult bulletin boards, telling them how to make money by fine-tuning their erotic services. Rimm even included an introduction dedicated to Bob Guccione, publisher of *Penthouse*, which read, in part:

> Therefore, Mr. Guccione, take this small gift in the spirit and lust for life with which I sent it. If you consider and read it diligently, you will appreciate my sincere desire to see you at last reap the great riches of the Information Superhighway. And if you will at some time turn your eyes from the summit of your plush office to these low places, you will see how undeservedly I endure a great and continuous malignity of fortune.

How eloquent! In fact, *too* eloquent. Mary Shaw, a faculty member at Carnegie-Mellon, realized that it had been copied wholesale from Machiavelli's introduction to The Prince, dedicated to Lorenzo de Medici:

> So, Your Magnificence, take this little gift in the spirit in which I sent it; and if you read and consider it diligently, you will discover in it my urgent wish that you reach the eminence that fortune and your other qualities promise you. And if, from your lofty peak, Your Magnificence will sometimes glance down to these low-lying regions, you will realize the extent to which, undeservedly, I have to endure the great and unremitting malice of fortune.

But the inside pages of Rimm's handbook made much juicier reading then its front matter. For example:

> When searching for the best anal sex images, you must take especial care to always portray the woman as smiling, as deriving pleasure from being penetrated by a fat penis into her most tender crevice. The male, before ejaculation, is remarkably attuned to the slightest discrepancy; he is as much focused on her lips as on her anus. The slightest indication of pain can make some men limp.

(A few weeks later, when Rimm complained he had been screwed by people circulating these writings over the Net, he was told to smile during the experience: "Otherwise, Marty, you know we can't enjoy it.")

But could this stuff be *genuine?* Was "John Russel Davis" a pseudonymous prankster who had invented the whole thing? Netizens speculated to and fro for a couple of days. Then Brock Meeks, Washington bureau chief for *Interactive Week* and self-publisher of an online news service titled *Cyberwire Dispatch,* settled the matter conclusively. He quoted a letter to him in which Rimm confessed, "The excerpts [from *The Pornographer's Handbook*] circulating around Usenet were stolen from my marketing book, Brock. You are the only one I'm telling."

The only one? *In your dreams, Marty!* Meeks was a journalist. There was no possibility—not the slightest, faintest chance—that he was going to remain "the only one" with this information.

The phrase "information wants to be free" was beginning to take on a whole new meaning. In fact, netizens seemed ready to add a coda: "If we find any information that *doesn't* want to be free, we'll soon take care of that!"

Many Net users felt that Rimm had gone out of his way to damage their environment. Just as a woman may feel justified using any method to defend herself against a rapist, netizens were ready to use any legal text weapon against Martin Rimm. And so he became the first major victim of a technique that had devastating implications for anyone with something to hide: total humiliation through total exposure.

Brock Meeks's *Cyberwire Dispatch* was copied into a Usenet group, where it became potentially accessible to ten million or more people around the globe. No doubt most of those Net users didn't bother to read the relevant newsgroups, but those who did were treated to some especially choice excerpts from Rimm's personal mail. "To say I'm pissed is an understatement," he wrote, regarding the excerpts from *The Pornographer's Handbook* that had somehow found their way online. "They all agreed not to photocopy it," he added. "I'm going to nail them for copyright violation." This seemed to refer to BBS owners who had received the handbook from Rimm under yet another condition of secrecy.

So what had really happened here? Rimm kept trying to do damage control; he claimed that the excerpts from *The Pornographer's Handbook* had been written to amuse several faculty members at Carnegie-Mellon before he ever considered writing his study of netporn.

Well, maybe, but his correspondence with Brock Meeks told a different story, so outrageous that it boggled the mind. The Meeks scenario ran like this:

First, early in 1994 Rimm had telephoned BBS owners and offered to analyze their data in order to help them target and fulfill the sexual appetites of their horny customers. Supposedly Rimm was ready to provide expert services to help any adult BBS refine its storehouse of pornography and make as much money as possible.

Some BBS owners seemed to fall for this offer. They allowed Rimm to inspect the images they offered online, and they supplied him with proprietary information about the viewing habits of their users.

The next step, according to Meeks, was that Researcher Rimm copied this privileged information into his Carnegie-Mellon study—where he concluded, with straight-faced objectivity, that adult-oriented BBSs were now using surprisingly sophisticated methods to enlarge their user base. Well, of course they were; they were using *his* methods, which he had created for them!

Finally Rimm treated the BBS owners to a handbook summarizing all the tricks of the trade that he had learned from his work. Simultaneously he submitted to the *Georgetown Law Journal* his study warning the public that online pornography was out of control and legislators should take heed.

No wonder he had looked nervous on *Nightline*. By failing to disclose to the *Georgetown Law Journal* his intimate relationship with at least one hardcore BBS, and by failing to disclose to the bulletin-board owners that he was planning to use their data for a study that would serve as ammunition for anti-porn crusaders, he was running a double game of deception.

Could this all be true? Rimm claimed that Meeks had quoted him out of context, quoted some comments that were meant to be sarcastic, and taken "considerable liberties." Still, Rimm didn't deny what he'd written to Meeks, and in his own study he acknowledged that he and his researchers had "rarely admitted" they were working on a study when they spoke to BBS owners. In other words, he had gathered the data under false pretenses.

Robert Thomas, co-owner of the Amateur Action BBS that Rimm had singled out as America's deepest porn pit, was now serving

prison time, but Mike Godwin eventually managed to interview him. Thomas remembered phone calls in which Rimm had sounded like a real porn fan. "He'd say things like, 'You never cease to amaze me. You're brilliant,'" Thomas told Godwin. "I was kind of an idol to him—at least, that's what I took it as. Some of his messages to me, he sounded kinda like he was in love with me or something. Or in love with the BBS. I thought he was probably a wanna-be."

Were Thomas's recollections fair and accurate? His wife, Carleen, was able to produce a piece of e-mail that Rimm had sent:

> I'll tell you, Robert, in spite of my few comments, I still think you're a fucking genius. Every time I run my list through your computer I learn new things that no one else in the business ever thought of. I'd like to help in any way I can. I hope you count me among your friends.

This from the man whose study exposed Thomas's BBS as a nightmare of female abuse, bestiality, and pictures of naked children! Rimm later claimed he was just trying "to sweet-talk Thomas into sharing information." He claimed that "in journalism and most business professions, this is perfectly ethical."

Godwin was not impressed. With Carleen Thomas's permission, he quickly posted Rimm's e-mail on the Well, an Internet site that maintains its own local discussion groups. Aaron Dickey at the Associated Press saw it there and helpfully copied it into Usenet so that it too could gain worldwide distribution.

When Rimm saw this, he wrote:

> Aaron, you're a prick. You and the others attack me for privacy violations, then you publicly post a message that was clearly marked private between Robert Thomas and myself.

Private? For Martin Rimm, the concept of privacy no longer existed, and he gradually seemed to realize this. "My lynching has been more savage and personal than any other in the history of the Net," he wrote. A couple of days later he stopped sending e-mail altogether.

But this vilification was only one part of the picture. There were other, more traditional forms of punishment.

The Academics Strike Back

Jim Thomas, the professor of sociology and criminal justice at Northern Illinois University who coedits *Computer Underground Digest*, has specialized in studying computer culture and, before that, prisoner and civil-rights law. He has taught more than a dozen academic subjects, some at graduate level, including methods of data gathering. When Thomas saw Rimm's study, he was so concerned that he wrote a whole paper on what he termed its "ethical lapses."

He accused Rimm of invading the privacy of users at Carnegie-Mellon by checking their Usenet access records without their consent. Also, Rimm had revealed private information publicly when he discussed Amateur Action BBS. And when dealing with bulletin boards generally, "there is sufficient evidence to conclude that the research team gathered data deceptively, perhaps even fraudulently." Overall, Thomas concluded, Rimm's use of the study "seemed more an exercise in media promotion than in intellectual inquiry."

Meanwhile, David G. Post of the Georgetown University Law Center had now seen the full text that student editors had refused to show him previously. Using words such as "preposterous," Post demonstrated that Rimm had made elementary blunders in analyzing his own data. As a result, his statistics were totally worthless.

Donna Hoffman, who had warned *Time* that the study probably contained flaws, wrote a thorough denunciation in collaboration with Thomas Novak—who, like her, was a tenured associate professor of management at Vanderbilt University. In relentless detail they attacked Rimm's work for being sloppy, vague, and incompetent. Most damning of all, they pointed out that the *Georgetown Law Journal* is not peer-reviewed; in other words, when

David G. Post of Georgetown University Law Center was appalled by Martin Rimm's sex study—when he was finally allowed to read it.

Rimm chose this particular publication, he was not compelled to go through the process of fact-checking that is routine at most academic publications.

It also turned out there was another study—by two Canadians, Michael Mehta, Ph.D., and Dwaine Plaza, B.A., M.E.S.—that totally contradicted Rimm's conclusions. Adult bulletin boards, Mehta and Plaza said, "do not usually post a statistically significant different amount of material [compared with the Internet] depicting illegal sexual acts, such as bestiality. . . . We never came across an image depicting a sexual act between an adult and a child/adolescent, or acts between children."

Whose study was more credible, theirs or Rimm's? Theirs certainly seemed more rigorous. While Rimm never explained how he chose his samples of images, Mehta and Plaza did the job right,

with a random-number table and proportionate random sampling. They explained the distinction between Usenet and bulletin boards, counted Usenet pictures that came from commercial and from private sources, and compared the numbers using a correlation coefficient, "a symmetric measure of association for 2 X 2 crosstabulations used when comparing non-parametrically distributed variables."

Their study was dry and precise, without a hint of voyeurism or sleaze. But most damaging of all, theirs had come out first. In fact, Rimm had actually called Mehta and asked for a copy of it.

Mehta said that when Rimm had spoken to him on the phone, the Carnegie-Mellon undergrad had claimed to be the leader of a fifteen-person interdisciplinary research team. He had sounded so authoritative, Mehta assumed he was a tenured professor. "He never corrected me," he said, "when I called him 'Professor Rimm.'" And Mehta went on: "I trusted Rimm, and he stole some of my ideas, lied to me, and distorted facts beyond belief." Declan McCullagh subsequently published a list of nineteen phrases from Rimm's paper that were almost identical to phrases in the paper by Mehta and Plaza. (Rimm later claimed that Mehta "was not at all truthful," although he didn't substantiate this claim.)

Worse still, it seemed that even Rimm's claim that he had counted actual downloads from bulletin boards might be unreliable. When Robert Thomas of Amateur Action was asked about this by Mike Godwin, he laughed at the idea. He pointed out that anytime his BBS software crashed, the download records would be reset to zero.

Rimm's Usenet figures turned out to be just as bogus. Brian Reid, who had gathered the data originally, is a Ph.D. employed as director of the Network Systems Laboratory at Digital Equipment Corporation. "Every professional is going to vomit when they see this study," he wrote. He added, "I am so distressed by its lack of scientific credibility that I don't even know where to begin critiquing it. The writer appears to me not to have a glimmer of an understanding even of basic statistical measurement technique."

While charting Usenet for more than nine years, Reid said, he had always warned everyone that the decentralized structure of the Net makes accurate measurement impossible. In fact, he said, his figures might be wrong by an order of magnitude either way. "In other words, if I measure something that seems to be 79, the truth might be 790 or 7.9 or anywhere in between."

Was Rimm aware of this? He should have been. Did his study acknowledge the problem? Absolutely not.

There was more. Reid said that Rimm had made "beginner's errors" that rendered his numbers "completely meaningless." He had measured people's access to Usenet newsgroups only inside Carnegie-Mellon, where 71 percent of the students are male, most of them oriented toward technology. In other words, Rimm had studied the sexual interests of an enclave of frustrated college-aged male technogeeks whose porn-ogling profile was likely to be high. Rimm then presented the figures as if they were typical for everyone on the Net.

Brian Reid, world expert on measuring Internet traffic, claimed that errors in Rimm's sex study rendered the numbers totally meaningless.

Moreover, when he talked about people "accessing" porn images on Usenet, he had never defined that term. In reality, according to Reid, Rimm's system only recorded whether a user checked the whole contents listing of a newsgroup. He couldn't tell if someone downloaded all the pictures, or just a few, or none at all.

No wonder Reid was furious. Naturally, along with the other academics, he circulated his comments online. Some enthusiasts then got together and set up a Web page where *everything* about Rimm was assembled for public derision, a chamber of horrors showing all the textual torments that an engineering student could expect if he was dumb enough to launch an inaccurate and seemingly malicious attack on freedom on the Net.

Was this the end of the story? Certainly not. The academics had responded fast compared with the print media. For the next month, magazines and newspapers explored the story. A Nexis search on July 8, 1995, found thirty-one news items mentioning Rimm's name during the preceding two weeks. The *New Yorker* ran a long piece by Jeffrey Rosen describing each step of the saga with playful delight, referring to it as "wonderfully bizarre." The *New Republic* included a full-page story about the scandal in which Rimm was described as "unrepentant and making things worse."

Faced with this blizzard of scorn, most of Rimm's associates quickly abandoned him. Carolyn Speranza, an artist and lecturer at Carnegie-Mellon, had been listed as an advisor for Rimm's paper. She was also credited as an illustrator for Rimm's *Pornographer's Handbook*, but she hastily informed Usenet readers that the credit had been given "without my knowledge or consent." Moreover, she said, she had never even seen the handbook. This was interesting, because in a letter to Brock Meeks, Rimm had said he was "pissed off" about Carolyn, whom he referred to as if she was an ex-girlfriend.

Another former Rimm associate posted this message on his Web page: "I've been told that I am listed as a 'contributor' in Martin Rimm's study. . . . I'd like to be able to say that this is completely untrue. In fact, I did unfortunately write a few primitive sed and awk

scripts which Mr. Rimm presumably used to sift through the data he collected. . . . If I had been fully aware of its nature, I certainly wouldn't have had anything to do with it."

Even *Time* magazine denounced its former guru of cyberporn. A one-page article written by Philip Elmer-DeWitt somehow managed to avoid blaming *Time* but had no problem blaming Martin Rimm. The article said that "serious questions have been raised" about Rimm's study. Just to make sure everyone got the message, *Time* included a photograph of Rimm looking shifty, pouting, and sullen, like a thinner, younger version of Alfred Hitchcock. It was captioned "A colorful past and two tawdry books have helped undermine the credibility of Rimm's sex research." In online discussions Elmer-DeWitt admitted that "I really did screw up by buying into the Rimm study."

Were any other punishments in store for Martin Rimm? Well, he was definitely uninvited to the Senate Judiciary Committee hearing on children and netporn. Also, his university formed a committee of investigation to examine his work, noting that "substantial criticism has focused on the study's scholarship and the methods by which data were acquired and used." It was even suggested that the academic credit that Rimm had received for his study could be withdrawn—which could cause him to lose the bachelor's degree that he had been awarded with honors during 1995. Would this actually happen? The committee's verdict was not expected till mid–1996. Until then, Rimm would have to wait and wonder about his fate.

Rimm Shots

In the meantime, he made a few attempts to salvage some remnant of his reputation, claiming, "I was viciously attacked by intellectually dishonest people." He wrote some specific responses to Hoffman and Novak, Mehta, and Reid. He said he hadn't tried to avoid peer review. He said that "numerous scholars" had read the first draft of his study in December 1994 (in fact, most

of them had seen only pieces of it). He claimed that his study "drew on the expertise of more than two dozen researchers, many of whom hold Ph.D.s in statistics, engineering, economics, management, fine arts, psychology, history and public policy." (Unfortunately, none of them was qualified in the more relevant field of sociology.) He complained that Hoffman had tried to "censor" the article before *Time* could publish it, he accused her and Novak of "seemingly personal attacks," and finally, with a straight face, he complained that they had "no previous research experience in the area of pornography."

As for the charge of plagiarism, he said that his own study had already been "in substantially complete form" in November 1994, a month before he had read the paper by Mehta and Plaza. Regarding his conversations with Mehta, Rimm claimed he "got no ideas" from them. "The charge of plagiarism," he wrote, "is part of a witch hunt of fabricated charges against our study."

He had a harder time dealing with Reid. "Part of the problem here," he wrote, "appears to be one of perception: the law journal did not want us to write a statistics paper. Some statistics and explanations, that may have alleviated your concerns, were left out." He added, "We had hoped that the statistics we inserted would be taken in a general sense."

A general sense? As in "83.5 percent"?

Hoffman and Novak responded to Rimm's response, but few other netizens bothered. They had already achieved their objective. As far as netizens were concerned, Rimm had become a nonperson.

His study, though, lived on. The Traumatic Statistic even found a place in the Congressional Record. Speaking in the Senate on June 26, 1995, Senator Charles Grassley stated that "83.5 percent of the 900,000 images reviewed—these are all on the Internet—are pornographic, according to the Carnegie-Mellon study."

Wrong! Most of the 900,000 images had *not* been on the Internet. They had been on private, adults-only bulletin boards. And the figure of 83.5 percent was based on hopelessly faulty data. No

matter; in the minds of politicians, journalists, TV viewers, and Americans in general, the statistic was lodged as firmly as Ronald Reagan's factoids about trees poisoning the air with carbon dioxide.

The Traumatic Statistic was powerful because it filled a valuable psychological need: It literalized an incoherent fear. People had been afraid of what their kids might find in this weird new medium, the Internet. Now someone had measured the danger from porn and put a number on it. It was like walking into a dark room, feeling afraid of what might be there—and then having some smart young scientist from a university switch on the light and count the bugs for you. A number—any number—was better than no number at all.

This, finally, was Martin Rimm's lasting contribution: The American public had had an inarticulate fear, and he transformed it into an inaccurate fact.

The Real Martin Rimm

The question still remains: Why did he do it?

In a footnote to his study he claimed that "the research team does not advocate or endorse any particular viewpoint or course of action concerning pornography on the Information Superhighway." Elsewhere, he even claimed to disapprove of Carnegie-Mellon for banning sexually oriented newsgroups: "I have publicly criticized the administration, and will continue to do so. They used me as a scapegoat for some peculiar agenda."

In a letter, he said that while some people would probably condemn his popular writing style as being "like Jerry Falwell," he considered himself a renegade artist and praised the Marquis de Sade as "a genius." This was an odd reference, because elsewhere he had referred to Robert Thomas of Amateur Action as the "Marquis de Cyberspace."

At best, this was muddled; at worst, it looked flagrantly dishonest. While Rimm was telling free-speech activists what they wanted to

hear, it now seems that his work was well-known to right-wing activists who were eager to censor the Net. Rimm claimed that his study had been accepted for publication "in substantially complete form" as early as November 1994, which suggests that his link with the *Georgetown Law Journal* was long-standing. The editor-in-chief of the journal has gone on record as saying that Rimm didn't submit his study directly; it came in via "an editor on the journal." Who could that editor have been? Well, appearing on the same *Nightline* show as Martin Rimm was a man named H. Deen Kaplan who is affiliated with the National Coalition for the Protection of Children and Families, formerly titled the National Coalition Against Pornography. Kaplan is believed to have been the one who gave James Exon the binder of pornographic photos that Exon brandished in the Senate. Kaplan also happened to be a third-year student at Georgetown University Law Center—and was an editor on the journal. Rimm has neither confirmed nor denied that antiporn activist Kaplan was the man who recommended the study to the *Georgetown Law Journal*.

Mike Godwin, legal counsel to Electronic Frontier Foundation, became obsessed with the Martin Rimm saga and gathered a mountain of evidence.

Meanwhile, John McMickle of the National Law Center for Children and Families—which claims to be an organization separate from the National Coalition for the Protection of Children and Families but shares the same address and phone number—became a congressional staffer for Senator Charles Grassley in January 1995. It was Grassley who chaired the Judiciary Committee hearings on children and Internet pornography. It was McMickle who asked Rimm if he would be interested in testifying at those hearings. While Rimm has denied any close links with antiporn crusaders, circumstantial evidence makes it look as if he was well-acquainted with them during the preparation of his study.

Using his skills as an attorney, Mike Godwin has researched this more thoroughly than anyone else, and he is now convinced that Rimm was actually assisted in writing his study by the National Coalition for the Protection of Children and Families, the National Law Center for Children and Families, and Enough is Enough, another antiporn group (which also testified in Senator Grassley's hearings). Godwin concludes that "there are numerous links between Rimm and antiporn groups that strongly suggest a team effort to create the perception of a pornography problem on 'the information superhighway.'" Rimm, meanwhile, has written in a letter to Mike Godwin, "I never had any contact with anyone who is affiliated with the 'Religious Right.'" Unfortunately, since Rimm doesn't say exactly what he means by "Religious Right," this is not a compelling rebuttal.

There's no evidence, though, that Rimm is a fundamentalist Christian with a personal desire to censor the Net. Christopher Reeve, a student at Carnegie-Mellon who wrote a section of Rimm's study surveying the World Wide Web, believes that Rimm was mainly in it for notoriety, plain and simple. "He wanted to be at the center of the controversy," Reeve said afterward. He added that Rimm realized his study might be used by the far right, and "we discussed how to avoid this. However, I think in the end, he actually did very little in the way of preventing it."

Reeve has a personal reason to be annoyed with Rimm, who had a bad habit of flirting with Reeve's girlfriend. Still, Reeve now tries to

shrug this off. "She thought he was kind of creepy," he says. "I think he just hit on her a couple of times." In fact, Reeve is one of the few people who will still say a few words in defense of Rimm. "I don't think Marty is extremely different from other Carnegie-Mellon undergrads, in that he started this project in hopes of making a name for himself (and really, I'm convinced that's about as far as his intentions go)." Reeve feels that Rimm simply wanted "to blitzkrieg the world as the new pornography expert."

Bret Pettichord, a former classmate, remembers Rimm as "a loner" who used to have an odd habit of pacing to and fro while listening intently to tapes of Jerry Falwell. "Not for the message," says Pettichord; Rimm was "fascinated by how Falwell was able to sway people with his rhetoric."

Rimm later disputed this, claiming that he studied Falwell because "I was reading Plutarch and some of the great Latin orators. I thought it would be creative to compare their rhetoric to someone contemporary like Falwell." The fact remains, though, that he later compared his own writing style with that of Falwell.

Certainly Rimm was interested in self-promotion—perhaps by unusual means. According to the Atlantic City *Press*, in 1990 Rimm was investigated by the New Jersey Division of Gaming Enforcement when fliers advertising his self-published book *An American Playground* were found on the windshields of cars in the parking lot of Atlantic City's Taj Mahal casino. The fliers promised that anyone who bought the book and showed it to Taj Mahal officials would be rewarded with $25 in coins for slot machines. This was news to the casino; no one knew anything about the offer. (Rimm later said it was news to him, too.)

Trying to assemble a picture from these fragments, we find, perhaps, a secretive, rebellious loner who had such a craving for notoriety that nothing else was important by comparison—not even freedom of expression on a global computer network serving millions of users. According to Mike Godwin, "I believe that he'd have been happy if *any* legislation had been passed as an outcome of his article—it would have been external validation of his importance."

Did Rimm want to damage Net freedoms? "I don't think that was his goal. It was always fame, the spotlight, and the sense that he had caused things to happen, even in the United States Congress."

Rimm categorically denies this. If he'd been looking for notoriety, he says, he wouldn't have pursued an engineering degree or served in the army. "Mike Godwin never met me," he points out, "and spoke to me only once during a one-hour conference call with *Nightline*."

Rimm also remains defiant about the value of his study: "I did not experience 'Total Humiliation By Total Exposure.' I and many of the people I worked with at Carnegie-Mellon are very proud of the study, of its quality, originality, power, and impact."

And yet this phrase is unintentionally revealing. By saying that he's proud of the "power and impact," Rimm confirms that he was, in fact, actively interested in affecting the status quo.

Rough Justice

Rimm's name has dropped out of sight in the national media, but Net users refuse to forget. In the fall of 1995 Rimm had planned to continue his studies in the Technology and Policy Program at MIT, where a place was waiting for him. When netizens learned of this, two of them visited a member of the admissions committee to warn him about Rimm. Evidently the committee member didn't need to be warned; he already knew some background. Either way, a few days later, without explanation, Rimm stated that his plans had changed. He would not be attending MIT in the fall semester after all.

In view of Rimm's distortion of data, maybe he didn't deserve a place at MIT. But there were some uneasy implications here. Netizens claimed they had merely told the truth about him, and the truth could only hurt someone with something to hide. But almost everyone has at least a few secrets that would be embarrassing or damaging if they were publicized, and on the Internet this means telling a potential audience of millions.

The truth can be a devastating weapon even where no actual crimes have been committed. Gay activists can wreck a macho movie star's career by revealing his private life as a homosexual. Journalists can ruin a political candidate by revealing incidents from her college days. Online, anyone can be a target. If people with unpopular views are aware that they can be instantly subjected to total humiliation through total exposure, won't this have a chilling effect on free speech?

Even where the technique seems fully justified, it's still a rough form of justice. When punishments are handed down by a judge, they usually include a cutoff date after which the offender has paid his debt and is free to go about his business. In the online world the cutoff date is undefined and may not exist at all. Some activists were trading tidbits and minor revelations about Martin Rimm six months after his study was published. Years from now, a few netizens may still be ready to warn any institution or employer that offers a place for Rimm.

Moreover, Total Humiliation by Total Exposure is a weapon that can point both ways. Imagine the Christian Coalition getting online and targeting a free-speech advocate who happens to have an embarrassing episode in his past. There's no way to prevent this. Indeed, under the Constitution, it *can't* be prevented so long as no direct threats or libelous statements are made.

Mike Godwin acknowledges the problem. "Let's suppose I want to damage your reputation," he says. "I have the power of the mass media on my desktop, I have no editor above me, and I can hide my identity by using a temporary account on America Online or Prodigy. I can broadcast my message to tens of thousands or maybe even millions, and even if my target tries to rebut the statement, his reputation is damaged in an irredeemable way."

Still, Godwin goes on, "We've had online communications for seventeen years, since the first BBS. And in that time there have been no more than half a dozen well-publicized libel cases based on online interactions. Let's assume that figure is just ten percent of the real total. Sixty cases in seventeen years is still nothing."

Godwin points out that in the online world, a statement doesn't necessarily carry the same weight that it would in print. "There's no default assumption of credibility as there is when you read the *New York Times*, especially if someone posts from an anonymous account."

Still, we should understand the power of the Net to destroy privacy, and we should recognize that some Internet vigilantes do have a tendency to hound individuals they dislike. The potential danger here is hard to predict, but it may be ultimately more significant than the supposed danger of downloading sexy pictures of naked people from Usenet newsgroups or computer bulletin boards.

Access, Content, and Distribution

Since Rimm's study has been discredited, we have to look elsewhere to find out how much pornography really exists online.

In mid–1995 Peter Trei, a highly experienced software engineer, did his own quick survey and posted the results on the Net. Basically he examined the Usenet feed at his local Internet service provider, counted how many newsgroups had dangerous-sounding names, and compared them with newsgroups that had safe-sounding names.

What standards did he use for "safe" and "dangerous"? Trei didn't use those words. Thinking back to Senator Exon, he tried to imagine what "might offend a certain retiring senator." Anything that fell into that broad category, or anything "which I'd feel uncomfortable about letting my five-year-old see or read," he labeled "Unexonian." Adding it up, 142 out of a total of 10,985 news groups had names that sounded Unexonian. This worked out to 1.3 percent.

But some groups are busier than others. To factor this in, Trei did what Martin Rimm chose not to do: He devised a program to count the number of actual messages in all the different groups. This

program didn't take a lot of time to write; in fact, it was a single line of Unix commands piped together. Using it, Trei counted a total of 591,783 messages, of which 16,288 were pictures in Unexonian newsgroups and 18,025 were text in Unexonian newsgroups. This meant that out of all the messages on Usenet, 5.8 percent might be unsuitable for a five-year-old, by Trei's rough estimation.

This figure is a lot less scary than Rimm's Traumatic Statistic, but according to Trei, it's still probably too high, for several reasons.

First, pictures are commonly split into two or more chunks of data. Trei's routine counted the chunks as separate messages when really they were subsections.

Second, picture newsgroups also contain text messages from people asking for, offering, discussing, or complaining about the pictures. There's nothing offensive in these messages—but they were counted as Unexonian by Trei's routine because they were sitting in Unexonian newsgroups.

Third, sexually oriented groups are often bombarded with threats such as "You will all burn in hell!" from religious fundamentalists and other do-gooders. Naturally, these threats generate an equal number of angry or mocking replies. Since this all happens in Unexonian groups, all of it was counted as being unsuitable for a five-year-old.

"Applying these caveats," Trei concluded, "it's likely that 'unexonia' actually occupies no more than 4 percent of Usenet traffic, in terms of 'things to be read or looked at.'"

How much should it worry us that maybe one message in twenty-five on Usenet is unsuitable for Senator James Exon or a five-year-old child? Trei suggested comparing the situation with a typical newsstand, where *more* than 4 percent of the titles on display might be unsuitable for five-year-olds. This seems reassuring—but is it? Usenet differs from a newsstand in three important ways:

Access: Newsstands are supervised; the Internet is not. Online, there's no one to say, "Sorry, kid, if you're under eighteen, you can't buy that."

Content: Material in some newsgroups is far more explicit than pictures or text in men's magazines.

Distribution: Newsstands in conservative areas of the country often choose not to carry "offensive" publications. Magazine distribution varies according to local tastes and community standards. By comparison, Usenet is equally accessible from any area of the country.

Access, content, and distribution are the three big problems afflicting free speech online.

Sex, Drugs, and Kiss My Ass

Another rough-and-ready study of Usenet was contributed anonymously to the Usenet newsgroup alt.censorship. Once again the author counted newsgroups that had names liable to worry moral activists. At his local site there were 4,283 available groups, of which 74 had the word "sex" in the title, 9 had the word "drugs" in the title, 1 was called "alt.irc.ops.kiss.my.ass," and so on. The total of potentially offensive group names came to 2.91 percent.

The author of this brief summary came up with his own analogy. Usenet is like a city: You're likely to get a very different impression of it depending on the neighborhood where you choose to hang out. He wrote: "If you stood in the 'Combat Zone' (an area where porno shops are concentrated in Boston) and looked around, all you'd see is pornography and strip joints and think what a filth hole this is and judge that city harshly. If, on the other hand, you stood in the Faneuil Hall Marketplace, all you'd see was all kinds of great restaurants and shops, historic buildings, street entertainers singing and doing magic acts, etc., and you'd judge that city quite differently. . . . Perhaps if 'investigative reporters' and paranoid hysterics didn't hang around exclusively in newsgroups with the words 'sex' and 'erotica' in the title, they'd see a lot of valuable and informative material being exchanged and the danger of censoring the system that carries it."

Here again, though, access, content, and distribution are different in a city compared with the Net.

Access: Young children can get access to all areas of Usenet, but they aren't so free to roam sleazy urban areas and wander into pornographic bookstores.

Content: The world online is far freer than the real world, even in urban areas.

Distribution: The Internet blasts urban-style material into quiet suburban backwaters. There's no clear division between neighborhoods, as there is in a city.

Suppose we could modify access, content, and distribution to make the Net more like the everyday world. Would this satisfy the decency activists? Would it outrage the libertarians? Is it technically feasible?

To answer these questions, we need more information on the Net itself—and Usenet in particular, since that's where most of the controversy has come from.

Origins of Usenet

Back in 1979 at Duke University in North Carolina, two graduate students named Tom Truscott and Jim Ellis were looking for a better way to distribute news about Unix, the operating system that controlled their minicomputers. Unix had been developed for internal use at AT&T; it was given away free on an informal basis to anyone who wanted it. No one took responsibility for maintaining Unix, updating it, and correcting things that were wrong with it. You used it at your own risk, and when you ran into one of its undocumented problems, you had to fix it yourself or find someone else who knew how. While you were doing that, your computer could be paralyzed for hours or even days at a time.

There were a couple of informal newsletters that offered useful advice on Unix bugs, but you obviously couldn't wait for one of

those updates when you had a real crisis on hand. Consequently, Truscott and Ellis suggested a scheme through which a bunch of sites would swap news with each other electronically. No single person would be in charge of this system. It would be run by everyone, for everyone, and anyone would be able to contribute. This, then, was the origin of Usenet.

Steve Bellovin, a graduate student at the University of North Carolina, put together a program that would handle the news-swapping. After some tests at the beginning of 1980, the program was given away to anyone who wanted it.

The system worked so well, people started swapping news that had nothing to do with Unix. The software was upgraded to handle larger volumes of information and sort it under subject headings. Finally, in 1986, Network News Transfer Protocol (NNTP) was established as a standard for packaging and transmitting the data. By this time the Internet was a reality, and the news transfer standard was finalized after a "Request for Comment" (RFC) from the Internet Network Information Center (InterNIC), which is the nearest thing to a centralized body administering the Net.

Now people started writing various news processors and news readers to make the system more friendly for the end user. Meanwhile, the number of newsgroups started growing wildly. Some system administrators felt that the whole thing had gotten out of hand, and they refused to offer the full range of groups at their sites. Other system administrators didn't approve of this; they felt that information should be available on every topic—it wanted to be free, right?—and they refused to censor anything.

In this way, Usenet evolved as a very flexible, totally decentralized system. No one owned it, no one ran it, and it quickly became one of the purest examples of anarchy that has ever existed. Anyone could say anything at all online. Peer pressure exerted a low-key moderating influence, but of course there were some troublemakers who took a perverse pleasure from being obnoxious, and there was no way to stop them. In the words of an anonymous aphorism: "Anarchy means having to put up with things that really piss you off."

Today Usenet still functions on this basis. The millions of people who use it seem pretty happy with it as it is, and hardly anyone online complains about its content. The activists who want to impose controls are almost all people who *don't* use it, which means that the inhabitants of Usenet are like citizens of a country whose laws are being written by a bunch of foreigners. In some ways the online environment in 1996 feels like Hong Kong in the last days of British rule: a very free community wondering what's going to happen as totalitarian forces start moving in.

Extreme Content

Usenet newsgroups focus on every conceivable topic, including job hunting, travel, humor, golf, and tropical fish. Most messages are as mundane as conversations you might over-hear on a city bus. How do you find the sexy stuff?

Most news-reading programs make it easy enough. Here's the result of searching for Usenet groups in the "alt.sex" hierarchy:

```
46279   alt.sex
 7326   alt.sex.anal
 8491   alt.sex.bestiality
   20   alt.sex.bestiality.barney
    2   alt.sex.bestiality.hamster.duct-tape
28088   alt.sex.bondage
    5   alt.sex.bondage.particle.physics
 1142   alt.sex.boredom
15103   alt.sex.breast
 2513   alt.sex.enemas
18886   alt.sex.erotica.marketplace
17263   alt.sex.exhibitionism
 6246   alt.sex.fat
10137   alt.sex.femdom
 4921   alt.sex.fetish.diapers
 3972   alt.sex.fetish.fashion
  357   alt.sex.fetish.feet
 3098   alt.sex.fetish.hair
 9492   alt.sex.fetish.orientals
 3754   alt.sex.fetish.startrek
 5329   alt.sex.fetish.tickling
```

```
   6418   alt.sex.fetish.watersports
   2089   alt.sex.first-time
   8885   alt.sex.homosexual
   2854   alt.sex.intergen
   6829   alt.sex.magazines
  21463   alt.sex.masturbation
   4412   alt.sex.motss
  22898   alt.sex.movies
      6   alt.sex.nasal-hair
  40360   alt.sex.pictures
   4138   alt.sex.pictures.d
  35886   alt.sex.pictures.female
  15919   alt.sex.pictures.male
    807   alt.sex.plushies
    273   alt.sex.services
   1753   alt.sex.sounds
   9652   alt.sex.spanking
  32296   alt.sex.stories
   3517   alt.sex.stories.d
  16585   alt.sex.strip-clubs
   8862   alt.sex.telephone
    698   alt.sex.voxmeet
   8604   alt.sex.voyeurism
  27352   alt.sex.wanted
   6821   alt.sex.wizards
   9324   alt.sexual.abuse.recovery
      1   alt.sexual.abuse.recovery.d
    597   alt.sexy.bald.captains
```

The alt groups were created as an alternative to more conventional groups that are often supervised by moderators. The alt hierarchy is the freest—and most troublesome—segment of Usenet.

In the list above, the number preceding each newsgroup shows how many messages have been posted since the group was last accessed by this particular user at this particular site. If you actually check the contents of a group, you're likely to find that many messages no longer exist; they've been erased to make room for new ones coming in.

Of course, sex isn't the only "sensitive" subject matter on Usenet. Nonsexual content can still be mind-boggling to consumers whose diet normally consists of TV, national-circulation magazines, and newspapers.

For instance, you may find . . .

Challenging experiments in high-school chemistry:

Imagine this. A great, inflated, green garbage bag slowly wafting down from a tall building. It gains some speed as it nears the ground. People look up and say, "What the....?" The garbage bag hits! *BOOM!!!* It explodes in a thundering fireball of green bits of plastic and flame!

"What is this?" you may ask. Well, this is the great "Acetylene Balloon Bomb." And here is how to make it.

(Posted to alt.2600)

Radical political statements:

Everyone remember when that idiot Martin Luther King was shot and killed? What happened after? Basically a bunch of losers running in the streets, burning and destroying things, and acting like the fuckheads they are. . . . It is time for whites to stop apologizing and get some pride. I have the words "white, straight, and proud" on my jacket, and just today some teenage girls were trying to tell me how "racist" I am. It is really sick.

(Posted to alt.politics.white-power)

True confessions:

It is a sad truth that fornication with negresses is a practice that is condoned, even encouraged, among southern white men. I can still hear the schoolyard sayings: "The blacker the berry, the sweeter the juice"; "I'm gonna get me some of that brown sugar"; and "Black absorbs heat."

It is also a sad truth that I, like many of my peers, spent many hours obtaining "knowledge" (in the biblical sense) of the bitches of that race of primates.

However, we certainly did not take the cows out in public....

(Posted to alt.politics.white-power)

Frank discussions of human biology:

Zits that hit the mirror then expel blood are not considered Streakers, only because their ejection system was aided, much in the way runners are wind-aided. These are called Cluster Bombers, more bang for your buck, or squirt for your squeeze, if you will. Have you noticed the way that this type of blood coagulates quickly? If you let the zit bleed for a bit, then wipe it, the blood on the top of Mount Pus is thick and comes in a clump. I thought of this when reading the menstrual coagulation posts earlier.

(Posted to alt.tasteless)

In-depth examination of substance abuse:

>What are the steps to separate the alkaloid chemicals from poppy sap?

Soak sap in kerosene and let sit for 5 minutes.
Add 1/2 cup of lime and let dissipate.
Mix with fertilizer and a cup of Drano.
Add a touch of pepper and ignite.

That should give you a mind-blowing experience you psychotic paranoid druggie buttlicker.

Hopefully this will sterilize you so society won't have to undergo the pain of seeing your mutant offspring.

Have a great day.

(Posted to alt.conspiracy)

Powerful statements of religious belief:

Groups are now being formed around the USA to celebrate the death or other personal tragedy of:

Sen. J. J. Exon   Sen. Jesse Helms
Sen. Phil Gramm   Sen. Robert Dole
[17 more names omitted for reasons of space]

For the past 2000 years, these jerks and their historical ancestors have killed, raped, butchered, tortured, mutilated, and suppressed more human beings than all the non-religious wars or diseases combined—all in the name of their GOD.

Now, when they die or suffer some other tragedy—
we will all meet throughout the USA at a common
time to toast the misfortune of these scum sucking
leeches.

(Posted to alt.politics.datahighway)

Exciting recreational diversions:

While checking the Prophone CD-ROM directory for
massage parlors in the northeast USA, I came
across "Salon d'Artiste" located in "Spreadeagle
Village," Stratford, PA, a little west of Philadelphia.
With a name like that and an address like that it
sounds exciting. Does anyone have any info about
this place?

(Posted to alt.sex.services)

Modern literature:

Janitor Dan Goats of Indiana paused to reflect on
his life-long obsession. "Sex," he proclaimed; "Sex
is SIN! It is foul! And disgusting!" He usually got
into these moods when he was fucking his pet goat
up the ass, because his dick would be all black and
brown afterwards.

(Fiction posted to alt.sex.spanking)

Products not available in stores:

I will sell my panties worn for an entire day for
$15, $10 for each extra pair ordered at the same
time. If you want me to wear my panties for more
than one day, then send me $5 for every day
extra you want me to wear them (but not more
than 7 days worth—or everyone will be able to
smell them!)

(Posted to alt.sex.boredom)

Most posts on Usenet are *not* extreme or offensive. On sci.medicine
you can ask questions and get authoritative answers on any topic
from circumcision to cancer. You can look for employment on
misc.jobs.offered or look for love on alt.personals. Cat owners can
exchange advice on caring for their pets; computer users can find
help that goes way beyond the typical support provided by a

retailer. People on Usenet are often selflessly generous and decent to each other. On the newsgroup alt.suicide.holiday (which was established to discuss why there are so many suicides on national holidays), participants have actively helped each other to cope with suicidal impulses.

But still the extreme material exists. Can it be controlled? Should it be controlled? And how do controversial newsgroups get started in the first place?

Canceling the Spam

In keeping with the spirit of decentralized anarchy, anyone with some technical knowledge can create a Usenet news-group. In practice, though, this would be pointless, because most sites wouldn't bother to offer the group to their users. So how do some groups get widely distributed?

It's surprisingly difficult to obtain a clear answer to this kind of question, because there's no official entity in charge of the situation. One starting point is to ask someone who's been involved as an activist on a volunteer basis.

Joel Furr fits that description. A longtime Net user, Furr has partici-pated in policy debates, has written one of the primary guides to online "netiquette," helps to publicize inappropriate use of Usenet, and became notorious when he got into an online fight with a couple of lawyers who took advantage of the system as a vast free advertising service.

Rapid-talking, sardonic, and irritable, Furr has developed a love-hate relationship with Net users. "A lot of people are determined to make up their own names for newsgroups," he says. "They've got the idea that they can do anything they want on Usenet, which is true on a local level but not globally. One guy wanted a newsgroup to talk about lifelong love. I don't know what there is to discuss on this topic that you can't discuss in alt.romance, but he was

Joel Furr does informal damage control on Usenet in his spare time (wearily).

determined to create this newsgroup and he wanted to call it alt.forever.linette because his girlfriend is named Linette and he was going to love her forever. He said he thought people would be interested enough to ask about it. Of course, no one ever did find out about his group because only five sites bothered to carry it, and no one was interested."

Businesses have made similarly misguided attempts to create their own forums for online discussion. "You get multilevel marketing operations," says Furr, "like Amway, who came in and said, 'We want to create a group named alt.business.amway.' There was in fact an Amway newsgroup, but no one ever posted to it, because hardly anyone carried it, and everybody knows that Amway is pond scum, and the newsgroup was only going to benefit one entity, which was Amway."

So what do you do if you want your newsgroup to be read? You have a choice. You can create your own alt group and publicize it on

the Net in the hope that people will nag their local Internet provider into carrying it. Or you can take a more formal approach, which means you write up your proposal for a new group and e-mail it to a man named David Lawrence.

Lawrence works for UUnet, a company that feeds news to 1,000 Internet sites. But Lawrence's day job maintaining the infrastructure has nothing to do with his activity creating newsgroups; like Furr, he does that kind of thing entirely in his spare time.

Every time Lawrence receives a request, he announces it on a special newsgroup named news.announce.newgroups. After twenty-eight days of discussion, a vote is held. Anyone on the Net is qualified to cast a ballot for or against forming the new group. If two thirds say yes, *and* if the number of yes votes exceeds the number of no votes by 100 or more, the new group is created. At this point, Lawrence notifies every Internet service provider that the group exists. This doesn't guarantee that all of them will add it to their list; as Lawrence says, "I don't really have any power; I just make recommendations."

Still, he acknowledges that people do often follow his recom-mendations, which gives him a kind of guru status. "I do have more influence than just about anybody else," he admits, "and some people get upset by the notion. . . . I'm not the only one with a vision of how Usenet should be, but I do believe I have a better understanding of how it works—and the implications—than the average user. So maybe I *should* have some influence."

Some libertarian Net users resent the voting system and accuse people such as Lawrence and Furr of being part of a "cabal" that wields censorious power over the Net. In fact, Lawrence is quick to point out that he has never failed to authorize a newsgroup because of its content; he only demands that there should be enough people to vote for it.

From his point of view, the problem on Usenet isn't control, it's "noise." This is the all-purpose term for time-wasting quibbles, off-topic rants, unfunny remarks, obscene insults, arguments that never end, accusations such as "You're a Nazi," and general stupidity. "We

used to notice a phenomenon every September," says Lawrence, "where kids would get into college, acquire Internet access, and do lots of stupid things. And now the saying goes, 'It's always September on the Net.' I have a lot of varied interests, but even in my passions, like motorcycling, I don't read the newsgroups anymore. There's too much noise."

The worst kind of noise is "spamming." Spam is defined as junk mail or other text posted to twenty-five or more groups simultaneously. Often it's some kind of advertising—maybe for "hot phone sex" or quasi-legal pyramid schemes with subject lines such as "Make money fast!" In the early days of Usenet this never happened, but in 1993 immigration lawyers Lawrence Canter and Martha Siegel sent identical ads for their "green card" legal services to *every one* of the thousands of Usenet groups that could be reached via their Internet provider, and other entrepreneurs were quick to see the potential in this technique. After all, many service providers charge a flat rate for Net access, so that it costs the same to send 1,000 messages as one.

Obviously, if every business started using the Net this way, the system would be overwhelmed. Netizens were predictably outraged; they mail-bombed the lawyers (sent them literally thousands of pieces of e-mail), ordered magazine subscriptions in their names, sent them pizza, called them in the middle of the night and yelled at them, sent them thousands of pages of faxes, and generally did everything they could to make their lives miserable.

Joel Furr started selling T-shirts with a message ridiculing Canter and Siegel. In response, they threatened a variety of legal actions against him, although they never actually filed a lawsuit, probably because dozens of other lawyers on the Net made it clear that they were ready to help Furr with free legal services plus a potentially lucrative countersuit.

Today some companies offer to spam your message across Usenet for a fee. Two of these organizations place regular classified ads in *USA Today*. Jeffrey A. Slaton of Albuquerque, New Mexico, came right out and called himself "Spam King"—prompting one newsgroup

moderator to call for massive retaliation. After publicly listing Slaton's address and home phone number, the moderator went on: "I'm doing a social security number trace on him now, and trying to find out where he banks. I'm not certain, but I think he has some other employment as well."

Not everyone feels comfortable about this commando-style retaliation. There is, in fact, an "approved" response to spam: cancellation.

Joel Furr comoderates the news.admin.Net-abuse.announce group, where cases of spamming are reported on a daily basis. This group also lists each piece of spam that has been canceled. Following another quirky, arcane system, a group of volunteers uses a complex mathematical formula based on how many groups have been hit by identical messages, or substantially similar messages, within a forty-five-day period. If the formula yields a high number, the volunteers cancel the offending message by issuing a special cancel instruction to all Internet sites, where news software responds by rendering the spam "unavailable" to anyone who tries to read it.

Canceling messages used to be considered a kind of crime against the totally open spirit of Usenet. But now, according to Furr, "In some groups spam constitutes most of the traffic, and if you didn't control it people would stop bothering to read those groups. As a result, canceling has become an essential function."

Really, this means that a form of Net censorship already exists. It is absolutely not based on content—but it could be.

What would happen if a Usenet censor started canceling "offensive" posts on a regular, methodical basis? His fate would be far worse than that of Canter and Siegel, worse even that the fate of Martin Rimm. He'd be a focus for unimaginably rabid hatred.

But suppose federal "decency" legislation puts the FCC in charge. Now a legally sanctioned government agency has the power to do cancels. This might be a First Amendment violation; but test cases can take years to reach the Supreme Court, and in the meantime, Usenet would be censored.

The consequences are hard to predict. Ornery system administrators might create some new protocol for swapping uncensored items, just as they created Usenet in the first place. They might work via sites overseas, beyond the reach of American decency laws.

There's a popular belief on Usenet—really, an article of faith—that the Net is so decentralized, no one will be able to censor it effectively, and the sheer volume of messages makes any kind of censorship impractical.

"There's no easy way to measure the traffic anymore," says Furr. "There used to be choke points where you could make measurements, but now there are some groups that cover the whole planet, and other groups at just one site, and no one really knows what's going on. It's at least a million messages a month, probably much higher, but that's the last figure with any reasonable accuracy."

Obviously, controlling the content of Usenet isn't going to be easy, and any institution that tries to do it is going to face legal problems, practical difficulties, and a major grass-roots rebellion.

CompuServe has already learned this lesson the hard way. Late in December 1995 it tackled the alt.sex problem by blocking all newsgroups with words such as "sex" or "gay" in their titles. Supposedly this was in response to a request from Bavarian officials, who informed CompuServe that many of the groups violated German pornography laws. According to a journalist who works for *Der Spiegel*, "Last summer, a kind of hysteria about Internet pornography broke out in German media. A few journalists had made their first steps in the Internet and discovered nasty postings in the alt.binaries.pictures.erotica Usenet hierarchy. . . . Then, the *Time* article about Internet porn was published and quoted by nearly every German newspaper." (This, of course, was Philip Elmer-DeWitt's cover story featuring Martin Rimm.)

Apparently a German task force managed to get a search warrant for CompuServe's office in Munich, and according to a public prosecutor, the service provider was "quite cooperative . . . We sat together talking about chances to kick pornographic contents out of

CompuServe's information system." Subsequently CompuServe was given a list of more than 200 newsgroups that could be problematic, and the groups were banned a few days later. CompuServe claimed that it was unable to provide different versions of its service in different countries, and consequently the ban affected every subscriber worldwide.

Like most censorship attempts, it produced some unintentionally absurd results. Brad Templeton, founder of the ClariNet news distribution system, noted that CompuServe didn't subscribe to his service but banned some of his newsgroups anyway—including clari.news.sex, which featured purely factual items such as "Vatican: Sex education not okay" and "China customs crack down on pornography imports."

Many netizens suspected that CompuServe was using the Bavarian complaint as a convenient excuse for getting rid of any material that could conceivably cause trouble at home. There were predictable shouts of outrage online, and some CompuServe members moved to services where the full range of Usenet was still available. Finally, after about a month, CompuServe was forced to back down. It lifted its embargo on almost all the newsgroups, although it still continued to block five that were suspected of carrying child pornography.

Shoot the Messenger

Throughout 1995 and into 1996, while federal legislation was being drafted, enacted, and then challenged in court, decency activists kept insisting on one basic principle: When an Internet service provider doesn't take proper precautions to protect children from viewing indecent material, it should be legally liable.

Some commentators saw this as a first step toward generally controlling the Net. Writing in *Boardwatch* magazine, editor-publisher Jack Rickard pointed out that it's "terribly inconvenient and expensive" for governments to prosecute thousands of separate individuals. "It would be much easier," he suggested, "to find some

pressure point, some mass control lever. . . . So every online service provider becomes a target. . . . We are scapegoating online services in an attempt to make them responsible for acts over which they have no control. The theory is, if we do it long enough and hard enough, they will find some way to control those acts and do our dirty work for us."

Well, if newsstands can keep sexually explicit material away from minors, why *shouldn't* Internet service providers do the same thing?

Leaving aside free-speech legal issues, it simply isn't practical to expect system administrators to check the content of a million Usenet messages a month, plus graphics, plus e-mail, plus online chat. Bearing this in mind, how can we accuse a site of being negligent if some pornography ends up on a child's computer screen?

Of course, sites could install software that scans text and recognizes "dangerous" keywords. Or a program could examine image files, check for the color and texture of naked skin, trace the outline of skin areas, and then look to see if there are any clothes covering the bodies. Farfetched? Not necessarily; a program of this type has already been devised by David Forsyth at the University of California at Berkeley. According to an abstract from his paper, his algorithm has "60% precision and 52% recall on a test set of 138 uncontrolled images of naked people, mostly obtained from the Internet, and 1401 assorted control images, drawn from a wide collection of sources."

Still, creative Net users will always find ways to fool censoring software. A simple way to thwart Forsyth's program would be to invert image colors before transmission. Taking this kind of approach to its simplest level, when Senator Exon first proposed to make it a criminal offense for people to say "fuck" online, Usenet contributors suggested using Exon as a four-letter substitute. No law against that, is there?

Robert Carr, a small software publisher in Boise, Idaho, started distributing a Macintosh program that would "exonize" *all* offensive text for transmission, then decode it back into its offensive form at

the other end. Called Hexon Exon, the program would input material such as this abbreviated excerpt from the newsgroup alt.drunken.bastards:

> Last night I got shit-faced and pissed in my pants. My girlfriend threw me out when I tried to grope her tits and ass. What a bitch.
>
> Fuck it! Life sucks.

The program would transform it into this safely "exonized" version, using names of suitable congresspeople:

> Last night I got NUNN-faced and BONDed in my pants. My girlfriend threw me out when I tried to grope her PELL and KYL. What a LUGAR.
>
> Exon it! Life GOREs.

Censorship always begins to look silly when it collides with humor. Back in 1988 Brad Templeton (who was then the owner of a small business named Looking Glass Software) became dissatisfied with a newsgroup named rec.humor, where the quality was often dismal. Templeton established a new group, titled rec.humor.funny, with himself as moderator, omitting jokes that he didn't find amusing.

Brad Templeton placed a joke in rec.humor that offended one Jewish reader. The consequences weren't funny.

Unfortunately, not everyone agreed with his judgment. Jonathan Richmond, a civil-engineering graduate student at MIT, found one of Templeton's jokes highly offensive. He caused so much fuss that Templeton lost his distribution site at the University of Waterloo, in Ontario, Canada.

News of this microscandal eventually reached Stanford University in California. After two months of vacillation, Stanford's vice president for information resources decided to enforce a ban on rec.humor.funny. This generated the usual student backlash, including a protest petition endorsed by 100 people, one of them the woman who had happened to mention the problem afflicting rec.humor.funny in the first place. Bay Area newspapers picked up the story and denounced Stanford's ban. The president of the university referred the issue to the academic senate. The academic senate's steering committee asked its committee on libraries for a recommendation. They responded with a statement saying that electronic media should be treated no differently from print media, and the ban should go. Ultimately, with bad grace, the administration followed the recommendation, and students were once more able to read rec.humor.funny. A couple of years later, the University of Waterloo came to the same conclusion.

But what was the offensive joke that caused all this trouble? Here's a transcript:

> A Scotsman and a Jew went to a restaurant. After a hearty meal, the waitress came by with the inevitable check. To the amazement of all, the Scotsman was heard to say, "I'll pay it!" and he actually did.
>
> The next morning's newspaper carried the news item:
>
> "JEWISH VENTRILOQUIST FOUND MURDERED IN ALLEY."

Jonathan Richmond, the MIT student who raised the initial objection, was Jewish. He found the joke offensive because it demeaned Jews.

Maybe it's hard for some of us to take it as seriously as Richmond did. But some Jewish-related speech online is no joking matter at all.

Tracking the Hate Groups

Rabbi Marvin Hier is dean and founder of the Simon Wiesenthal Center and its Museum of Tolerance, located in the Los Angeles area. In May 1995 he testified before yet another Senate group discussing "dangerous" netspeech. This time it was the Senate Subcommittee on Terrorism, Technology, and Government Information.

According to Hier, the Wiesenthal Center regularly monitors more than 240 hate groups, from neo-Nazi and Klan groups to Holocaust revisionists and Christian identity groups. Supposedly more than fifty of these groups were found "utilizing various elements of cyberspace—from electronic bulletin boards to sophisticated Web sites on the Internet. . . . Cyberspace has suddenly empowered marginal local groups, be they overt white supremacists or militias with racist ties like the Northern Regional Militia of Michigan. These groups market nationally, inflammatory videos and computerized files which fuel a conspiratorial, rabidly anti-government and often violent world view."

It's true that white supremacist views are easy to find online, in newsgroups such as alt.politics.white-power. Rabbi Hier wasn't suggesting that these discussion groups should be banned, because he realized this would be unconstitutional. Instead, he urged that large Internet service providers should refuse to carry the groups, just as CNN or the *Washington Post* would refuse to carry advertising from "avowed racists or Nazis."

No one paid much attention to this suggestion, so the Wiesenthal Center escalated its attack. At the beginning of January 1996 it circulated a letter to hundreds of Internet service providers pressuring them to block access to any Usenet groups or Web pages

that were spawning grounds for hate speech. The center even offered to assist service providers "in drafting a code of ethics."

Bearing in mind that the Internet functions like a telephone system allowing people to exchange personal views, this call for a crackdown was like suggesting that AT&T should refuse to transmit phone calls from racists. Still, the Wiesenthal Center's press release attracted some sympathetic publicity, which faced Internet service providers with an unpleasant choice: impose a form of censorship, or be named as purveyors of anti-Semitic propaganda.

Most sites still refused to censor themselves. Some of them pointed out that the racist newsgroups actually serve a useful purpose, providing a forum where Holocaust revisionists can be debated and refuted. Even a group such as alt.politics.white-power usually contains dozens of messages arguing for tolerance and mocking the bigots.

There was a more fundamental issue, though, which no one mentioned: Is hate speech really as widespread as the Wiesenthal Center chose to imply?

At the Museum of Tolerance there is a map of America flagged with literally hundreds of "hate group" locations. By pressing numbered buttons, a visitor can call up more information about the groups. In many cases, this information reveals that "hate group" is not an accurate label. A group in New Jersey, for instance, turns out to consist of two alleged skinheads who burned down a warehouse more than five years ago and haven't been heard from since.

Online, maybe three or four out of more than 10,000 Usenet groups have a racist agenda. There are also some Web pages, the best-known being sponsored by Ernst Zundel, who has spent a large part of his life trying to debunk the Jewish Holocaust. In January 1996, shortly after the Wiesenthal Center circulated its press release, one of two telephone networks in Germany was persuaded by the German government to block access to Zundel's American Web site so that his writings could not be viewed by German citizens. Since German law prohibits certain forms of speech about Nazism, the action was legally justified. Within a day, however, American free-

speech activists such as Declan McCullagh (who had organized the anti-Rimm demonstration at Carnegie-Mellon University) started "mirroring" the Zundel site—duplicating its entire content on their own Web sites, even though they disapproved of what Zundel had to say. The message was clear: If one Web site was blacked out, half a dozen would take its place. A couple of weeks later, German authorities were forced to admit that their effort at censorship had been a failure.

Here again, though, most press reports omitted to mention a pertinent fact: Most German citizens didn't bother to investigate Zundel's theories. One of the Web sites that made his text available logged fewer than 200 hits in a one-week period, even though the site had received national publicity. Most people simply weren't interested.

In fact, racism is a much smaller problem on the Net than in the everyday world. Netizens are generally uninterested in all forms of physical difference: age, disability, ethnicity, nationality, or race. It's common for people to swap messages without knowing any personal details about each other—even gender. Bearing this in mind, maybe it would make better sense for antiracism activists to forget about the Internet and concentrate on racism in the physical world, where it is a very legitimate cause for concern. Likewise, since bomb recipes and incitements to violence are extremely rare online, law enforcement would deploy its resources more effectively on the streets of any American city.

Of course, some senators refuse to see it that way. In the Senate subcommittee hearings on terrorism, technology, and government information, subcommittee chairman Arlen Specter suggested that some material on the Net—bomb-making information, in particular—poses a "clear and present danger" to American life. Since speech of this type would not be protected under the Constitution, Specter seemed to be finding a rationale here for censorship.

The Department of Justice respectfully disagreed. Robert Litt, a deputy assistant attorney general from the Criminal Division, told the senators what they should have already known: A bomb recipe, on its own, is protected speech. Moreover, when Litt was asked

if he had any statistics or direct knowledge of any crime resulting from someone getting information from the Internet, he had to admit that there had never been a case of this kind. The "threat" of terrorist information on the Net was being exaggerated even more than the "threat" of hate speech or online pornography—and there was no way to pass a constitutional law against it, anyway.

In the words of Scott Charney, the leading expert on computer crime at the Department of Justice: "Speech that incites imminent lawlessness or incitement to riot may not be protected, but generally speaking you cannot punish people even for reprehensible speech. As soon as you start talking about regulating speech, you have to ask who regulates it and where do you draw the lines, and you realize it's completely unworkable."

Probably Charney was speaking in legal terms when he made this statement, but controlling online content seems unworkable in practical terms, too. The German government couldn't figure out how to do it, CompuServe gave up after just a few weeks, and even if federal decency legislation survives legal challenges, there are some obvious ways to evade such restrictions.

The challenge of regulating the content of netspeech seems thorny at best and insoluble at worst. Could it be any easier to control access and distribution?

Community Standards

Amateur Action, the adult bulletin board run by Robert and Carleen Thomas and immortalized by Martin Rimm, was based in Milpitas, California. For several years it served users who were mostly located in that general area.

In 1993 a postal inspector named David Dirmeyer in Memphis, Tennessee, joined the BBS under the pseudonym Lance White. Using a long-distance phone connection, he downloaded a bunch of pictures, then handed them to a local federal prosecutor. Ultimately

a jury decided that the pictures violated local Tennessee community standards, and the Thomases were sentenced to three years in jail.

The Supreme Court has ruled that obscenity is a relative concept. The same picture that's legal in San Francisco may not be legal in a conservative part of the country where different values apply. Maybe there's some sense to this, so long as physical objects such as photographs or magazines are involved; but online communication shatters geographical barriers. A BBS can be accessed by anyone willing to pay long-distance phone charges. Usenet is freely available all over the world. Does this mean that all online speech must be censored to the point where it will not offend someone in, say, Georgia—or Iran? Alternatively, must small communities put up with a torrent of salacious material that they find horribly offensive?

Internet service providers in conservative areas can block any Usenet newsgroups that are known to contain explicit material, just as CompuServe chose to block a whole class of groups. This will placate some users—but will anger others. Even in small-town USA, for every antiporn activist there's at least one person who resents having his decisions made for him.

There's another possibility, though. The American Civil Liberties Union (ACLU) and the Electronic Frontier Foundation both filed amicus briefs on behalf of Robert and Carleen Thomas seeking (unsuccessfully) to overturn the guilty verdict. The ACLU made an interesting argument: "Computer technology has created new 'communities' or groups of individuals who communicate among themselves, sharing thoughts, ideas, and values. These communities do not exist geographically, but they exist nonetheless. The district court should have instructed the jury to apply the standards of the community involved, that of the members of the Thomases' bulletin board."

In other words, forget the whole concept of geography. Amateur Action created a new kind of community in which pictures that David Dirmeyer downloaded were *not* obscene. In fact, Dirmeyer was an outsider who intruded into this community. Since he ignored warning messages when he chose to go poking around there, it was his own fault if he didn't like what he found.

Extending this concept further, large service providers such as Prodigy, CompuServe, and America Online have created cyberspace communities that are just the opposite of an adult-oriented BBS. They're designed to be as wholesome, safe, and family-oriented as Disneyland. In fact, on Prodigy subscribers are simply not allowed to use "inappropriate" language (such as four-letter words).

This seems an excellent answer to the problems of access and distribution. A large service provider can even allow varying levels of access that are established by a child's parents when the account is opened. Adult chat groups can be locked out; in fact, all of Usenet can be excluded if necessary.

And yet in practice, this hasn't worked.

One problem is that regardless of what people *claim* they want, a lot of them really want to sample some online sex. Another problem is that service providers have an incentive to make as much money as possible by attracting users of as many different ages and tastes as possible—not just a narrow special-interest group. Also, censorship is hard to enforce when there are hundreds of thousands of users generating millions of messages.

Consequently, even on a big family-oriented system such as CompuServe, which runs and monitors its own teen chat areas, you still find adult-style material. The following transcript (in which fictitous names have been used to identify the children) was contributed by a CompuServe user in Canada:

Tommy, my 12-year-old brother, is a Compuserve teen chat-forum devotee. We never knew what he was up to with his 12-year-old friend Dave until he accidentally left one of his chat transcripts lying around.

Sandra:	hey guys
Tom and Dave:	Hey baby!
Sandra:	whats up?
Tom and Dave:	the sky what else
	baby
	How old are you sexy thing
Sandra:	15 u 2?
Tom and Dave:	7 & 8 momma

Sandra:	hey
	your 7 and 8
Tom and Dave:	17 18
Sandra:	my friend Angie is here with me
Tom and Dave:	Cool two Babies
Sandra:	what do u want 2 talk about?
Tom and Dave:	want to go on a sex date
Sandra:	sure
Tom and Dave:	How about tonight sex thing
Sandra:	ok
	where u from?
Tom and Dave:	Where and when?
Sandra:	where u from?
Tom and Dave:	my house
Sandra:	what state?
Tom and Dave:	sexy state
Sandra:	what state in the us?
Tom and Dave:	Sex town
Sandra:	what part of the world?
	smart asses
	hahaha
Tom and Dave:	look hows mommma is talkin
Sandra:	what????
Tom and Dave:	Are you deaf sex things
Sandra:	u 2 r crazy yet sound fun
Tom and Dave:	We are fun
Sandra:	where u from?
Tom and Dave:	sexy Montreal
Sandra:	CANADA!!!
Tom and Dave:	Yah sexy things
Sandra:	thats far
Tom and Dave:	from your sexy things
	Hey grovey chick
Sandra:	r u 2 my babies?
	r u 2 comedians?
	cause u 2 r funny
Tom and Dave:	no we are sex machines
Sandra:	r u gonna go 2 work on me?
	and Angie?
Tom and Dave:	Yah with our cross bone
Sandra:	lets talk about sex babie
	lets talk about u and me
	lets talk about all the good things
	and the bad things that may be
Tom and Dave:	you and me can have some sexy
Sandra:	sexy what???

Tom and Dave:	sex
Sandra:	sexy sex?
	ohhhh
Tom and Dave:	yah baby
Sandra:	i miss chris
	ha ha ha
Tom and Dave:	He he he
Sandra:	u guys crack me up
	i love you 2
	ha ha ha
	he he he
	ho ho ho
Tom and Dave:	yah we are going to crank you
	in to high gear
Sandra:	we we we
	oh really?
	says who?
Tom and Dave:	tommy and dave
Sandra:	i know a guy name tommy
Tom and Dave:	so do I
	di
	d
Sandra:	duh
	but my tommys really hot
Tom and Dave:	lets fuck now because I am
	getting tired
Sandra:	i dont do small favors
Tom and Dave:	Heh I have a big faver for you
	sexy
Sandra:	ok
Tom and Dave:	goodbye sexy thing se you
	next time
Sandra:	bye
	why did u leave?
Tom and Dave:	sorry got fuck someone else
	to night

Should this chat have been censored? Yes, according to CompuServe terms of service. But what would censorship achieve in this case? If Tom and Dave were stopped from indulging in their sex fantasies online, maybe they'd get bored and go back to reality. Wouldn't it be more hazardous for them to play these roles in the real world, with a real fifteen-year-old girl? Online, no one gets molested, pregnant, or raped. Doesn't this mean that the online environment is actually safer, even if it remains uncensored?

Charles Platt

Pedophiles' Playground

Of course, the situation changes drastically when kids are no longer just interacting with other kids but start communicating with adults. The environment seems to be an ideal stalking ground for pedophiles.

America Online (AOL) is the largest family-oriented service provider, selling itself as a nurturing environment for children. AOL has also attracted a lot of publicity for installing safeguards against bad behavior. Yet when a leading antiporn crusader had to select a single Internet service provider as a nest of child pornography and pedophiles, AOL was the one.

Barry Crimmins is a left-wing activist who makes a modest living doing antiestablishment comedy routines. At the same time, Crimmins has also become one of the loudest voices denouncing the traffic in online pornography. More effectively than any other person, he has publicized the dark side of AOL and demanded action to protect its young users.

Crimmins was sexually abused when he was a child. "My sister witnessed my abuse," he says. "Years later I published a story about it, and a social worker read it and knew the time period and got ahold of me, and in 1989 the person who had abused me was arrested and jailed for the third time. What he did was rape little boys, and he died in prison in 1991. He was—I'll just say he was an adult male in my baby-sitter's life."

As a result of the case, Crimmins became a contributing editor for *Moving Forward*, a news journal for survivors of sexual abuse. He started speaking out on the subject. In 1994 he learned that child pornography was being "openly traded" on America Online. Crimmins became an AOL member, sampled the chat rooms for himself, and was horrified by what he found.

A few months later he was invited to testify at Senator Charles Grassley's hearings on children and netporn. John McMickle of the National Law Center for Children and Families—the same

Senator Charles Grassley held hearings on children and netporn. Martin Rimm found himself uninvited, but Barry Crimmins told shocking tales about AOL.

man who approached, then disinvited Martin Rimm—picked Crimmins after receiving an endorsement for him from the publisher of *Moving Forward*.

Crimmins later said he felt terrified speaking at the hearings. Still, he made a strong, impassioned speech. "I came upon numerous atrocious rooms [on AOL]," he told the senators. "Many were obviously created by, and for, pedophiles. There were rooms promoting rape, incest, the exchange of child pornography, hate crimes, and every possible, and in some cases impossible, sexual activity. The first time I found the Abuse Survivors' room, it was located between a room called 'DadsNDaughtrs' and another entitled 'lilboypix.'"

Like other large service providers, AOL divides its system into many different areas. In the "People Exchange" area, members can create and name "rooms" where they can share messages with anyone else who visits the room after being tempted by its name.

There are two tiers of rooms: public and private. Crimmins used the system for a couple of months before he discovered the private tier. AOL offers parents the option of making this tier inaccessible for their children, but many people fail to do this—because they don't understand how, or they don't realize the potential problem, or they forget, or they simply don't bother.

When Crimmins saw what was going on, he complained to the management of AOL. When his complaints seemed to be ignored, he created a new online identity for himself as a twelve-year-old and lay in wait for the pedophiles. He didn't have to wait long. At the Senate hearings, he claimed he had been sent more than 1,000 pornographic photographs of children by people he met online. "At one point," he said, "a particularly sick individual sent me (in my guise as a twelve-year-old) so much child pornography that it took eight and a half hours to download it."

Crimmins forwarded this contraband to AOL and told them they should reimburse him for the online charges he incurred while receiving it. He didn't get a reply.

He felt that the pornography was dangerous for three reasons: It was being used to entice children, it encouraged adults to think of kids as sex objects, and real children were needed in order to create the kiddie porn in the first place. "The law of supply and demand is kicking in," he later wrote. "The increased demand for child pornography directly translates into an increased number of sexually abused children. You cannot have child pornography without abused children."

His testimony received a mixed reception. Civil libertarians were angry with him for giving new ammunition to decency crusaders, but he also annoyed conservatives because on topics outside of child pornography he maintained a permissive attitude. At the Senate hearings, for example, he endorsed the idea of chat rooms for gay and lesbian teens. "I'm concerned about them," he said later. "They're the group that has the highest rate of suicide. But Grassley turned purple when he heard me say that."

Crimmins is a hard-liner on child abuse partly because he feels it's not receiving the attention it deserves. "Take the Susan Smith case," he says, referring to the woman who drowned her two infants. "It may be in the *National Enquirer*, but how much space does the *New York Times* spend on it—especially the fact that her stepfather sexually abused her for years, and was active in Pat Robertson's presidential campaign?" Crimmins sighs. "There's your family values for you."

Is he a Christian?

"I have no problems with Jesus; he was a socialist among other things, and he wasn't a hypocrite. But I do think that Pat Robertson is a hypocrite. And I think that what's going on online, unless people of good conscience act, will provide the excuse for the Pat Robertsons of this world to destroy the whole deal for all of us."

According to Crimmins, liberals should clean up the Net so that conservatives don't find an excuse to do it for them, far more sweepingly. He fully realizes that this doesn't go down too well with civil libertarians. "If everyone's worst fear comes true," he says, "and Big Brother takes over the Internet, I'm certain that people like me will be blamed for it."

But why did a family-oriented service such as AOL become such a prime pedophile hangout? Several factors seem to have been involved:

First, millions of AOL disks were distributed through direct mail and as inserts in magazines. This made it easy for anyone, of any age, to log on and receive hours of free connect time. Moreover, people were free to use fictitious names.

Second, access was easier on AOL than on other providers. By developing its own point-and-click software, AOL became one of the first systems that could be handled by naive users . . . such as young children.

Third, partly because of its free disk distribution scheme, AOL experienced explosive growth, with all the problems of management and control that this implies.

Crimmins admits that by mid–1995 the service had improved its internal security compared with the time when he first started monitoring it. "To some extent they've cleaned things up," he says. "But at one-fifteen A.M. last night there were fourteen private rooms, and I found 'XXfamilyXX,' which is an incest room, and 'Dad's Home,' same thing. Another room was titled 'PbRoEyTgEiEfNs' which, if you read it carefully, says 'preteen boy GIFs.'" GIF stands for Graphic Image File format, the most common way of storing photographs online.

AOL runs a program that checks room names. According to one AOL user, the word "boy" has been totally banned, along with "girl" and "hacker." But it seems easy enough to fool the program by misspelling words, scrambling letters, or adding a few X's here and there. In this way, users have defeated the scheme just as easily as Robert Carr's Hexon Exon program would defeat a federal decency monitoring program.

Crimmins feels the only answer is better human supervision. "AOL claims they are going to have fifty people on their staff," he says. "When I first logged on there were four people. In those days it was running unchecked. AOL now says that ninety-eight percent of the rooms are *not* related to child pornography. Well, all I can say is that last night, one hundred percent of the people who wanted to traffic in child pornography found where they wanted to go."

America Online has since made further attempts to restrict and monitor its members. At the beginning of September 1995, president and CEO Steve Case sent a letter to all users asking them to "report any unusual or improper behavior that you see immediately. If you're in a chat room, notify our Terms of Service advisory unit by using keyword GUIDEPAGER. E-mail, Instant Message, and Message Board violations should be reported to keyword TOS."

These attempts to protect the innocent may have achieved some results but have also caused the inevitable backlash. Complaints about AOL tend to be censored by AOL itself, so angry users go outside the system and post their rants to groups such as alt.censorship on Usenet. Here, a woman who works as a prostitute

and used the name ACallGirl on AOL reported that she was constantly hassled about it. "They even went so far as to suggest I not go into the chat rooms. Frequently arguments would erupt in chat rooms about my name."

Maybe this seems reasonable on a family-oriented service—except that ACallGirl says that she came across other names far worse than hers, including FistFuk, FukU2, BitchKillr, BooEatShit, and NiggaKill.

Eventually a group of militant AOL members caused such a fuss that they prompted an AOL guide to send them a list of recent user names that had been judged acceptable, and another list of names that were unacceptable. The lists were a rare treat for anyone who savors the intricate absurdities of censorship:

Acceptable Names	Unacceptable Names
a362438	acdc69
a501bulge	advisor1
a9inchnail	akinkyboy
acidflash	allsex
acpeker	alwayswet
ahaard	amybianal
akaclymax	aolstaffpw
alfredo69	arcangel69
allpink	aroused
alwayzhard	ass123
alwayzwet	aswhipe
askme24u	auburnbtch
autofellat	autococker
	azcumman
babysitme	baldcrotch
balls9	ballcock
batsguano	barfbag
bdchats	bastabasta
beaver8786	bengetsoff
beaverhill	bentover69
bigbskt	betternbed
biginnh	bhole
bigjim10	bigfag69
bigmike69	biggenital
bigniner	bignipps
bigsmacker	bigot
bigthickie	bite69
bills2hi	bitemetoo

Acceptable Names	Unacceptable Names
bitravel2	bjguy
bixxx	bjsstud69
bjgun	bksydspnkr
bjstud	bloatedsac
bmtoy	blowbuddy
bono69	blowupdoll
boobashay	bluepuss
booby30835	blueroks
bootybutt	bobfxu
bornstiff	bofo
borntodv8	boner69
bottomsup	boner6in
bronzbunz	bonerboy69
bttmman	bonghit13
bullsize12	boobalay
buttman290	boobed
buttoid	boobsmom
butts1	boobsrme
butx	boobster
	bootyboy
	bottomteen
	boytoboy
	breasts474
	brian8r
	bstoned
	btche1
	buckmuff
	bukknekid
	burgerbutt
	bushtrimr
	busty36d
	bustychick
	buttgravy
	buttheadb
	buttlooker
	buttmun280
	buttpuppet
cahones	cahardon
can69	cap
cazzo2	catpoo
centel	chengdu
chas69	cls69butt
cheese4me	cltplzr
cherry	cmep

Acceptable Names	Unacceptable Names
christklr	cock4two
chuckacker	comeinme
chucker3	copul8
chuckqear	couplesexe
ckuntzman	crabass
ckup	crapage
clintonsux	ctoris
commiescum	cumback
creepbud	cummer1
crip1999	cumn
cruiser101	cunnling1
cumundone	
dafuca	damlesbian
dano11214	damnit
dbldee	davidsex
dealerfred	dcutecocky
deathurge	dickdem
deboner330	dicked
degrademe	dickhertz3
dewmenow	dickishard
dickdial	dicknude
dinktwo	dikhard
doctorwad	dikhed99
doggydoo	dimebag6
doitdoit	doggydoo
domin8tor	dogmaster4
donnabi69	domenow388
donnad19	donkydick
dough61878	doobie4u
drbadxxx	dooche
drerotik	doubled38
drmscumtru	douchebag1
drron69	dr4skin
drugfairs	dragonass
duane6969	drsx
dv8tion	drtysmthng
	dungi8
	dungman
	dykeslave
	dyperboy
easykatie1	eatme001
eater	eatme2430
eatsemhot	eatmeup1
ellesdee	eatmycheez

Acceptable Names	Unacceptable Names
eroticus	eddie69er
erotkman	eightinche
ezrider69	ez269
	ezlickher
fabulust	faghater69
farkface	fartman007
farooqueq	fartman510
firmrod	fck
flylester	firmbooty
fonefunguy	fkcu
foneman69	fkngruven
fonestud	flslaveboy
footkisser	foetusruin
foreverwet	foixqueue
forfun69	fongule
freewyfary	fooku92
fsteddy69	foreplayou
ftlong5408	friggin1
fuco	fsbush
funkthat	fskinlover
furrymonk	fukushima
	furburger
	fuusob
	fuzzyballs
g8phattttt	getspanked
gabe7ucct	gifs4swap
garyho	gimmedix
gaschamber	gmikeuide
gaspass384	gonjasnif
ghassert	goodtime69
glenda69bf	grasshigh
godofpain	gspotfindr
goingdeep	gspotlickr
gradstud69	guidelj
grwnr	guido4a
guidodude1	guidoa
guidoL	guidoo0000
	gutfahrt
	gvsgdhead
hacker3398	hairpi647
hacktwo	hard4u85
hairyone	hardlikker
hamrtime	hardnipps

Acceptable Names	Unacceptable Names
hard4ever	hardone069
hard8m	hardone452
hardblonde	hardonguy
hardbody3	hardonyou
hardj	hardstick
hardloverr	harrybutts
hardone104	here269
hardwoody	hhhhhot69
harryone	himaroids
hashn	hndjob
highheels1	hnrynjun69
hoffy	hoemoe
honeypott	hoofharted
hophead718	hooterman
hot4u35	horneebear
hot4urlove	horneyj
hotbabe703	hornline
hotbabexx	horny17162
hotfoxx	horny17f
hotnfun	horny1ii
hotnhairy	horny63706
hott2chat	hornydevel
hottalker	hornyette
hottime282	hornyguy1
hottool4u	hornyinfl
hotygboy	hornyl
howard069	hornym16
hugehose	hornyman4u
hungry4it	hornytode
	hornywun
	horsecock
	hot2bbottm
	hot42dd
	hot469
	hot4sex669
	hot4unow2
	hot69rod
	hotandpink
	hotboytoy
	hotnhornym
	hotnwet4u
	hotpoop
	hotpussy02
	hottngue4u
	hottpanz

Acceptable Names	Unacceptable Names
	hotxmuscle
	houcpl
	hrddriver
	hrnydave4f
	hung
	hung9innyc
	hungdave
	hunghunk
	hunglow777
	hungnhard
	hungsolo
	hungtough
	hvyfknmtl
i12leiu	i69er
iam2big4u	iam2busy2p
iambarfing	ieatpuss
iamrigid	igetnude4u
icupking	igrowsoft
icustrip	ihave8in4u
im2sxe4u	ilik2fuk
imlicker	iluvitwet
in2deep548	im69hunter
in2u	imacumen
indystud1	imhot69696
intactteen	inedsex
	irishphuck
jacksrwild	j10inches
jazzlicks	jackmeeoff
jeff9in	jacme
jerixxx	jbhooters
jimtoole	jenny4sex
jnasty1	jewdie
jock30	jimtoke
joeg6900	jizm
jockitch	johnnypee
jockitch0	joorlando
jon69er	jsass
jrw696969	juggs44
junkie3628	
kathyjim	karnhorney
kevorkian	killamig
kicker69	kingof69
kilrgrnbud	kinkie69

Acceptable Names	Unacceptable Names
kinkymind	kinky69
kotekese	kinkyfag
kraka40oz	kinkygent
kydeptedjo	klitykat
	kyke
laurieX69	largenlong
lcktysplit	libid0boy
leathrdyke	lickingu
leerassi	lickme576
lesbefrien	lickmewet
likemthick	lickquest
lisabi69	like269
lisahot4u	like2muff
lloyd69	likkme
longlean17	lilsexchik
lorifunks	lindais469
love69	longniner
lovembig	longone013
lovesatyr	longprong
lovesword	lorox
loveurod	love4skin
lovsmuscle	love69ing
lsdee	lovehotgif
lubeman	lovelick
lustchaser	lovetodoit
lustful1	lovetoocum
lustladie	luv2suxone
lustomatic	luvmuf69
lustplus	luvmusclef
lustyL	lvmuscle
lustymaria	lvs2licku
luv2watch3	
luvemhard	
majorbuzz	makemehard
male4u2nv	mamajuicy
manboy	marklsd
mandy69mmm	massingill
manmuncher	masterb8
marketpsy	mediawhore
marvinm699	megahung
maryjane2	mobysdick
masokist	mofo147297
max696965	morethan9
meatpkr	mrballsout

Acceptable Names	Unacceptable Names
mebeup	mstdbter
meunderu1	muffdiv569
mhaycock	muffdiving
mlibido	muffdve285
mofriggin	muffdvrr
monkeebutt	muffydiver
moundrider	muflovr
mrmouthful	munchme
mrsmack	my4play
mrstudnine	myload4u
mrthrust	
mytfine69	
nakedlunch	n24skin
ndeep	n24skin479
ninefory	naked4u69
nudebchbum	nakednancy
nudistgal	nastyboy11
	nastygspot
	ne1469now
	nicebox
	nippieman
	nipplefat
	nudestang
	nympho1010
olcock	ohmyrod
oldr4yngr	oildup4luv
olock	oraphus
onlinesux	orgasming
opiatelvr	
orallover	
oralsax	
orasis	
orlcouple	
pandass	pantygirl
patty169	pantypudin
phish4me	passgass
phonelover	patmaweeny
pigtop	patty694u
pilloman	peckerlick
pissow	peehead94
poofta	peepee18
poonty	pervert678
poopyrus	perverto

Acceptable Names	Unacceptable Names
prodigyguy	philmycrak
prozactome	pimpall
pucker4me	pimpz
pudd	pissboy
pussycatte	pisserb
putzing	pixelwhore
	plezureman
	poodgussy
	poonlicker
	poopooman
	poopystank
	pornoman
	pudyanker
	pumpit69
	pusygalor
quik2lick	qtbutt
	quaylewd
	queerbate
radioscrap	ratbastrd
rassm	ready469
raw969	readyass
rcfuchs	redpanties
rimtool	reeffer
rkhard	restroom
rmh	rheasuck
rockhar64u	rik6969
rockhardx	roachclip
rodya	roxxoff
roidfixer	ru469im
rollafatty	rubbrhood
ronnywad	rumppumper
rubberface	rushisjerk
ruburight	
rugsuckers	
sallyohhh	sadistman
schitzy	schmeckle
screwdoink	seekingfem
sergeant69	semourbutt
sexygal696	sex4all
sexylovers	sexbag
sexymalemd	sexbyter
shakabra	sexcaliber9
sillycybin	sexexpert

Acceptable Names

sirhoser
sirstoney
sixty9dude
slambamer
slambang
slave2bitc
slickmenow
slo4u
slowtease
smegghead
soltan963
sooogoood
spandex530
sphinxor
squeeky969
staffdude
stickitin
stiff11949
stoners
studentboy
studm97856
studnhand
submisfem
suca
suelust
sueneedsit
sundrops
sweetdeath
sweetme69
swmvox
swrdswalor
sxulfantzy

Unacceptable Names

sexgod696
sexhealing
sexitivity
sexkitten9
sexlover2
sexme469
sexmonger6
sexnrock69
sexplor420
sexrocket
sexslave
sextacy
sexual4u2
sexy69guy
sfqueerboy
shaved
shavedlee
shthpns
shvdbvr
sillyass
sitonit69
six9
sixty9iron
sixty9king
skrumig
skyhor
slipnme
slittylikr
sloandhot
slotdoctor
smardass
smegmahead
smoothbutt
softandwet
spanks4u
spanks4us
spanksalot
sphincterx
spredem
spunknbuf
spurtzfar
sshole
stiffwilly
stinknsnif
stlhacker

Acceptable Names	Unacceptable Names
	stonerbabe
	studpleasr
	swallow812
	sweet2eat
	swtyjock
teatman87	tatooonass
techsup	tbos4sx
thedonger	teenbutt
theerotic	teetsnarse
theguido	teninchone
thejoker69	the69king
thepimp456	thickwik
theramrod	thistuds4u
thick	ticklmyclt
thicknhott	tightholes
thrusterr	tihsyloh
tieittight	tool4u5022
tienspank	topguy4u
tight501ss	topless586
toni69	tossalad
toosaxy4u	travel4sx
total69	trojansd
troyjen	twat160
tryallonce	twatts
tskmstr	twohomos
turkweiner	twohot4u
	tyemupp
uc9plus	u2canchu69
udrugby	uallsuck
underconst	ubendmeovr
unity69	ucum2
upanddown	uncutbutch
	uncutfan
	uncutrob
	upncumming
	upnhard1
	uwannablow
	uwillbeg
valium5mg	vibr8or
velvetbox	violntlust
vendejo	
vhou812	
voxs	

Acceptable Names	Unacceptable Names
wantinmen	wanasxuup
wetlevis	wankers
woodie69	wannarideu
woodyhuge	wayhunglow
wopgun1	wellhung4u
	wetbeever
	wetdiper
	wetndep
	wetnwld69
	wetone4u
	wetpussy19
	wetsex
	wettpantys
	whipme104
	whipnpost
	willdou2
	wnt269u
	woodie6969
xxxlarge	x69696969x
	xlibidocpl
	xslibido
	xxbonerxx
	xxxposed
	xxxsecxxx
yngman69	ynghrny
	yngnstiff
	yngpuslvr
	ynme69me
	youcome1st
	zenphuck
	zoner69

Subsequently it was reported that the guide who sent this list is no longer employed by the service provider. AOL did not respond to attempts to confirm or deny this story.

Language in AOL chat rooms remains an equally sensitive topic. Guides can instantly eject anyone who uses forbidden words. The following dialogue was transcribed and circulated through the Internet and even earned a mention in *Playboy* magazine. Note that TOS is an acronym for "Terms of Service," and the :) symbol is meant to suggest that the person using it is smiling.

SPIDERM540: todd is the REAL problem, you see he hasno *genitalia*.... asexual...get it?

Guide GO: SPIDERM540 vulgarity is a violation of the Terms of Service. Please stop NOW. Read at Keyword TOS.

Mary5913: Wait......what was the vulgarity? Can you tell us which of Spiderman's words were vulgar?

Guide GO: Mary I suggest you go read your Terms of Service

Stpfljes: may i suggest that you read the constitution of the united states of america

Guide GO: I am just talking about the Terms of Service :)

Trout Esq: fascist

Stpfljes: which are vague therefore void and unenforceable

Trout Esq: agreed

Guide GO: Not really :)

ToddT38799: and we appreciate that but are you monitoring conversation.

SPIDERM540: response......loving, heartwarming response.....i love you guide go..... :)

ToddT38799: aint he wonderful

SPIDERM540: CENSOR>>>>TOS>>>>

Stpfljes: well i think the room is in agreement

SPIDERM540: i said love.........oops .....typo.......

Stpfljes: yes watch it love is four letter word

SPIDERM540: mary, what's your take on this....tyranny...

Stpfljes: marys gone

Guide GO: Well I have to be GOing now. If there are any TOS problems and you need a guide..... Please use Keyword GUIDEPAGER.

Stpfljes: guide did u dump mary

ToddT38799: what happened to mary

Kids4sale: She left

Stpfljes: or the guide had her dumped

Yet according to Barry Crimmins, the real lawbreakers on AOL still find ways to do what they want to do. Is it really reasonable to expect AOL to maintain total control over everything that's said in all its chat rooms? Shouldn't parents take some responsibility, especially since AOL has made it possible for them to lock out some areas if they will just take the trouble to do so?

Crimmins disagrees. He points out that child abuse is often perpetrated by the parents themselves.

Crackdown on Kiddie Porn

If we can't trust parents to protect their children, who *can* we trust? According to Crimmins, the answer is law enforcement. "We need more cops on the Internet to enforce existing laws against child pornography and stalking, and they should be undercover. If they start trying to bust people for other reasons, I'll be right there with the ACLU. Civil liberties are extremely dear to me. But with freedom comes responsibility. Nobody has the right to trade pictures of an eight-year-old with semen on his or her face. An epidemic of child abuse is going to result from this. People will say, 'I've thought about it, but I've never thought about *doing* it.'"

Pictures, he says, are a stimulus that encourages new crime, and the FBI seems to agree with him. On September 13, 1995, agents raided approximately 120 homes of AOL users nationwide. According to a report from the Associated Press, computer equipment was seized and there were "at least a dozen arrests." Other reports stated that AOL had been cooperating with the government for two years, supplying names and addresses of users suspected of trading child pornography and/or luring children.

Pam McGraw, a spokesperson for America Online, admitted that the service had monitored e-mail and private messages exchanged between people in chat rooms. Wasn't this a violation of the Electronic Communications Privacy Act? Evidently AOL felt that the law didn't apply to communications that never left its own computers. Department of Justice guidelines have suggested a similar principle.

Attorney General Janet Reno praised the raids in a statement that should have warmed Barry Crimmins's heart. "We are not going to permit exciting new technology to be misused to exploit and injure

children," she said. In February 1996 a man in New York State was sentenced to five years in prison for sending sexually explicit pictures of children via his AOL account.

But after all the publicity had died down, what did it add up to? According to the Interactive Services Association (of which AOL is a member), major Internet service providers had a total of more than eight million members when the raids took place. Of these users, AOL claimed more than three million. If child pornography and pedophilia were such a problem on AOL, why did a two-year investigation of this huge membership base yield only *a dozen* arrests, with no guarantee that these cases would yield convictions?

Nationwide there are at least a million cases of sexual abuse of children each year, according to a 1995 Gallup survey that based its figures on statements from a sample of 1,000 parents. Bearing this in mind, imagine what a huge number of offenders the FBI could grab if it could snoop into people's lives as easily as AOL was able to monitor its members online. Evidently the real world is far more hazardous for children than the online world.

True, the Net attracts some people who like to talk dirty to children; but judging from the disappointing results of the AOL raids, these people are more interested in talk than action. Anyone who seriously wants to molest children will obviously get better results hanging out at shopping malls or schoolyards. Wouldn't it make more sense to deploy FBI agents there rather than online, where fantasy is a relatively harmless substitute for reality?

Child Pornography: Pest or Plague?

Turning back to Usenet, a quick scan of the relevant news groups shows many pictures of solo children at nudist camps and very few photographs of kids with partners in sex acts. In fact, according to an attorney who has been actively involved in

pornography litigation, penalties against creating hard-core kiddie porn are so severe that virtually none has been produced in America since the 1970s. Pornographers naturally prefer to make money marketing pictures that are legal.

Still, child pornography is abhorrent to almost everyone—which makes it an ideal scare topic for conservative legislators, right up there with Communism and drug use. A senator can condemn it in the comfortable knowledge that almost everyone will agree with him.

On September 6, 1995, standing before the Senate, Orrin Hatch did exactly that. "It is impossible," he said, "for any decent American not to be outraged by child pornography and the exploitation of children. Such material is a plague upon our people and the moral fabric of this great nation." Hatch said there was an overwhelming bipartisan belief "that there is no place for such filth even in a free society and those who produce or peddle this reprehensible material must be made to feel the full weight of the law and suffer a punishment reflective of the seriousness of their offense."

The reason for this diatribe wasn't immediately clear, since there's already a federal law against producing or possessing erotic photographs featuring underage models. But this law is limited. Its purpose is to protect children who might be used in the production of pictures. Thus, a crime only exists when a real child has been used as a model. Federal law does not cover text or visuals created purely from the human imagination.

The snag is, computer graphics software can now create simulations that are almost indistinguishable from the real thing. Hatch talked about the case of a twenty-year-old Canadian, Joseph Pecchiarich, who had used retouching software to process a picture of a child in a bathing suit. Pecchiarich artfully erased the clothing and put the child "in a sexually provocative position," according to Philip Enright, an assistant crown attorney associated with the case.

Since no real children had been harmed, Hatch believed that "this type of repulsive conduct" would be legal if it ever occurred in the United States. Worse still, "computers can also be used to alter

sexually explicit photographs, films, and videos in such a way as to make it virtually impossible for prosecutors to identify the individuals, or to prove that the offending material was produced using children." A pornographer could conceivably sell unretouched photographs of real children having real sex but could claim that the pictures were computer-generated, and no one would be able to prove otherwise.

So what's the answer? A new law, obviously. Hatch introduced a bill that would criminalize *any* form of art or graphics (including paintings as well as digitized photographs) depicting children indecently. The new law would prohibit not just sexually explicit pictures but also the depiction of the buttocks and breasts of children under eighteen, and it would ban any advertisement or description worded "in such a manner that conveys the impression that the material is or contains a visual depiction of a minor engaging in sexually explicit conduct." This seems to mean that if you see some kiddie porn, you'd be committing a crime if you describe it to someone.

Hatch's proposal sparked a heavy debate among Net users. Even hard-core libertarians couldn't claim that real photographs of children having sex should be legal—but they feared the consequences of a crackdown all the same. On Usenet, Joseph H. Allen wrote: "Pedophiles have been with us since before the beginning of recorded history—certainly before computers, photographs, or even printed books. Most child molestations occur in the home or local community and are usually instigated by a loved one. Censorship of any kind is not going to make any difference whatsoever in the incidence of this permanent part of the human condition."

Allen digressed into a brief paean of praise for free speech online, then finished up: "Yet this achievement is to come to an abrupt end by a man and a mind-set so replete with suppression and domination that he and it would go so far as to censor public libraries. It is to be replaced by a forum based on a lie—perhaps the lie of Western culture: that sex is the last thing on the mind

of any given human. The new Net will be occupied with stale Disney characters instead of real humans, but will certainly be convenient for shopping."

Others were deeply skeptical of legislators' motives. A woman who signed herself "Joan" suggested that "the badness of child porn is something everybody can agree about. Which makes it the perfect tool for a power-greedy government to grab control over a new medium . . . just use your word processor to substitute 'witchcraft' for 'child porn' and 'witches' for 'pornographers,' then re-read the messages. Just try it and see what you think. Then try 'transsexuals' . . . then 'Catholics.' Think of it as a game . . . your leaders certainly do."

Joan went on to say that she found it hard to believe there was an active market for child pornography or businesses actively supplying it. "I'd like to see some REAL DATA before going off in a half-cocked hysterical panic . . . or is that wishful thinking?"

Well, what *are* the figures? Kiddie porn on Usenet certainly does exist; it's right where you'd expect to find it, in alt.sex.pedophilia. And a few of the pictures are almost certainly illegal under *current* federal law. This raises another question: How do people get away with posting them so openly?

An anonymous contributor to the newsgroup explained precisely how it is done. "I suggest chaining multiple remailers (at least 3) together. . . . Also if you're going to post here I suggest using a dummy account [at an Internet service provider]—one in which you paid by money order with a bogus name and address—and ONLY use this account for 2 months! Because they can do a trace back to see where you're calling from. But by the time it takes to subpoena different remailers from all over the world you won't be using that account anymore!"

What's a "remailer"? Simple: a computer on the Net that receives messages, automatically strips off the name and address of the sender, and forwards the message to its destination. Anonymous remailers are run by people who believe that anonymous speech is

an important liberty, shielding people who have unpopular views. Indeed, the Supreme Court has found that anonymous speech is protected under the First Amendment. In McIntyre vs. Ohio Elections Commission, a woman named Margaret McIntyre had distributed anonymous pamphlets in violation of Ohio elections law. By a 7–2 vote, the Supreme Court found the law unconstitutional and stated that anonymous pamphleteering is protected speech.

What if you don't know how to find an anonymous remailer? No problem; like most useful nuggets of information, it's available online. Lists of remailers are stored at a couple of Web sites:

```
http://www.cs.berkeley.edu/~raph/remailer-list.html
http://www.replay.com/staff/usura/chain.html
```

And just to make the situation even more interesting, in February 1996 Joel Grasty, a self-described "cypherpunk," announced that you no longer need to be a Unix programmer to set up a remailing operation of your own. Grasty developed a program that can turn any PC running Windows into a remailing system, and he started giving away the software from his Web page:

```
http://www.c2.org/~winsock/
```

Under Senator Exon's decency amendment, of course, anonymous remailers could be penalized for knowingly allowing porn to flow through their computers onto screens that might be seen by children. But since most of the sites are located overseas (Hacktic, for instance, is in Holland) it's hard to see how they could be prosecuted under American law.

Even so, remailers are not totally secure. The Church of Scientology shocked Net users in 1995 by successfully persuading police in Finland to raid a site and break open its shell of anonymity. Still, the system does provide reasonable security if multiple sites are used and the person who sends the message maintains a fake ID. Usenet participants certainly feel quite confident about posting illegal photographs. They also enjoy discussing their "forbidden" pleasures.

On alt.binaries.pictures.erotica.children, one person described precisely the photo he was looking for: "A young couple (mf)

together naked, the boy with an erection, obviously stimulated by the sight of the girl, and the girl admiring it. Anyone else have this (also known as 2TEENS.JPG or maybe that's a different one from the same series) please post it. Or anything similar. I get a bit fed up of the 7-year-olds sucking off 'Dad.' Much rather see two youngsters enjoying themselves together."

Naturally, this kind of post is matched by an equal number of apoplectic rants. PPkiller warned everyone on alt.sex.pedophilia: "you fucking sick bastards should have your genitals scrambled . . . this newsgroup is not natural. you are all stricken with a disease . . . you all need help."

And there were some typical Usenet conspiracy theories: "The 'regulate the Internet' people are posting the photos here in order to justify their cries of 'pedophiles are all over the Net.'"

Some moralists vowed to take personal action. In response to a woman who had posted a bunch of pictures, one man wrote: "I have taken the liberty of downloading approximately 25 examples of your sickest work, and sent printouts, along with your header and the name of your access provider to the local FBI office. It is child predators like you that are giving the Net a bad name, besides harming the most innocent of our society. I hope they find you and nail you for everything that they can."

But the target of this letter was cheerfully defiant. She replied to it in detail: "I freely and merrily admit that I made those posts! What saddens me is your narrow mindedness . . . you just rush forward and attack like a knight in shining armor, without even thinking that you may be attacking someone who hasn't done anything wrong. Mr. H, not only did I post this material, but if you've read the newsgroup even a little, you'd know that I've made occasional mention of my daughter and of my past relationship with my mother. Now, let me ask you a simple question of logic: seeing that some 30–35 years ago, I was supposedly one of the children you are protecting, and that I feel in no way harmed or molested by the love my mother had for me . . . don't you think I have a say in this? Also I wish to note, *if* you could touch me (and believe me you can't), you'd not only be

putting me in prison, you'd also be ruining my husband's and 8 yr old daughter's lives, how chivalrous, don't you think?"

So here was a decency crusader's worst nightmare. Perverts were trading kiddie porn openly on the Net, for all the world to see. And as if that wasn't bad enough, they were indulging their perversions with real children and then *bragging about it*, challenging anyone to try and stop them!

It was only natural that this kind of thing would provoke a man like Orrin Hatch to stand up and start ranting about "the moral fabric of this great nation." But wait a minute—some of the pictures online were already illegal! If existing laws were having absolutely no effect, why should new laws do any better?

Perhaps Barry Crimmins was right: The real answer was to enforce existing laws more vigorously. But the FBI had been able to arrest only a dozen offenders after a two-year investigation of AOL, where they had full access to the names and locations of members. How can they even begin to tackle the hordes of Usenet, safely shielded by multiple layers of anonymity?

Cruising Channel #littlegirlsex

In America Online's chat rooms, speech can be censored legally because everything happens inside a privately owned system. On the Internet, there's a much bigger online chat arena where supervision is impossible and law enforcement is virtually unknown.

Internet Relay Chat (IRC) is a huge global service divided into thousands of topic areas. The system resembles Usenet, except that you don't have to wait a day or two after posting a message in order to read other people's replies. On IRC, everything happens in realtime.

The mind-boggling scope of the system is made clear when you log on:

```
*** Welcome to the Internet Relay Network
*** This server was created Sun Sep 24 1995 at 12: 12:11 PDT
*** There are 6990 users and 4879 invisible on 87 servers
*** There are 129 operators online
*** 2859 channels have been formed
*** This server has 471 clients and 6 servers connected
*** Current local users: 471  Max: 601
*** Current global users: 11868  Max: 12206
```

If you want to chat with people on IRC, you have to master a horribly confusing vocabulary of commands. The system was originally put together by hard-core Unix geeks and is definitely not a user-friendly environment. But the word **list** is all you need to find room names. Here's what you see in response to the command **list *sex***, which means "Display all room names containing the word **sex** regardless of other letters before and after it." (The number following each chat area indicates how many people are currently using it.)

```
*** #SexyTalk    1
*** #100%%sex    1
*** #sexpix      1
*** #cybrsex     1
*** #dirtysex    1
*** #kinkysex    2
*** #sexjpgs     1
*** #allsex      1
*** #SEXINDIVI   1
*** #sextoy      2
*** #Sex-STuf    2      Sex Pics, Sex Talk, Cybersex!
                        C'mon in!
*** #sexydaugh 2
*** #PlushieSe   1      Sex with Large Soft Stuffed
                        Animals! (18+ Only)
*** #Fantasyse   1      Master looks around the net
                        for fun......
*** #EnderSex    1
*** #cybersex2   1
*** #sex_i_nor   1
*** #peesex      2
*** #sexo        1
*** #wildsex     4
*** #toiletsex   3
*** #fantasy_s   1      ladies drop by we can get
                        horny and satisfy each other
```

```
*** #sexydaugh 3      rude people not welcome
*** #40+sex    1      Cougar2 is MALE/27 that
                      likesolder woman. CUM with
                      me ladies.
*** #lespeesex 4      GIRLS just wanna have fun
*** #%%%%frees 2
*** #texassex  1
*** #dallassex 2
*** #dogsex2   1
*** #daughter_ 2
*** #tru-sex-  5
*** #sweetsex  3
*** #freesex   5
*** #extacysex 1
*** #FinSex    1
*** #DolphinSe 2      Sex with Marine Mammals!
                      (18+ Only)
*** #gayteense 4
*** #tvsex     12
*** #!!!SEXPIC 4
*** #sexier    3      SeXIer..tHe Bar iS OpEn.
*** #blacksex  2
*** #netsex    35     Have something to say...
                      then say it...but it had better
                      be good...
*** #hempsex   1
*** #bifemsex  17     Nobody home
*** #beastsex  12     Sex and your Beasties ||| All
                      Zoos and Zoo Curious Welcome
                      (18+ only)
*** #softsex   5
*** #sexgifs   23
*** #rapesex   32
*** #cuseemese 19
*** #3waysex   22     CUM ONE CUM ALL...
                      BUT JUST CUM!!!
*** #30+sex    20     Visit #30+sex homepage!!!!
*** #sextalk   10     We Respect Intelligent Women !!!
                      Now, can we see your breasts ?
*** #cybersex  58
*** #gayboysex 20     Where is Ishamael when
                      DarkAngel needs a good man...
*** #littlegir 38
*** #gaysex    54     OJ must die
*** #llamasex  6
```

Suppose you select the chat area named #littlegirlsex. From this point on, things get confusing, as IRC displays at least six things on your screen concurrently:

1. **Messages from the system (preceded by three asterisks) explaining who's online, who's just arrived, and who's just left**

2. **Messages that you type, automatically preceded with a > mark**

3. **Messages from other people in the room, tagged with online names in a format <like this>**

4. **Messages from people in the room describing what they imagine themselves doing; these lines begin with a single asterisk**

5. **Personal, private messages from you to someone in the room; these lines begin with /msg**

6. **Personal, private messages from someone in the room to you; these lines begin with the sender's name inside asterisks, formatted *like this***

Just to make things even more confusing, there may be three or four conversational threads running simultaneously.

People who hang out on IRC soon learn to disentangle the text as it scrolls up the screen, but for the sake of clarity in the transcript below almost all the system messages have been removed and the text has been reformatted to make it easier to read.

```
*** Platt has joined channel #littlegirlsex
*** Users on #littlegirlsex: Platt Viper2 BobG
pepsi01 louie14yr @PhaRxMer +cessna BigMack
_Gred smash Lump mrhugz Xcalibre roberto
shagnasty cyggie +Stalker sts6 Nocturnal sally
crazybob RedEagle Sandbar Zanth LNDSHRK
horndog +Gretchen trader Roamer dvi Amy_13
YngDaveB Heintz Ritchie Picman @_Robyn
+@_Clarissa lilgrlpix kuroth @FNorris

* Platt looks around
> quiet place for 38 people
> are you all msging or asleep?
<horndog> cya later gretchen......hope i didn't
make you too wet!
/msg horndog so is this place for real? i mean are
```

there really like little girls here?
horndog yes
horndog why
/msg horndog lookin' for some
horndog do you like little girls
/msg horndog don't you?
horndog talk to gretchen shes 15
horndog 14 i meant
horndog she's hot too
/msg horndog yeah but i mean do you do anything
or just talk?
horndog love them....but i gotta go
<Karina> Hi
/msg horndog i'm new to all this
<RedEagle> i am still awake...!!!!!!!!!!!!!
horndog finish her off for me
/msg horndog um okay
horndog gets dirty
<louie14yr> hello pepls!
> but is it safe here?
<louie14yr> safe! yessssss!
<lilgrlpix> just dont trade with roamer, he is a leech!
> but—how do I know if any of you guys are from law enforcement or whatever?
<Xcalibre> Are you trading pics
* zen laughs
<lilgrlpix> you both send at the same time, that way you are safe
> no i'm looking for people not pictures
<lilgrlpix> no laws against chatting
> so people don't really meet in person? Like if i found someone in my area who i really wanted to get together with
<LNDSHRK> You'd have to decide that for yourself Platt... now wouldn'y ya ...
> it just seems... i dunno... why would a 14-year-old girl join a channel called #littlegirlsex?
<LNDSHRK> Of course .. if you're not breakin' the law ...
<LNDSHRK> you have nothing to fear ...
> well, no one seems to be saying much, and I have to go soon because my father will be home
<mickey> Hello!!!!
> hi mickey

<mickey> Hi Platt!
> is this all you do?
<mickey> What are you guys talking about?
> it doesn't seem very... titillating
[long period elapses with no message activity]
> oh well
/leave
*** Platt has left channel #littlegirlsex

(Note: since people on a channel can swap messages privately with each other, there could have been a lot of action among the thirty-eight participants that didn't show up on the screen.)

*** Platt has joined channel #rapesex
*** Users on #rapesex: Platt dugbug female Avan
ggreg Bronson mark1 random +nahwk RedEye
hotm4f Fantasi Xcalibre @PhaRxMer Sup-rnova
Sherilyn joebob +calkid roberto Pirate2 TheSuper
barbi valerie daisie bevrly Maniac- Reamer
+StarDustR Psych MikeJB Jeet @RapeMe @JackDRipr
@Stalker_

* Fantasi struggles...uselessly
<dugbug> Hi Fantasi!! :)
<MikeJB> hi female
<female> just fine, maniac,U?
> hello
* Psych starts to push his cock in your tight ass
<female> hello mikejb
<barbi> ohhh, Psych, it won't fit
<Maniac-> i am doing OK, where ya from female?
<random> not mine i hope
<Fantasi> Hey dugbug
<RedEye> Female are you really F or a guy
in disguise???
* joebob rubs his cock over fantasi's clit
<Pirate2> hey fantasi..why ya ignoring me?
* Platt blinks
* Psych pushes slowly... a little deeper
* MikeJB watches with a sense of satisfaction as
fantasi gets raped....... ;)
<Alicia> hi!all
<Maniac-> Hi Alicia
<female> i am very much a female
<Avan> fantasi- hiya...
* TheSuper helps out Fantasi and kicks Mikes ass

<RedEye> Oh okay...
<TheSuper> Hey alicia
<Avan> alicia- hi!
* barbi groans as psych pushes in
<female> i am from Virginia does anyone here
want to meet me in real life?
<Adidas> cool
<random> why don't any women ever rape a man?
<Adidas> Cuz you can't rape em idiot!
* Psych pushes in deeper.. going all the way in,
deep against the base of my cock
<random> sure you can asshole
<Avan> female- where in virginia are ya from?
<Avan> adidas- you damn well can!
* barbi moans and tries to hold still
<female> Avan:Williamsburg
* Adidas moves closer to Fantasi
<Avan> female- my brother and his wife live in
[location omitted]!
> so is this like a discussion group or something?
* Psych reaches around and grabs your tits,
sqeezing your nipples as he begins to move his
cock in and out of your ass
<Adidas> Avan..how would you know?
<random> it would not be too difficult with me,
and the right woman
* Adidas Gives Fantasi a single red rose
<female> AVAN: really, what part of [location
omitted]?
* barbi squeezes tighter inside as her nipples
are pulled
> Frankly this is not what I expected at all!
<Adidas> Platt...these guys are just horny
<Avan> adidas- it's all theory, as far as I'm
concerned.
* Psych pulls his cock to the tip, then slams it
back in deep
> Well, I may be horny too, but that wasn't what
was on my mind.
<Adidas> Surprised? Theoru? Explain
* barbi gasps and nearly falls over
<Avan> female- my bro and his woman live down
around [location omitted]. My mother lives in
[location omitted].
> This seems a bit silly to me. I mean if I wanted to

have sex, I could go to a pickup bar.
<RedEye> Platt: Try the love channel
* Psych starts to move in and out faster
<Adidas> Shreri left idiot!
<Adidas> M or f Platt
> Why bother with this? I mean do you people ever
do anything for real?
> Adidas: i'm female, why?
<RedEye> Platt: are you sure about that???
<Avan> this is for rape fantasies
<RedEye> Platt are you sure your F
> I suppose this is a good healthy way to get out
aggressions.
<Avan> Platt– it's for doing things that you DON'T
want to do for real.
> Thanks for the information.

On IRC, just the same as on Usenet, *most* areas are *not* full of sexual fantasies and perversion. IRC functions mainly as a way for lonely or isolated people to find other people who share interests such as pets, gardening, literature, or movies. Thousands of people have met in real life after chatting online via IRC. I personally know of two couples who ended up getting married.

The problem posed by the minority of sexual-oriented chat rooms still boils down to the same old story: access, content, and distribution.

Filters

Content-filtering programs are now available, enabling parents to lock out various areas of the Net in just the same way that AOL allows some of its own features to be selectively disabled.

SurfWatch, one of the most widely publicized packages, "comes ready to block more than 1,000 sites containing material we would not want our children to see," says Ann Duvall, president of the corporation. Customized lists are also available, blocking only certain types of Web sites or newsgroups.

The Internet Filter goes further and automatically eliminates "specific types of messages within any newsgroup" (presumably, messages containing offensive words). The Internet Filter boasts "silent installation, without any indication to the child that it is installed." And it automatically e-mails a warning message to the parents if any "access violations" occur.

Net Nanny, marketed by a Canadian software developer, allows parents to specify "dangerous phrases" that the program should look for—such as "What's your name?" or "What's your phone number?" If the program notices one of these phrases, it logs off immediately.

Meanwhile, in June 1995 Netscape, Microsoft, and Progressive Networks, Inc. formed the Information Highway Parental Empowerment Group "to work together on coordinating standards for technology that would give parents greater control over what their children are able to access on the Internet." According to a Netscape spokesman, "The technology for filtering content is easy. The hard part is deciding what to filter."

But if that's true, why does AOL have such a hard time filtering just the names of its chat rooms, let alone the chat itself? Word-oriented or phrase-oriented programs such as the Internet Filter and Net Nanny must check for countless "danger signals" in online text—and will be instantly defeated if a security-conscious pedophile merely transposes some letter pairs or sprinkles a few X's here and there. Also, the list of forbidden sites in software such as SurfWatch will have to be frequently updated to keep pace with new Usenet groups or Web sites that come online. And many parents won't be computer-literate enough to grapple with the complexity of all this filtering. In many homes, the kids are more computer-literate than the adults.

Bearing all this in mind, another tactic has been suggested: a rating system. The Recreational Software Advisory Council (RSAC) is an independent, nonprofit organization established in September 1994 with funding from various trade associations, which in turn

are financed by corporations in the computer business. It was established after a previous round of Senate hearings sounded the alarm about excessive violence in video games.

Stephen Balkam, executive director of the RSAC, reports that more than 200 software titles from nearly eighty software companies have now been rated using a scale that was developed in conjunction with parents, pediatricians, and Dr. Donald Roberts, chairman of the Department of Communications at Stanford University. This working group developed objective criteria to measure violence, nudity/sex, and bad language in video games, boiling it all down to a number from 0 (totally safe) to 4 (totally outrageous).

But the RSAC doesn't evaluate software itself. Video games tend to have dozens or even hundreds of hidden levels; there's no way they can be thoroughly examined in the same way that it's possible to view and evaluate an entire movie. As a consequence, RSAC requires manufacturers to rate their own games by answering a questionnaire on the content of each new product. It then spot-checks games at random to make sure that nobody cheats.

Like parental advisory labels on music CDs, RSAC game ratings now exert a subtle force encouraging manufacturers to sanitize their products. There's also a strong incentive for all game manufacturers to participate in the scheme: Wal-Mart and Toys R Us have both announced that they won't sell unrated games anymore.

Could the RSAC rating scale be used online? Definitely, says Balkam. He feels that "many hundreds if not thousands of Web sites and home pages could be rated and regulated."

Moreover, adult material could be blocked automatically. Each transmission from a Web page or Usenet group would commence with a few bytes establishing its rating. Software at home or at every Internet site would sense these bytes and lock out material exceeding the level specified by the consumer. Any source that misrated its material would find itself rerated or blocked for a penalty period. And sources that refused to rate themselves would automatically earn the maximum adult rating by default.

Does this sound like the final, equitable answer to the problem of access, content, and distribution? Even Stephen Balkam admits that the scheme would be useless for online chat, where content is totally unpredictable. Balkam suggests a system such as Surfwatch for that—or he says parents can block *all* chat areas if they want to be totally secure.

But even if the rating scheme is just applied to Web sites and newsgroups, it still raises problems. Will the authors of Usenet posts have to rate every message that they write? Will smaller Internet service providers play along and participate in the scheme, even though they have resisted every attempt at censorship in the past? Participation could never be compelled by law; that would be a clear violation of the First Amendment.

In March 1996 Microsoft endorsed the RSAC's rating system and pledged to incorporate filtering capabilities into the next version of its Internet Explorer software. It's still hard, though, to see how such a system can ever be enforced. With thousands of new Web sites constantly coming online and the content of current Web sites constantly changing, who's going to do the random sampling to check that everyone's following the rating scheme? Who's going to deal with the bad sites that need to be rerated or blocked? Who's going to process the arguments, complaints, and appeals from people who claim that they did rate themselves accurately and are now being unfairly penalized? Who's going to administer this nightmare of censorship, and who's going to pay for it?

According to Balkam, about 2,000 new video games are published each year—and he admits that even this volume creates a sizable amount of work for the RSAC. But it's a tiny fraction of the ratable material on the Internet.

And so, no matter what kind of cunning tactic is proposed or who bears the burden of it, online content seems uncontrollable, distribution can't be contained, and access can't be effectively restricted.

Angels Online

There's one more possible approach for controlling the Net. In 1995 a bunch of Net users decided to take matters into their own hands by giving peer pressure a new and more sinister meaning. They became the first decency vigilantes of cyberspace.

The Guardian Angels started out as a citizens' group in New York City, patrolling subways and bad neighborhoods in an effort to discourage crime. Wearing distinctive T-shirts and red berets, the Angels have become a well-established feature of urban life, although they have never been regarded as particularly useful or desirable by the New York City Police Department.

Curtis Sliwa, founder of the Angels, has his own daily show on talk-radio station WABC. In 1995 he announced that he'd acquired an Internet address. Soon he found himself talking to listeners who were worried about netporn, hate speech, and pedophiles online. Soon after that, Sliwa came up with his inevitable response. If the Internet is just another "bad neighborhood," it's up to him—or citizens like him—to patrol it.

In June he issued a preliminary press release signed by himself and Colin Hatcher, who called himself Gabriel and was appointed coordinator of the project to police the internet, called Netwatch. They appealed for volunteers who would spend two to eight hours a week "looking for places where they believe there may be unacceptable activity" on the Internet.

The main targets seemed to be Usenet, IRC, chat areas in major Internet service providers, and "any sites providing material/discussions/images/contacts of a sexually explicit nature (there are thousands!)."

This raised some interesting—and unanswered—questions. Were the Angels suggesting that sexually explicit material was illegal? They seemed a bit vague about this. "We are not trying to abolish free speech," they said in a press release, "but we believe that freedom

of speech should not be exercised if by exercising it you are violating someone else's basic rights."

What rights? Gabriel didn't say.

Another unresolved issue was discipline. Sliwa freely admitted that he wouldn't even try to control the online conduct of his vigilantes: "None of our volunteers is qualified to represent our organization. They are simply people who have contacted us and said they will keep a lookout."

Colin Hatcher, leader of the Guardian Angels decency vigilantes, prefers to call himself "Gabriel" online.

For what? Sliwa offered the following hit list:

a) Hate crimes (like racist postings, hate mail) etc.
b) Sexual harassment (eg Online stalking)
c) Sexual abuse of children
d) Kids access to pornographic material
e) Anything where Service Providers Terms of
   Service are being violated.

Of course, it's no crime in the United States to publish racist tracts. As for sexual harassment, it's tricky to define and hard to prove. But the Angels seemed to feel that they'd know it when they saw it, and if a volunteer found some stuff she didn't like the look of, she should "report the violations to us at Netwatch, and also to the System Administrators, or Service Providers, of the cybercriminal." Cybercriminal? This suggested that as far as the Angels were concerned, hate speech and sexually explicit text and pictures *were* crimes, no matter what the Constitution and federal laws might say.

How would this decency crusade actually work in practice? Later in 1995, one Net user received the following not-very-friendly, not-very-literate warning, sent via an anonymous remailer:

The Net is out of control, sex crimes, hate crimes and felonies.

Just as on the streets, CyberCrime is committed by a minority of criminals who destroy the quality of life for an innocent majority. And just like on the streets the Guardian Angels will combat it.

We have good reason to believe that you are involved in unlawful, harmful, hateful, threatening and/or harassment, particularly relating to minors. We will be watching you.

The netizen who found this in her mailbox was baffled and irritated. She had no idea what she'd done to provoke the warning, and since the message was anonymous, there was no way to *find out* what she was supposed to have done.

By November the Angels claimed they had volunteers working for them, busily searching for bad guys on the Net. "We have reported a number of Child Pornographers (50) to Sysadmins [system

administrators] this month," Colin Hatcher noted, although he was no longer signing his real name to his progress reports, perhaps in fear of reprisals from angry pedophiles. "Letters we have received back all share our concern and promise stern action. Remember, each electronic image represents a real life destroyed."

The Angels now had an international reach. When Hatcher found a message from a sixteen-year-old girl on alt.teens that was "extremely nasty (obscene)," he contacted the site from which the message originated—which turned out to be a girls' school in England. According to Hatcher, "I wrote to the Sysadmin and asked the question, 'Are you aware that one of your girls is posting this kind of material to this newsgroup?' He investigated the matter, and it turned out apparently that the postings came not from a 16 year old girl at all, but from an older, MALE, member of the teaching staff."

When Hatcher told the system administrator about the teacher's secret online persona, did this also result in a "real life destroyed"? Hatcher didn't say. In his righteousness, it didn't seem to occur to him that he could seriously injure an adult whose only "crime" was fantasizing. Hatcher made it clear, though, that in his universe some topics were so taboo they shouldn't even be mentioned. For instance, he was outraged by the idea of free-speech advocates suggesting that conversations about pedophilia were a form of protected speech:

> Like environmental granola terrorists who will injure loggers or bomb hunting retreats to save the spotted owl, these Champions of Cyber feel that freedom of speech as proposed by the founding fathers was intended to allow child rapists to hold public gab sessions, discuss their disgusting deeds and depraved desires and just generally work themselves into a pedophilic lather. Personally, I prefer a little preventative medicine, a little stitch in time that saves sending out the blood hounds to try and locate a snatched 5 year old before she ends up in a garbage bag in a dumpster.

According to Hatcher, his force of 200 volunteers was ready to administer this medicine. "Basically there are more law abiding

Users on the Internet than law breaking Abusers," he wrote. "It's just a matter of the good guys working as hard as the bad and the ugly."

Some Net users wondered, though, if Hatcher was qualified to draw a dividing line between good and bad, let alone ugly. They also worried that decency vigilantes might have a chilling effect on freedom of speech. A student at Rutgers University complained that some of the Angels' public statements "are threats to violate the civil liberties of users of the Internet." In addition, he said, "the record of the Guardian Angels suggests that they will step over even the bounds that they publicly set for themselves."

Still, he had an answer. "The idea is to use one problem (the 'CyberAngels') to counter another (Net-abuse such as spamming). Simply forward copies of spamming . . . [to the Angels] . . . and ask them to deal with the problem."

Was this a polite way to mail-bomb the Angels into oblivion? The writer didn't come right out and say so, but he did admit he was "hopeful that the volume of mail received on this count will be great enough that they will be unable to carry out any improper actions."

So here it was again, the Net community's strange powers of instant, universal communication, ready to be invoked at a moment's notice for purposes of self-defense. But in this particular case, the call for action created barely a ripple of interest. Netizens weren't very impressed by Gabriel and his team. They just seemed a bit weary and annoyed, like elephants harassed by a passing swarm of tiny biting flies.

The State of the States

Decency groups such as the Christian Coalition or Enough Is Enough are far more powerful than vigilantes such as the CyberAngels because they're well organized and savvy about political power. Not only do they maintain paid lobbyists in

Washington, but in some cases their members work as aides to conservative legislators. If some sort of federal online decency law ultimately survives constitutional challenges, almost certainly it will have been drafted with the aid and advice of fundamentalist Christian activists.

Still, it may take a while. Federal lawmaking is a slow process. By comparison, state legislation can be passed far more rapidly—and with far less publicity. Back in the summer of 1995, when Senator Exon had only just begun waving his famous binder of bestiality pictures on the nightly news, many states had already pushed through laws of their own to control content online. In fact, some of these laws at the local level went even farther than Senator Exon wanted to go.

In Kansas, for instance, a law now exists to prohibit netizens from making "indecent comments" via their computer keyboards.

Connecticut, Georgia, New Jersey, North Dakota, and South Dakota have all broadened existing laws covering phone calls to include computer communications. As a result, in these states it is now a criminal act to send e-mail that is obscene, vulgar, offensive, or liable to cause "annoyance" (the exact wording varies from state to state).

Even if you live elsewhere, you could still be prosecuted for sending a message *to* someone in a state that has Net-decency legislation.

The new state laws controlling online speech have attracted hardly any attention. Most netizens remain blissfully unaware of what was happening, and there have been no test cases yet to make people aware of the legislation. But local prosecutors have already taken advantage of preexisting obscenity laws worded so loosely that they could be applied to computer graphics just as easily as to printed magazines.

At the local level, the effects have been traumatic—especially for BBS owners. Even family-oriented bulletin boards can be fair game for local decency crusaders if the boards happen to contain some Penthouse-style pictures. It's simple enough for a local district attorney to get a search warrant and seize the equipment, and the

payoff is obvious: TV coverage in which the district attorney can show himself fighting the good fight against cyberporn. Conservative voters feel reassured, and the DA gets reelected—while the system owner loses his computer and is forced to defend himself in court.

A Lawman's BBS

Lorne Shantz learned this the hard way. For years he operated a BBS out of his home in Phoenix, Arizona. He was careful to stay within the law; in fact, Shantz *was* the law. He worked for the Arizona Department of Public Safety, in the Highway Patrol. Many of his colleagues in law enforcement used to log onto his system, and so did at least one judge and one prosecutor.

All this changed abruptly in November 1994 when Shantz's computer was seized because it allegedly contained obscene materials and child pornography. Shantz protested that he had maintained a strict policy prohibiting pornographic uploads. Still, he was immediately suspended from his job.

Four months later he was indicted by a grand jury. The day after that, county attorney Rick Romley held a press conference claiming that his office was "cutting new ground" in the war against cyberporn.

It turned out that three pictures on Shantz's BBS were of women under eighteen years of age—according to the prosecutor's office. The age was estimated by using the Tanner Scale, a rule of thumb devised by doctors to estimate a woman's age by measuring breast development and pubic hair. Shantz objected that the scale was vague and was based on Caucasian women, while the pictures on his board were of Asian women, whose sexual characteristics (according to Shantz) mature later. His objections were ignored.

His BBS also contained some pictures of bestiality. Shantz readily agreed that those should not have been there, but he said he had never seen them. They were included on a CD-ROM that he had

bought by mail order. It was labeled "BBS-ready," so Shantz assumed it was legal. He had sampled a couple of pictures, found they were no different from poses in *Penthouse*, and didn't bother to check the other thousands of images on the disk.

The prosecutor's office ignored this defense also. "We're talking hard-core obscenity," said Barnett Lottstein, special assistant to the county attorney, speaking on the nightly news. "Mr. Shantz had an *obligation* to know what was on his bulletin board."

Well, did he? The grand jury agreed to press charges, but Shantz's lawyer complained that Shantz had never had a chance to explain himself. The prosecutor had somehow forgotten to notify him of his right to testify. When a second grand jury was convened, they had an opportunity to listen to Shantz; they believed he had acted in good faith, and they let him go free.

"Almost every BBS around here used to have an adult section," commented Jonathan Gillies, thirty-one, a networking engineer and former BBS owner. "Lorne actually took more trouble than most of them, posting notices warning people not to upload certain types of picture and demanding proof of age."

According to Gillies, the real value of Shantz's board had nothing to do with its erotic content. "This was one of the best information resources we had in Phoenix. I made some valuable contacts with people using the message base, and there was an enormous amount of shareware programs. Plus he had Internet connectivity."

If the grand jury hadn't thrown out the charges, Shantz would have found himself in court in the spring or summer of 1996, during the run-up to the November elections. According to Gillies, "Everyone suspected that this whole thing was done by Rick Romley to get back into office."

Shantz certainly believed this. "The only reason they picked on me was they thought it would help Romley get reelected," he said. "What happened to me was an abuse of prosecutorial power." (A spokesperson at the county attorney's office refused to comment on the case.)

Shantz ended up beating the charges, but he endured six months of anxiety and unemployment, he ran up $30,000 in legal fees, the police held on to his computer equipment until they were legally compelled to return it, and to get his job back Shantz had to start a new court battle. As of May, 1996 that battle was still in progress, costing still more money.

Meanwhile, even though the charges had been thrown out, a spokesperson for the prosecutor said he hoped the case would send a message to all BBS owners in the area. And that's exactly what happened. According to local observers, half a dozen BBS operators shut down their systems after they saw the fate of Lorne Shantz, and many others who stayed in business closed their adult sections, just to be on the safe side.

This is the real danger posed by a local prosecution: Its effects spread far beyond the site that is actually hit.

An Exercise in Paranoia

Robert Carr, who circulated the Hexon Exon program to "exonize" offensive speech, also runs a small BBS in Boise, Idaho. He used to offer a huge library of counterculture files, including erotic stories and his own video games mocking religious fundamentalists and the hard-core right. In August 1994 Carr's picture was published in *Wired* magazine as a defiant anarchist, armed and dangerous.

One year later Carr was still armed but no longer so dangerous. The erotic stories had gone from his BBS, along with most of the games. "The final straw," he said, "came when the local police were looking for some kids who had been setting off pipe bombs. The kids hadn't actually hurt anyone, but the police announced they were going to come online, find the source of the bomb recipes, and eradicate it. Also, a year previously, a couple of boards had been shut down where teenagers were trading GIFs. I couldn't risk getting raided because my neighborhood is so conservative, the publicity could cost me my job."

Robert Carr ran a subversive bulletin board in Boise, Idaho, that was chock full of goodies—until police action prompted Carr to censor himself.

Carr took everything that he regarded as potentially dangerous off his system. He now feels that the BBS scene will never be the same again. "When I first started my board, it was fun. You could put anything online and nobody cared. These days, I have to examine every upload to make sure no one's planting something. Running a board has become an exercise in paranoia."

At One BBScon, the national BBS convention that took place in August 1995 in Tampa, Florida, similar stories were told by sysops from all over America. Many of them had toned down their libraries of erotica or had removed them altogether. There was a mood of

caution tinged with fear—not because of federal legislation, but because of local harassment.

The most shocking example of state law enforcement running amok occurred in Cincinnati. Here was a classic case of systematic intimidation in the online world, chilling free speech and shutting down businesses with complete disregard for anyone's constitutional rights.

Self-Taught Sysop Loses All

Bob Emerson is a big, friendly, cheerful midwesterner who looks like Santa Claus without the hair and the beard. Bob says that one of his guiding principles in life has always been to make a living by doing things that are fun, and he's succeeded pretty well at putting his principles into practice. He had a weakness for hot-rodding, so he opened an auto accessory store specializing in high-performance parts. He got interested in video in the early 1980s, so he opened the first video rental store in Cincinnati. It was the same kind of thing with his computer bulletin board: He was one of the pioneers, starting it out of his own home in 1984, and he built it up as a labor of love.

Like most of Bob's ventures, the board was successful. He had no formal training in computers or electronics, but he taught himself what he needed to know, and for a total investment of around $45,000 he ended up with a Novell network of twenty-three computers serving about 6,000 subscribers over twenty phone lines. Bob even added Internet access, with e-mail service and a Usenet feed.

In 1995 he lost it all.

He was working in his auto accessory store with his son one Friday morning when the phone rang. "It was one of my neighbors," he says, "calling to tell me that it looked like a SWAT team was in the driveway outside my home. I assumed someone must have broken

into the house, so I jumped in the car and headed over there. I found eight or ten cops, two or three police cruisers, and a big black sheriff's van parked in the street. And they were all waiting just for me."

Emerson found himself served with a search warrant.

"There was nothing I could do to stop them. They went in the house, and the first thing they did was pull out all the phone lines. Then they asked me to show them where everything was at on my system. I asked them if they would let me keep my computers if I did what they wanted, and they said no. I said the heck with that, I wasn't going to show them anything. So they took it all away, twenty-three computers, and the monitors and hard drives. Plus they even took my grandchild's multimedia machine, which we just use for running games."

The search warrant listed forty-five graphics files that the police believed were obscene, but Bob claims he had gone out of his way to be discreet and stay on the right side of the law. "The adult area of the board wasn't even listed on the main screen," he says. "To get access to it, people had to come to me *in person* so I could make sure they were of age. I made absolutely no extra charge for the adult section; it was just an extra free service for people who wanted it. I estimate that it only amounted to three percent of the total usage."

A longtime active member of Bob's BBS who describes herself as a Christian churchgoer confirms that this was his policy. "I was given access myself," she says, "and I looked around. What he had and what I saw was what you'd see in *Playboy* and *Penthouse*. I decided it was not for me, so I simply stayed away from that section in the future."

Most users had no idea that the X-rated pictures were available. "I used the board for about a year and a half," says Steve Guest, who runs a network consultancy business named PC Plus. "I hadn't a clue that there was an adult area. There was no way for the average user to know that it existed." Guest says that he used Bob's board

mainly for its e-mail and file transfer facilities. "We have five engineers," he explains, "and almost ninety percent of our business is outside the local area. The BBS was basically our mailbox. Ironically, I selected the board because it was among the cleanest, most family-oriented that I could find. People on the system didn't use any bad language, and I never found any pirated software."

So why was Bob's equipment seized? One simple answer: local politics.

Bob Emerson's computer bulletin board in Cincinnati was seized by smut-busting sheriff Simon Leis. Emerson spent more than $17,000 to replace his equipment, and he sued the sheriff.

The Sheriff of Hamilton County

In Cincinnati, a museum exhibition of photographs by Robert Mapplethorpe was shut down by 125 sheriff's deputies in SWAT uniforms, carrying automatic weapons. The subsequent trial created national publicity.

In Cincinnati, *Hustler*'s publisher, Larry Flynt, had to fight in court for the right to distribute his magazine through local vendors.

In Cincinnati, there are no adult bookstores. One by one, they have all been driven out of business.

The man who takes most of the credit for this relentless campaign is Simon Leis, sheriff of Hamilton County, which covers a large part of the Cincinnati area. Sources close to Leis report that he is a devout Catholic who attends church every day. (Leis himself refused to accept phone calls in connection with this investigation, and no one from his office would comment.) Without a doubt, moralistic behavior is an entrenched tradition in Leis's family: His father, a judge, used to fight smut back in the 1940s.

Leis lost in the Mapplethorpe trial, and he lost the case against Larry Flynt. In fact, according to local attorneys, Leis has lost every obscenity battle that has gone to appeal. But still, he has won the war. His policy of raiding bookstores and seizing the merchandise has discouraged anyone from running similar businesses in Cincinnati.

To understand the connection between Leis and Bob Emerson we have to go back to 1982, when Bob started his video rental business. It included an adult section, which he ran just as discreetly as his BBS. "The adult stuff was not displayed," he says. "If you wanted it, you had to pick it off a list of titles, and it was given to you in a plain black box."

There was a Catholic church on the opposite side of the street, and members of the congregation rented tapes from Bob's store all the time—because most of his stock was family-oriented. Patty Volz

has been a member of that church all her life and was one of Bob's first customers. "I never had a problem with the adult section," she says. "You could bring anyone into the store, your grandmother or a child, and never be ashamed, because nothing offensive was displayed. I was raised in a strict Catholic environment, but I believe that what people choose to watch in the privacy of their own homes is no one else's business. This is freedom of choice, and that's what's America is based on. Personally, I don't even like to see people rent violent movies for their children. That to me is offensive. But I have no business telling them what they should or shouldn't spend their money on, and I don't think Simon Leis has any business doing that, either."

Where Bob's store was concerned, Leis had a problem. The store was located just outside the sheriff's jurisdiction.

Still, Leis had a friend: Charles H. Keating, a Cincinnati native and lifelong antismut crusader (later imprisoned in connection with the savings and loan scandal). Richard Nixon appointed Keating to the Commission on Obscenity and Pornography back in 1969, to add a conservative voice to the basically liberal group.

In Cincinnati during the late 1980s, Keating created Concerned Citizens for Community Values, and they compelled the prosecutor in that county to act on their complaint against Bob Emerson's video store. The prosecutor charged Bob with violating state obscenity laws, took him to court—and lost. He tried again and lost again. He kept trying and kept losing, seven times in a row.

Bob was told by his attorney that Simon Leis had offered to help the local prosecutor on an informal basis. Having cleaned up Cincinnati, the sheriff wanted to extend his reach into the suburbs. Unfortunately for Leis, officials in neighboring counties were reluctant to cooperate with him and insisted on running their own antismut campaigns; but in 1995 something happened to change all that.

Cyberporn had become a hot issue. News coverage had been so intense, many people were under the impression that the online world was a cesspool of smut threatening the safety of their

children. Meanwhile, it happened that the Cincinnati area was well supplied with bulletin boards—more than 200 of them, serving more than 20,000 users, according to one estimate—and many of the boards had adult sections featuring explicit photographs.

Sheriff Leis finally had his opportunity for a vote-getting crusade that no elected official could afford to ignore. He put together his coalition, a Regional Computer Crimes Task Force containing personnel from two counties in Ohio and one across the border in Kentucky (Cincinnati sits right on the state line.) It was a great new way to reach out and bust someone; and with so many tempting targets, the only problem was deciding whom to hit first.

Bob Emerson was the obvious choice. His video store had defied Leis's ideas of decency for more than a decade, and unlike Cincinnati bookstore owners, Bob had refused to be intimidated.

The sheriff could now teach him a lesson.

Net Users Strike Back

On the day when the task force confiscated his computers, Bob recalls one of the cops telling him that he seemed to be taking it very calmly. "What do you expect me to do?" Bob said. "Jump up and down?"

Indeed, Emerson describes himself as an amiable, laid-back kind of guy. "I don't start anything," he says. But then, thoughtfully, he adds: "If somebody pushes me, I do push back. I love my country and the freedom that it stands for. To me, these people are trying to take away my freedoms, and that pisses me off."

The very next day after the bust, Bob Emerson went out and bought $17,000 worth of hardware. By Sunday he had his board up and running again.

Then he hired Louis Sirkin, president of the local First Amendment Lawyers Association. One week later Sirkin filed a suit on behalf of

Bob Emerson against Simon Leis and a long list of other city employees and departments. Citing violations of constitutional rights, the suit requested $250,000 in damages.

This wasn't all. Steve Guest, the networking consultant, decided to push things a step further. "I'm not a political person," he says. "I never get involved in political crusades. But in this case, I just got angry. I put out a message asking if anyone was interested in helping with a lawsuit on behalf of the users, and I got 200 messages in the first day. So I hired a local lawyer to look into it, and he found some other attorneys who were experienced in this area."

Guest still sounds surprised that he got involved. "You have to understand," he says, "I'm a conservative kind of guy, I'm not a liberal. But Simon Leis—how can I put it nicely? I guess I can't. Leis is a Nazi. He has to pay for forcing his beliefs on everyone else. He's violating the basic principles on which this country was founded."

Guest is now the first person listed in an unprecedented class-action suit filed on behalf of *all* Bob Emerson's BBS users who were deprived of access and had their e-mail illegally seized. The suit demands the statutory maximum of $11,000 compensation *per person*, plus punitive damages. Bearing in mind that Bob's system served at least 5,000 people, the total compensation could be over $50 million.

The filing of this suit was good news for Bob Emerson and his online community, but Bob was not the only one who had been targeted by the task force. Four other BBS owners had been raided on the same day—and they didn't have his ability to push back.

Steve Brown, age forty-four, is married with two daughters and lives in a neighborhood that he modestly describes as working-class. Daytime, Steve has a full-time job as a salesperson. He started his BBS as a hobby, serving 520 people via just one phone line and a single 486SX computer. He kept the computer and a couple of CD-ROM drives sitting on a Ping-Pong table in the basement of his suburban home.

He was at work when his wife called to tell him that police were taking his BBS apart. "I got a sick feeling in my stomach," Steve recalls. "I spoke to the cops on the phone, and they asked me which computer ran the BBS. I told them. Then they asked me where the CD-ROMs were. I told them that, too. Then they went to my personal system, which requires a CMOS password to get in. I explained that it had nothing to do with the BBS. I gave them my password so they could see for themselves. But the guy mistyped it, and he got mad and just said, 'Take it.' So they seized that as well. And it's got my finances, my tax records, my whole life in there."

Steve says he was shell-shocked for days afterward. "It was a nightmare, except that each day I woke up and it was real." He was afraid he would lose his job because the police released his photograph to local newspapers and TV stations, and they alleged there had been kiddieporn on the BBS.

Like Bob Emerson, Steve had allowed users to upload material freely. He had no idea what people put there. This meant he couldn't even respond to the police allegations, because he hadn't seen what they claimed they had found. He still doesn't know what the pictures portray.

In the months since the bust, Steve has not tried to replace his BBS. He says he's through with it; he doesn't want any more hassles.

The experience has deepened his general distrust of government. "I feel they have gone far beyond their duties, to the point of malicious persecution of me and my family," he says. "I just don't understand what's happening in this country. There's always some law coming out that doesn't make a whole lot of sense. You know, they just passed a law here that if your teenager is found smoking, they can come and arrest the parents. Incredible. The fact is, Americans are not as free as we think we are."

Lorne Shantz, whose system was seized in Phoenix, feels the same way. "Let's face it," he says, "our judicial system is ill and needs curing. We have to make sure that the government remains accountable to us, the people. The federal situation is bad enough,

but what's going on at the state level is more frightening—because they're getting away with more than the feds. Big Brother has got his nose where it does not belong."

This from a man who spent fourteen years as a law-enforcement officer.

A Chilling Effect

There is a plus side. Scott Greenwood runs a Cincinnati law firm (Greenwood and Associates) concentrating on constitutional law. He coauthored the class-action suit on behalf of Bob Emerson's BBS users, and from Greenwood's perspective, Sheriff Leis's men have created a golden opportunity. "We're suing the hell out of the sheriff's department," he says with cheerful relish. "What the police did was totally outrageous, like walking into a post office and taking all the mail because one person receives hard-core magazines from Denmark. The police didn't need to take anything away; they already knew which files they wanted on the BBS. They could have copied them onto a few floppy disks. If the government can shut down a computer system because one individual sees something he doesn't like, then the whole communications system of the country is under attack. You could just as well shut down a phone switch because organized crime is using it."

Collaborating with Greenwood on the suit is Peter D. Kennedy of George, Donaldson, and Ford, a law firm located in Austin, Texas. The firm has defended major media clients such as the *Wall Street Journal* and Time-Warner. Kennedy is their resident expert on computer law and has also consulted for nationwide Internet service providers. He was the lead trial counsel in the case of Steve Jackson Games vs. U.S. Secret Service, which ended in 1993 with the Secret Service being fined for seizing e-mail illegally.

Kennedy is not as emphatic as Greenwood. He has an erudite, low-key manner. Still, he's openly scornful of Cincinnati officials and can

Peter D. Kennedy warns that state prosecutors have a strong incentive to stage crusades that play well on the nightly news. [Photo by Guerrero Photographic Group, copyright 1993.]

itemize a dozen deficiencies in the way that the search warrant was requested, issued, and applied. And yes, he says it all comes down to politics. "A lot of state prosecutors are elected," he says matter-of-factly. "Federal prosecutors are not elected. That can make a big difference in how they behave over issues such as cyberporn."

In other words, when there's a vote-getting issue, a state prosecutor has a strong incentive to do stuff that will play well on TV.

"Compare what happened in Cincinnati with the federal investigators who went looking for child pornography at America Online," Kennedy goes on. "Investigators didn't seize computers at AOL, they didn't

take e-mail, and the system stayed up. They used legal process to order AOL to produce particular information about particular suspected users. This is what is required under the Electronic Communications Privacy Act: You have to state precisely what you're looking for. Federal law enforcement is now getting the message, slowly. But there are fifty states with hundreds of county prosecutors apiece who are way behind on the learning curve. We're now trying to teach them the lesson that the federal people learned in the Steve Jackson case."

In fact, Greenwood and Kennedy are trying to set an additional precedent, claiming that messages exchanged semipublicly in forums on Bob Emerson's system should be protected under a separate, noncomputer law, the Privacy Protection Act of 1980.

"This act traditionally protects a reporter's news notes," explains Greenwood. "Our theory is that sending messages via Usenet or a BBS conference is the functional equivalent of publishing. After all, companies like Lexis refer to themselves as being in electronic publishing, when all they do is send formatted data."

Unfortunately, this kind of civil suit can take a year or more to reach trial; in the meantime, Sheriff Leis shows no sign of changing his ways. At the end of August 1995 his task force raided and seized several *more* boards—this time, systems that were being used by alleged hackers and phone phreaks.

Commenting on this, Greenwood's voice takes on a tone of amazement bordering on awe. "The sheriff just doesn't know any boundaries," he says. "Some kids were shaken down who are just users of these boards. The sheriff has already prompted two lawsuits, and if he continues doing this—well, there will be more."

Greenwood agrees that state officials are far more worrisome than federal law enforcement. "The Exon amendment was horrifying," he says, "but it's worse on the state level. For instance, the overwhelming majority of obscenity prosecutions are brought by state prosecutors—and given the hysteria over cyberporn, we're going to see more activity of this type."

Also, when new laws are created, it tends to happen faster at the state level than in Congress. While Senator Orrin Hatch was introducing his bill to criminalize the "repulsive conduct" of producing simulated child pornography using image-retouching software, similar legislation had already been signed into law in Illinois and Nevada, making it a crime to create, distribute, or possess sexually explicit computer representations of minors even if real children have not been harmed. These laws could be applied to BBS owners and Internet service providers, even if they are genuinely unaware of the material on their systems.

Introducing his bill, Mr. Hatch remarked that online services have evolved so fast, the law "has failed to keep pace with technology." But on the local level this simply isn't true. State legislators have moved far faster than most people realize, and one gung-ho antismut crusader like Simon Leis is all it takes to activate the new laws, terrify service providers, and eradicate constitutionally protected speech literally overnight.

In Cincinnati the BBS raids have had a massively chilling effect. Bob Emerson estimates that more than twenty local boards have stopped operating rather than risk being raided, and other sysops have reacted as Robert Carr did, removing any material that might possibly offend a decency crusader.

Users also have felt the impact. "Have I been chilled?" asks one person who prefers not to be named but lives in the Cincinnati area. "I certainly have. . . . What happened where I live may seem to be an isolated incident to most people. But . . . the mind-set that brought it about is not. This will occur in other parts of the U.S. It's a shame, but our own local law-enforcement authorities are a greater threat to our free-speech rights than are any of the politicians and bureaucrats in Washington."

Bob Emerson fought back, and by spending a large chunk of money, he kept his BBS up and running. Even so, it has been affected by the raids. Many people have chosen not to renew their memberships, and there's a new air of caution even in text messages in the chat

areas, where citizens now feel that anything they say may be monitored and possibly used against them.

Sheriff Simon Leis may lose this battle in court, just like all the others he has lost over the years. But outside the courtroom, once again he has already won the war. The Cincinnati BBS scene has been radically altered, and the freedoms that have been lost will be hard to restore. Worse still, each time there's a local crackdown, other system operators scattered across America will be tempted to censor themselves. In January 1996 a site in Wisconsin claiming to be the largest BBS in America announced that it was eliminating about 50,000 files containing adult material. Its founder was quoted in the *Tampa Tribune* as saying that "since it is only seven percent of our service and it could result in the 100 percent loss of our business, the risk is not worth it."

And so, calmly and quietly, with hardly any publicity, the retreat from free speech continues.

The Loyal Opposition

The only organization fighting for online freedoms through affiliates in all fifty states is the American Civil Liberties Union.

"Where we have had some time to react," says Ann Beeson, ACLU's Net expert in New York, "we have been generally successful in defeating state bills. We are now considering constitutional challenges to bills that passed this year."

Beeson joined ACLU in February 1995 to fill a new position that had been established for an activist specializing in First Amendment issues in cyberspace. In less than a year she became a central figure in the fight for free speech online. During 1995, working as an attorney and as a public-relations spokesperson, she helped students whose universities censored Net access, organized lobbying efforts opposing the Exon amendment, cowrote a statement opposing

key-escrow encryption, launched a biweekly online cyberliberties newsletter, and worked with ACLU affiliates to fight several state bills that threatened to impose Net censorship locally. In New York State and Washington State, the bills were stopped.

"Ann has definitely taken the lead in bringing the voice of the ACLU to the Net," comments Mike Godwin, legal counsel at the Electronic Frontier Foundation.

The ACLU is located on West 43rd Street, in Manhattan's theater district, which rubs elbows with the sleaze district, in which can be found probably the greatest gathering of peep shows and adult video stores in America. The ACLU building has an old, gray facade, and the ground-floor lobby has a low-rent look, bare and dimly lit, with no air-conditioning, just a massive old 1930s-style fan pointing at a guard behind a desk. For no obvious reason, on the day I visited the building twenty cartons of C-fold paper towels were dumped in one corner of the lobby beneath the fierce gaze of Roger Baldwin, the principal founder of the ACLU, who is immortalized in a large oil painting on the brown marble wall. A plaque above an old leather couch explains that after Baldwin established the ACLU in 1920, he spearheaded battles for free speech during World War II and subsequently during the McCarthy hearings.

The building's upper floors have been renovated, but they still have a utilitarian feel. One hallway is crowded with old four-drawer file cabinets. Another stores a stack of five-gallon water bottles. There are frequent reminders of liberal causes: Near the elevator a sign points to the Lesbian and Gay Rights Project, and above a recycling bin a poster says, "You don't need to have a home to have a voice. Every American citizen has the right to vote—including homeless people."

Beeson seems a little less politically correct than this. Her office doorknob bears a little sign that says "Come on in, relax, take your clothes off." Beeson herself is slim, dark-haired, and stylishly dressed, looking more like a Fortune 500 employee than the media stereotype of a dowdy rights activist.

Her personal passion for free speech turns out to be quite complex and slightly paradoxical. "Before I went to law school," she says, "I did a masters in cultural anthropology. As you can imagine, this means I am a cultural relativist. I believe in the legitimacy of every culture and set of beliefs. Consequently I am well aware that our notion of free speech is a particularly American value. To say that it's supposed to be the supreme value that trumps all others is a culturally situated point of view."

By this logic, if Americans impose free speech on other cultures, they're guilty of cultural imperialism.

"But," Beeson goes on, "if there are all these different belief systems out there, what are the fundamental goals that *allow* all that diversity? One of them has to be freedom of speech." In other words, free speech is necessary in order to *permit* cultural diversity.

Ann Beeson of ACLU has become a vital figure in the fight for online freedom.

Religious conservatives, of course, don't see it that way. They feel that some forms of speech are powerful enough to erode Christian principles and family values.

Beeson totally rejects this. "To talk about something is never to destroy it. What if we tried to prevent conservatives from talking about *their* values? It should be possible for everyone to speak freely and still protect particular points of view. Minority communities would actually be better-protected in a world in which everyone's speech is allowed rather than one in which a majority point of view is imposed."

Should there be any limits at all on free speech?

"I think I would stick by the famous test that there should be no penalties unless the speech is an immediate incitement to imminent personal violence. Imminent assault."

But surely the new technology of the Net changes everything. It has the power to cross boundaries and invade communities more intrusively than any other communications medium.

Beeson rejects this argument, too. "This battle has been fought with every new form of communication," she points out. "The ACLU has seen it in their entire history, a new medium coming along which people want to censor. Allowing freedom to flourish has never yet caused those conservative communities to fall apart. Somehow they still manage to thrive."

Does she see anything bad about the Net?

"The positive aspect of free peer-to-peer communication is also the negative aspect: There's a lot of junk out there. But it's truly the most democratizing medium we've seen."

Beeson speaks rapidly and seems businesslike. Her mannerisms are pure New York—but her accent is southern. "I come from a very conservative Republican family," she explains, "from Texas originally, where ACLU is a four-letter word." She laughs happily. "In fact, I think my dad's the one who coined that phrase. My

parents are very supportive, but when someone asks them what their daughter does, they say it under their breath."

Before she signed on at the ACLU, she was an activist at Human Rights Watch, where she was "working on global free-expression and cyberspace issues." She moved to the ACLU partly because she liked the idea of having some influence over the evolution of Net law. "These are cutting-edge legal issues, a chance to be involved in precedents which are just now being fought in the courts. I never even considered the alternative of a job in corporate law; I've always been involved in public interest issues."

When asked why, she shrugs. "I like to advance the cause of what I see as justice and fairness."

Ann Beeson's enthusiasm and idealism are infectious. She comes across as an exceptionally smart, decent, caring person. But when she makes general statements such as "more speech is always better than less speech," she creates a mental image of serious debate that isn't always an accurate reflection of online behavior. Sometimes Net speech can be so extreme that it offends just about everyone—including some liberals.

The Four Little Pigs

Late in October 1995 four male students at Cornell University amused themselves by compiling a deliberately offensive document titled "Top 75 Reasons Why Women (Bitches) Should Not Have Freedom of Speech." Subtitled "Let's Go Back to the Good Old Days When Men Were Men and Women Were Ribs," the list began like this:

1. She doesn't need to talk to get me a beer.
2. If she's in the kitchen like she should be, no one can hear her anyway.
3. If she can talk, all she'll do is complain.
4. Because she won't say "I will" instead of "I do."
5. No man wants to hear "first down" during a basketball game.

It ended like this:

71. Hell, if I wanted your opinion, I'd give it to you.
72. "Where've you been?" Who the fuck are you, my mother?
73. Women on radio? You can't see them, do you really want to hear them?
74. Unless the words are "Doctor, can you make these bigger?", shut the fuck up.
75. Big breasts should speak for themselves.

The list wasn't posted on Usenet and wasn't widely distributed. Each of the students sent it to a few friends, and under normal circumstances, that should have been the end of it.

But circumstances aren't normal anymore. One of the people who received the list didn't think it was funny. She circulated some extra copies as an example of sexism run amok. The copies generated more copies, and within a couple of days—well, it was the same old story. The information just wanted to be free.

The boys who wrote the original version had signed their real names but omitted their e-mail addresses. This omission was soon rectified, which was easy enough, since a single Unix command to the site at Cornell would reveal the e-mail address of *any* student or faculty member.

Now the backlash began. The students were bombarded with hundreds of angry messages, including hate mail and death threats from outraged feminists. The university itself received countless complaints, and the "75 Reasons" list was condemned as a form of sexual harassment. Many people wanted the students suspended or expelled.

Vanessa Hosein, a senior psychology major at Boston College, said that she and her friends at the Women's Center were considering whether to crash the entire Cornell e-mail system in retaliation against the four students. "These people are incredibly stupid," she said. "We want them to pay for what they did."

In discussion groups such as alt.feminism, there was more outrage. "Your list was not funny," wrote Tracey Spiegel, a student at

Wellesley. "The celebration of violence against women is abhorrent."

And since the Internet was involved, naturally the national media picked up the story. "The young men are learning the price of offensive behavior in an era of instant communication and heightened sensitivity," wrote Michael Grunwald for the *Boston Globe*.

The university had to respond, but how? Cornell's judicial administrator, Barbara L. Krause, circulated a public statement that explored the various options. First, she pointed out, Cornell didn't have a hate-speech code; "therefore, in order for our office to take disciplinary action against the four students, we had to find either that they engaged in sexual harassment or that they misused computer resources. Either of these findings would constitute a violation of Cornell's Campus Code of Conduct."

But since the students had circulated their "75 Reasons" only to "a handful of people they knew and whom they did not believe would find its content offensive," they hadn't tried to harass anyone, and they hadn't misused computer resources, because their distribution list had been so small.

Krause's statement had an apologetic, frustrated tone. It almost seemed to be saying, "These naughty boys really should be punished, but we can't find a legitimate way of doing it!"

Still, she came up with a face-saving solution: "The students recognize that they have caused great anger and hurt to many people. They deeply regret their actions and want to begin the process of restoring their reputations and the community's confidence in them." Consequently, she said, they had offered to attend a sex education program sponsored by Cornell Advocates for Rape Education (CARE) and the Health Education Office at Gannett Health Center. Also, each student had agreed—voluntarily, of course, since this was *not a punishment*—to perform fifty hours of community service. "If possible," said Krause, "they will do the work at a non-profit agency whose primary focus relates to sexual assault, rape crisis, or similar issues." And finally the students agreed to meet senior Cornell administrators to "express regret

for their actions and for the embarrassment and disruption caused to the University."

Dutifully the four students circulated their own official apology. They wrote: "Our original intention for writing this list was as a joke to send to some of our friends, male and female. These are people that know us and know our personalities. They know it was a joke. As individuals, we are in no way sexist or discriminatory against any group. . . . We had no idea that we were really being taken seriously and seriously offending people until we received a letter from a young woman who had been sexually assaulted. At that point we realized exactly how far this has gone. To think that our names were being connected with people who condone or even accept this type of violent behavior made us all sick to our stomachs. . . . Our only hope now is that every person who has read this list can see that we never meant these things and can forgive us."

But wasn't this a little odd? The students had sent private e-mail to a few friends, telling some tasteless jokes. Wasn't it typical—normal, even—for college students to make tasteless jokes? And since when did someone have to do fifty hours of community service and apologize publicly for statements made in private correspondence? If the material had been widely read, wasn't that the fault of the people who had chosen to circulate it?

Robert B. Chatelle, the political-issues chair of the National Writers Union, sent an open letter to Barbara Krause complaining about her attitude and correcting her on some legal issues. According to Chatelle, it didn't matter whether the students who wrote the "75 Reasons" chose to send the document to one recipient, 100, or 100,000. It was constitutionally protected speech; therefore, said Chatelle, they had "the legal right to distribute it as widely as they wish."

Chatelle also scolded Krause for mentioning that the students hadn't intended to anger or offend anyone. "This again is irrelevant," he said. "The courts have been crystal clear that offensive speech is protected."

He finished up: "Finally, I express skepticism that the four students will be attending the rape-education program and doing community service 'voluntarily.' This, frankly, reminds me of accounts of political dissidents in repressive Marxist regimes who attend re-education camps 'voluntarily.' I suspect the students were placed under tremendous pressure. Their understandable acquiescence, unfortunately, will have a chilling effect on speech, not only at Cornell but at all college campuses."

So here it was again: an institution trying to maintain a facade of moderation and respectability, trying to control wild excesses of netspeech, and finding itself attacked by liberals for whom any compromise was unacceptable. Cornell had handled the fracas more adroitly than Carnegie-Mellon University, which simply shut down dozens of newsgroups. Krause was careful to make her letter evenhanded, scolding not just the students but also the people who had sent hate mail and death threats. The right way to deal with the situation, she said, was to *explain* to the boys why their words were "so hurtful." This way, she said, it would be possible "to turn a very negative incident into a positive learning experience."

Well, nice try, Barbara, but it wasn't going to work. There was *no possible compromise* on these issues of netspeech. Cornell was going to make people mad no matter what it did. The MacKinnonesque feminists weren't going to be placated by anything less than a real crackdown, and the civil libertarians weren't going to settle for anything less than a ringing endorsement of everyone's right to say anything they damn well pleased, regardless of whom it might offend.

The situation was never really resolved, because it couldn't be. This became evident a few days later when a radical group calling itself Online Freedom Fighters, Anarchists, and Libertarians (OFFAL) sent 21,132 copies of an e-mail message to almost every member of the faculty and student body of Cornell, ridiculing Krause and satirizing her. OFFAL concocted an imaginary memo from Krause and put her name at the top of it, although since the e-mail originated from an Internet site in New York City, it was clearly a spoof. The full text of the message read:

Memo from Barbara L. Krause, Judicial Administrator, Cornell University

to the Ad-Hoc Disciplinary Advisory Committee

CONFIDENTIAL

I would like to extend my heartfelt thanks to the many faculty members who advised me regarding the unfortunate matter of the "75 Reasons" letter that was circulated via electronic mail. Your recommendations for dealing with the foul-mouthed "four little pigs" (as I think of them) who circulated this filth was both apposite and prudent.

Now that we have had time to evaluate the media response, I think we can congratulate ourselves on a strategy that was not only successful in defusing the scandal, but has actually enhanced the reputation of the university as a sanctuary for those who believe that "free speech" is a relative term that must be understood to imply acceptable limits of decency and restraint—with quick and severe punishment for those who go beyond those limits and disseminate socially unacceptable sexist slurs.

I am especially pleased to report that the perpetrators of this disgusting screed have been suitably humiliated and silenced, without any outward indication that they were in fact disciplined by us. Clearly, it is to our advantage to place malefactors in a position where they must CENSOR THEMSELVES, rather than allow the impression that we are censoring them.

Personally I wish I could have inflicted a more severe response such as suspension or perhaps a public "debate" in which we would have paraded the little pigs in public, for their humiliation. But in some cases (and this is one of them) a subtler approach yields higher dividends on the broad stage of public opinion, even though it provides less gratification for those of us who enjoy the vigorous application of punishment.

Once again, my thanks to you all for participating in this highly successful public-relations exercise, which has kept Cornell safe for those who wish to

live in a nurturing environment free from offensive speech and degenerate behavior of all kinds.

Yours sincerely

Barbara L. Krause
Judicial Administrator Cornell University

The letter reaped a bizarre range of responses. Many students were fooled by it and believed that Krause really had written it. Some people were outraged by the smug tone, but others said they heartily agreed with every word.

The author of the text granted an interview after he was assured that his identity would be protected. He will be referred to here as John.

Why did he perpetrate the hoax? "I don't see it as a hoax," he says. "I see it as an exercise in verbalizing the real mind-set of the worst kind of censor—the kind who wants to suppress free speech but pretends to be evenhanded and *nice* about it. This kind of person can be just as oppressive as a Stalinesque demagogue, but she's more dangerous, in a way, because she wears camouflage."

Does John really think that Cornell wanted to suppress free speech?

"Of course they wanted to. There's nothing unusual in this. Most people have something they hate to hear, because they're afraid of it. That's where censorship comes from: fear of concepts that may drag society in directions that make people nervous."

John dismisses the idea that Cornell had to compromise for fear of alienating feminists on one side or libertarians on the other. "When they compromised, they annoyed everyone. If they'd taken a strong stand—if they'd said, 'Free speech is one of the fundamental principles of this country, and our students can say whatever they like, and no one should have to apologize for his opinions,' I think most people would have respected that. But Cornell has this agenda to impose goodthink."

Isn't it true, though, that swamping students and faculty with 21,000 pieces of e-mail isn't going to help? It's more likely to give new ammunition to people who want some control over the Internet.

"A freedom isn't worth much if you're too scared to use it," John replies. "If we daren't take advantage of the Net to disseminate a point of view for fear of giving Senator Exon a new excuse to crack down, that means we've been intimidated, doesn't it? It means he's got what he wanted. You have to remember, people in Washington have total contempt for people who lie down and do what they're told. So we have to fight back. It's the only way. And I fully intend to continue doing so."

"John" sent 21,132 copies of a bogus memo to students and staff at Cornell University. College administrators were not amused.

Threats Online

Cornell's list of seventy-five reasons was offensive—no doubt about that—and some people sincerely believed that it was a form of violence against women. It didn't come close, though, to the real limits of offensiveness and violence. That honor had already been won by another young, college-age male, this time located at the University of Michigan.

On October 3, 1994, a nineteen-year-old linguistics student named Jake Baker posted a story titled "Gone Fishin'" on the Usenet newsgroup alt.sex.stories. Baker preceded his text with a warning: "The following story contains non-consensual rape, torture, and snuff of a teenager by her brother and his friend. Consider yourself warned."

Was there a difference between ordinary, everyday rape and "non-consensual" rape? A linguistics student should have known better—but semantic quibbles like this soon seemed irrelevant when you started reading the story.

It was told in the first person, as if Baker were recounting events that had actually happened to him. Near the beginning was a conversation between himself and his friend Pete:

> See, several weeks ago we admitted to each other that we both thought more about rape than girlfriends; more about sticking hot needles through girls' tits than sucking them, more about abusing them than loving them. So we started to refer to girls in derogatory terms. It turned us on. "Girl" or "woman" makes you think of them as people. "Whore," "bitch," "cunt," "slut" makes you think of them as what they are—fuck toys for the men of the world. Only the bitches've convinced most men they have rights, and so most men don't take advantage of them as they should.

Was this the posturing of a shy teenager who felt hurt or rejected by women and was using semifiction as an outlet for his anger? Baker's

petulance and resentment toward smart, beautiful females was underlined when his narrator said he wanted to rape and punish Pete's sister because she was "a true bitch, and didn't like either of us. She was smart, got good grades in school, so Pete's mom liked her and not Pete."

The message seemed to be that if a smartass girl commits the unforgivable crime of ignoring a teenage boy, she has to be punished. But Baker took the punishment farther than any reader could have expected.

In the story, Pete and the narrator follow Pete's sister into the woods, where they catch her with her boyfriend. The narrator drowns the boyfriend, then he and Pete rape the girl anally and vaginally, stick hot pins through her nipples, whip her with electric cord, force her to give oral sex, torture her with pliers, force tent stakes into her vagina and anus, burn her thighs, hang her upside down and use her as a punching bag, cut her with a knife, urinate on her, amputate her nipples, repeatedly throttle her till she passes out, and then revive her. Pete thrusts his entire arm up into her rectum and rips at her intestines. "Then, she died, and we spent the night fucking and abusing her dead body before burning her in the morning."

Woven through the various atrocities is a homoerotic thread. Pete is the older boy; Jake, narrating the story, defers to him. They have an unspoken bond of trust and affection. The girl that they lust after is seventeen but has an abnormally youthful, boylike body, with breasts that haven't developed. Pete's penis is described with more visual detail than the girl's genitals, which are barely mentioned. And when the narrator has a choice of vaginal or anal sex, he chooses anal.

It didn't seem to occur to Baker that this story could get him into any kind of trouble. He submitted it under his own name, via a university e-mail account, to a newsgroup that could be accessed by millions of people. Presumably he did this because he wanted a response, and since women were unlikely to enjoy the story, he seemed to want his response from men.

He got it. A Canadian named Arthur Gonda made some positive comments. On November 29 Baker wrote back to him, saying, "I'd love to meet with you. There's no one else I can share my thoughts with." This turned out to be the beginning of a two-month correspondence.

Meanwhile, Baker wrote another story titled "A Day at Work," which he posted on December 15, 1994, this time with a different introductory note: "Comments and criticism always welcome. Enjoy."

Enjoy?

"A Day at Work" was told in the first person, like the first story, but in this one the protagonist is a school custodian. He traps a young female Korean student, ties her, beats her, bites her breasts, whips them with his belt, pounds her head against the wall while she is impaled on his penis, pauses for a dinner break, then hacks the girl's breasts with a knife, pours bleach into the wounds, tears her breasts entirely off, ejaculates in her face, and kills her.

Once again the victim is childlike, and the first preference is for anal sex.

On January 7, 1995, Baker struck a third time. This story featured yet another anal rape of a teenage girl. Titled "Going for a Walk," it was prefaced with a more plaintive note: "For those of you who do, I write this to turn you on. For those of you who don't, I write this to annoy you. Either way, have an opinion. The greatest insult to a writer is not to have any feelings for his work."

And the greatest insult to Jake Baker was obviously being ignored. Well, he needn't have worried; he soon had more notoriety than he could have ever wished for.

On January 9, 1995, Baker posted the story that changed his life. "The premise," he wrote, "is that my friend Jerry and I have broken into the apartment of this girl . . . whom I know . . . and are proceeding to have a little fun with her."

The story described another rape-and-mutilation sequence. This time the victim is tied and gagged, fondled, slapped, and forced to

kneel. Bizarrely, Baker describes himself forcing his penis "as far as it will go into her ear."

Next she is suspended from a ceiling fan by her long hair, so that her feet kick helplessly in midair. Her breasts are beaten with a hairbrush, her labia are held open with superglue, a clamp is applied to her clitoris, and her buttocks are whipped till they bleed. She is moved to a chair, tied, and forced to perform oral sex while a hot curling iron is thrust into her anus. One of her nipples is cut off. She is anally raped, then doused in gasoline and burned to death.

This was comparable to Baker's previous fiction—yet there was a crucial difference. This time he gave the victim a name; indeed, he used it as the title of the story.

The name just happened to identify a real-life female student enrolled at Baker's college.

"I need to DO IT."

Phil Watson, who runs a computer system for a defense contractor, was eating lunch when he browsed through alt.sex.stories. He didn't vomit when he read Baker's latest effort, but to use Baker's phrase, he did "have an opinion."

As he said later to a reporter from *New York Newsday,* "It was the grossest thing I had ever read online." From his office in Washington, D.C., Watson sent an e-mail message to the University of Michigan, warning them that one of their students might be dangerous.

Meanwhile, the global reach of the Internet included a sixteen-year-old girl in Russia. She read Baker's latest work and showed it to her father, who passed it to Richard DuVal, an American attorney who happened to be working in Moscow. By coincidence, DuVal was an alumnus of the University of Michigan. As he later said to a reporter, "There's something here that crosses the line from bad taste to pathological." He sent his own message to the college authorities.

On January 20 university security officers visited Baker's dorm room. Did he admit writing the story? Sure he did. He saw nothing to be ashamed of. He waived his right to call an attorney, and he willingly divulged the password to his Internet account so that officials could read his e-mail. As FBI special agent Greg Stejskal later told journalists, "It would have been private, except that he signed a waiver."

The e-mail included all of Baker's correspondence with his Canadian pen pal, Arthur Gonda. In some ways this turned out to be even more incendiary than the material Baker had posted to Usenet, because it seemed to cross the boundary between fantasy and reality.

In the excerpts below, typographical errors and punctuation have not been corrected.

On December 1, 1994, Baker wrote to Gonda, "I highly agree with the type of woman you like to hurt. You seem to have the same tastes I have. When you come down, this'll be fun!"

Less than twenty-four hours later Gonda wrote to Baker, "I would love to do a 13 or 14 year old . . . once tey are tieed up and struggling we could do anything we want to them."

By December 9, Baker seemed to be evolving some specific plans: "I don't want any blood in my room, though I have come upon an excellent method to abduct a bitch— As I said before, my room is right across from the girl's bathroom. Wiat until late at night. grab her when she goes to unlock the dorr. Knock her unconscious. and put her into one of those portable lockers (forget the word for it). or even a duffle bag. Then hurry her out to the car and take her away . . . What do you think?"

Two days later Baker wrote: "Just thinking about it anymore doesn't do the trick . . . I need TO DO IT."

The next day Gonda replied: "My feelings exactly!"

The two of them swapped more than forty messages between November 29, 1994, and January 25, 1995. During the same period Baker also corresponded with other people who had read his

stories. But his letters to Gonda were the ones that galvanized college officials. Clearly (in their minds, at least) two men were plotting to kidnap, rape, and murder a student on campus. Which student? Well, Baker had already chosen her, hadn't he? Her name was right there in the title of his most recent story.

On January 26 the university notified the FBI.

On February 1, emerging from a class, Baker found himself collared by a plainclothes university police officer and two housing department officers, who told him that university president James Duderstadt had suspended him without a hearing. Baker was taken to his dorm room so that he could pack some clothes, and was then escorted off the campus. "He was asked to leave, and he's outta here," said Captain James Smiley, of the university's Department of Public Safety, speaking to a journalist from the *Ann Arbor News*.

Baker still didn't seem to understand what all the fuss was about. "I'm more than willing to make up whatever harm I've done, but not to leave the university," he said in a public statement. On February 7 he offered a compromise: to undergo therapy, live off-campus, and only visit the university for classes. But college authorities were in no mood to make a deal, and neither was law enforcement. Two days later Baker was arrested by the FBI at the home of his lawyer. He was charged with violating Title 18, U.S. Code, Section 875 (c), which prohibits threats to injure or kidnap a victim and carries a penalty of up to five years imprisonment. Baker was the first person ever to be charged with making interstate threats via the Internet.

By this time, the story was national news. Baker's mother, Vilma, launched a fierce publicity campaign in defense of her son. Age fifty-six but pictured in the national press as a youthful woman with shoulder-length shaggy blond hair, wearing a colorful sweater, sweatpants, and sneakers, Vilma turned out to be a spirited woman who taught creative writing to high-school students. She had separated from Baker's father, a dentist from Kuwait, six years previously.

Borrowing a phrase from Rush Limbaugh, Vilma condemned university officials as "femi-Nazis" and said they had picked on her

son because they nursed a "hatred toward men." (This could have been an oblique reference to the fact that famed antiporn crusader Catherine MacKinnon just happened to be affiliated with the university and had wasted no time contacting the girl whom Baker had named in the title of his story.)

Vilma claimed that Jake had never intended the girl to see what he wrote. In fact, said Vilma, when college authorities insisted on showing the text to the girl, Jake "couldn't eat for a week. He cried and cried and cried."

Regarding Baker's correspondence with Gonda, she said: "I thought it just sounded like a bunch of boys trying to outdo each other. I didn't take it very seriously."

To complete her picture of Jake Baker as a decent, respectable young man, Vilma released a photograph of him dressed up in a tuxedo, playing the violin. *People* magazine published it alongside Baker's mug shot from the U.S. Marshals' office—but oddly enough, he came across the same way in both pictures, as a shy, fragile, nerdy teenager looking a little bit lost.

The ACLU quickly made a public statement. "The FBI needs to go after people who commit violence against women, not college students who fantasize about it," said Howard Simon, executive director of the Michigan chapter. "His stories may have been disgusting and vile, but I have seen nothing that would appear to be a threat to any person."

One of Baker's attorneys, David Cahill, told reporters that not only Baker's stories but also his entire sex life were a fantasy. "He's a virgin," Cahill claimed. "He just has an active imagination."

And when journalists spoke to Baker's eighteen-year-old roommate, Jesse Jannetta, he told them, "I had a hard time recognizing the person who wrote that story. I've never seen any indication that Jake is a threat. He is not violent."

Really, though, it didn't matter how many endorsements Baker received or whom they came from. They couldn't compete with

the deranged sadism of the text that Baker himself had written. In the court of public opinion, he had pronounced himself guilty; the only question was whether the same thing would happen in a court of law.

A Ticking Bomb

Prosecutors seemed to feel they had a clear and simple case. Thanks to the wonders of e-mail, the FBI didn't even have to gather any evidence; it had all been collected for them, time-stamped, date-stamped, and archived on the hard drives at the university's Internet site.

In his correspondence with his Canadian friend, Baker had emphasized that he was no longer willing to settle for fiction; he needed to "do it." He had named his proposed victim publicly; she was a student in a Japanese class that he attended at the university. According to an affidavit sworn to by FBI agent Greg Stejskal, the girl was "aware of Baker's transmission concerning her and is frightened and intimidated by it." What more could a jury ask for, in order to convict?

Federal magistrate Thomas Carlson referred to Baker as "a ticking bomb" and provisionally ordered him to be held without bail. The next day, February 10, the case was formally assigned to federal district court judge Bernard Friedman, who presided over a detention hearing—and he too refused to free Baker under any circumstances. This was highly unusual; almost all defendants charged with federal crimes other than treason or murder are normally granted bail.

Maybe things would have been different if Arthur Gonda had stepped forward and testified that he and Baker were just fantasizing online and had never had any intention of following through. Unfortunately, though, Gonda had disappeared without a trace. His name wasn't listed in Ontario tax records and seemed to be a pseudonym.

Baker's criminal attorney, Douglas Mullkoff, appealed the no-bail ruling to the Sixth Circuit Court in Cincinnati, but on March 7 they too refused to free him before his trial.

Then the situation changed. On March 9, after a month in jail, Baker appeared for a hearing before federal judge Avern Cohn.

Cohn had played a highly publicized role in another case involving the University of Michigan, in which he had struck down a code limiting student speech. Originally appointed by Jimmy Carter, Cohn was an old-school liberal who frankly admitted his bias in favor of free speech. On the other hand, he wasn't predictably pro-defendant. One court observer characterized the judge as "demandingly tough. Even if he likes your case, you're not necessarily going to have an easy time."

At the hearing, Cohn learned that the university had conducted their own psychiatric evaluation of Baker more than a month earlier. The evaluation had determined that Baker displayed no risk factors for potential violence. Another evaluation on February 7 yielded the same verdict. Still another evaluation, on February 9, concluded that Baker "presented no clear and present danger to [the student named in his story] or anyone, at the time of the interview."

Cohn decided that there should be a fourth and final psychological evaluation, and prosecutors agreed to be bound by the results. Two days later, when this evaluation turned out negative like all the rest, Cohn released Baker on $10,000 bail. He told him to stay away from the university, not to associate with anyone involved in the case, and not to post any more stories online. Apart from that, Jake Baker was at liberty pending his trial.

But would there actually be a trial? Mullkoff said his next step would be to demand that the whole case should be thrown out for lack of evidence.

Lack of evidence? This seemed to make no sense at all. But the situation was turning out to be far less straightforward than most people had expected.

A Losing Battle

Statutory law offered three main choices for prosecuting Jake Baker.

1. Publication of obscene literature. His stories were certainly shocking and might be obscene—but the most appropriate federal law, 18 USC 1465, was interpreted in 1987 by the Tenth Circuit Court of Appeals as "restricted in its terms to the transportation of tangible objects." Usenet posts obviously didn't fit that description.

2. Making an obscene communication by telephone. This looked more promising—but since Baker had given his fiction away, he could be accused only of disseminating obscenity on a noncommercial basis, and the sentence for that was a maximum of six months. The case had acquired so much visibility, prosecutors wanted more.

3. Making threats to kill or kidnap. The relevant federal law is worded as follows: "Whoever transmits in interstate or foreign commerce any communication containing any threat to kidnap any person or any threat to injure the person of another, shall be fined under this title or imprisoned not more than five years, or both."

The key word here is "threat." In 1976 a Second Circuit federal appeals court ruled that a threat must be "so unequivocal, unconditional, immediate and specific as to the person threatened, as to convey a gravity of purpose and imminent prospect of execution."

This created some new problems. Had Baker and Gonda actually named the person they were threatening to kidnap and rape? Not precisely; Baker had only used a girl's name in a work of fiction. Had Baker and Gonda decided on a specific plan of action? No, Baker had just talked vaguely about grabbing a girl in the bathroom opposite his dorm room. The female students who used that bathroom had been frightened when they learned what Baker wrote, and they'd put a notice on the door reminding each other to lock it; but in the famous words of Supreme Court Justice Louis Brandeis, "Fear of serious injury cannot alone justify suppression of free

speech. . . . There must be reasonable ground to believe that the danger apprehended is imminent."

Tacitly acknowledging these problems, on March 15 federal prosecutors dropped their initial charge against Baker and charged him with five other counts based on his e-mail with Gonda. Reading this e-mail carefully, prosecutors claimed, it became clear that Baker was plotting to abduct various other victims, in particular the daughter of a neighbor in his hometown of Boardman, Ohio. The latter charge was based on the following exchange:

> **Gonda:** "By the way, how about your neighbor at home, you may get a chance to see her?"
> **Baker:** "She might have moved. But she'd be a great catch."

Would these new charges against Baker turn out to be more plausible than the rest? There was only one way to find out.

Words Constitute the Crime

On May 26, 1995, Judge Cohn presided at a hearing to consider Mullkoff's motion to dismiss all charges. According to two observers who were present at the time, it was a memorable session.

Cohn, seventy-one years old but looking more like sixty with his full head of neatly combed white hair, was in a typically impatient, irascible mood. He did not project a friendly manner.

Mullkoff, in his forties, was an unimpressive figure, below average height, clean-cut, conservatively dressed, not at all like a stereotypical flashy, boisterous criminal defense lawyer. He was very low-key.

Ken Chadwell and Christopher Yates were the prosecutors. Chadwell, tall with a dark mustache, was a zealous law-and-order type, eager to protect society from a dangerous threat and liable to get excited at times. In a previous brief he had warned that the rape

Douglas Mullkoff defended Jake Baker's shocking online sex stories, claiming they could not possibly constitute a legal threat.

and murder of women and children would follow if Baker was released. By contrast, Yates was more deliberate, measured, and thoughtful. Described by one observer as "the intellectual of the Detroit U.S. Attorney's Office," Yates was definitely not prone to emotional outbursts. This gave him a better chance than Chadwell at getting along with the judge.

Baker, meanwhile, was totally unobtrusive, a shy, frail, timid twenty-year-old peering through thick-lensed wire-framed glasses. Throughout the whole legal ritual, he didn't say a word.

"Hi," said Judge Cohn as he sat down.

"Good afternoon, Judge," said Mullkoff.

"I have a couple of questions to ask for some clarification," said Cohn, turning to the prosecuting attorneys. He then spent ten minutes grilling Chadwell relentlessly about witnesses who would be called if there was a trial. He seemed skeptical that many of them were relevant, especially parents in Boardman, Ohio, who were supposedly worried sick after reading excerpts from Baker's e-mail that had been published in local newspapers.

Finally Cohn zeroed in on his first specific point. Prosecutors were claiming that a threat had been made jointly by Gonda and Baker, but no one knew where Gonda was, or how old he was, or even whether he was a man.

"I think it's fair to say it's a man," said Chadwell.

"Why, why?" Cohn snapped back. "Arthur Gonda could be a twelve-year-old boy, couldn't he, or an eighty-year-old woman?"

"I guess theoretically," Chadwell said.

This was relevant because there is no way to evaluate a threat without knowing who made it. If a five-year-old kid threatens to punch someone in the face, no one can regard this as seriously threatening. If a 200-pound bodyguard says the same thing, it's a different matter.

Suppose Gonda turned out to be an eighty-year-old-woman who had just been playing a game with Baker. Wouldn't that force everyone to view the e-mail in a completely different light? Wittingly or unwittingly, the judge had picked up on the uniquely ephemeral, impersonal quality of online communication.

There was some more to-and-fro in which Cohn got the prosecutors to admit that threat analysis experts at the FBI and the Secret

Service had never been consulted to determine whether Baker was a danger to anyone.

Cohn then proceeded to teach the attorneys some history. According to his research, in 1932, after Bruno Richard Hauptmann had sent threatening letters to the Lindbergh family demanding ransom money, Congress passed a law to prohibit threats by mail. Two years later the law was broadened to include threats by phone. "And then," said Cohn, "in 1939 they amended it and said, people now are not only extorting money and things of value, but they're doing other things, they're threatening to blow up the Capitol in South Carolina unless somebody is released. So we have to broaden its language. Now, would you agree that the way it's being applied in this case is a substantial broadening from that?" Cohn paused for an instant. "Just out of curiosity," he added.

Chadwell didn't seem to like this question. He simply said that the way he was applying the law was consistent with the way it had been applied in other recent cases. Cohn was ready for this, pounced on it, and rejected it. He didn't want to know about recent cases; he wanted to determine the original intentions of the lawmakers. Personally he didn't believe that anyone in Congress had ever intended the law to apply to e-mail messages between a student and an unknown correspondent, talking about doing something unstated to a woman who wasn't properly identified.

Judge Cohn moved on to his next point, which he addressed to Yates. Suppose Cohn was walking down the street and saw a good-looking woman, and he said to his companion, "'I would really like to F the broad whether she wanted it or not' . . . would that be a threat?"

"Probably not," admitted Yates.

Now that Cohn was dealing with Yates, he focused on the question of who, precisely, had been threatened.

Yates was thoroughly prepared for this. He quoted the e-mail from Gonda: "By the way, how about your neighbor at home, you may get a chance to see her?"

And Baker's response: "She might have moved. But she'd be a great catch."

And then later, according to Yates, Baker had written: "I HAVE to make a bitch suffer! . . . All I think of before I sleep is how I'd torture a bitch I get my hands on." Didn't this make it seem that the girl next door was in jeopardy?

Cohn wasn't impressed. "All he's doing is telling the thoughts that go through his head. We're not punishing him for having lustful or evil thoughts, are we?"

"No, we're not," Yates agreed.

"What are we punishing him for?" Cohn persisted.

Yates quoted some more of Baker's e-mail: "Just thinking about it anymore doesn't do the trick . . . I need TO DO IT."

"He's expressing an inner need," said Cohn, "like he's talking to his analyst. How is that a threat?"

Chadwell took over from Yates and insisted that the e-mailed statements were perfectly clear in their meaning.

"I'm not going to go through that one again," said Cohn. "I went through it with Mr. Yates. I don't think he did very well, and I don't believe you're going to do much better. No offense, but I just think you're not going to clear up the ambiguities. It's perfectly clear, Mr. Chadwell, there are some ambiguities in these words."

To Chadwell, this seemed intolerable. He was a federal prosecutor. He possessed correspondence between two men who were clearly plotting kidnap, rape, and possibly murder. For heaven's sake, how clear did it have to be? "They're planning a crime!" he protested.

"Well," said Cohn, pouncing again on his unfortunate adversary, "planning a crime isn't what they're charged with."

This was true: The prosecutors hadn't charged Baker with conspiracy because there wasn't enough evidence for that. Barker was charged with making a threat, and in that case, as Cohn put it, "The words themselves [must] constitute the crime."

Finally Cohn finished tormenting the prosecuting attorneys and told them to sit down. He invited Mullkoff to speak and took a far more lenient line with him.

The defense attorney cited a precedent that said for a threat to be a criminal offense, it had to be unequivocal, immediate, unconditional, and specific. By comparison, the statements in e-mail had been vague, the threat had not been immediate (a month had passed without anything happening), and no person had been specified.

Cohn seemed to agree. He turned back to the prosecutors and gave them one last chance. They had five days in which to find a case that had been tried in the past and seemed similar to Baker's.

"Thank you, Your Honor," Yates said dutifully.

That was the end of the hearing.

The Undefined Menace

Judge Cohn delivered his final written opinion on June 21, 1995. He stated that he did not regard the e-mail as a threat, and he was scornful of the prosecution's case. He wrote: "The government's enthusiastic beginning petered out to a salvage effort once it recognized that the communication which so much alarmed the University of Michigan officials was only a rather savage and tasteless piece of fiction."

Naturally, a lot of people were outraged. Susan McGee, executive director of the Domestic Violence Project in Washtenaw County, released a statement complaining that the ruling "shows the judicial system in the United States is more interested in men's rights to torture, beat, and harass women than it is in women's rights to live their lives in peace and safety." Catherine MacKinnon vowed to bring civil charges against Baker on behalf of the woman he had named in his story.

But these were impotent rants. Like it or not, Cohn had affirmed Baker's right to fantasize publicly—globally!—even though he had used the name of a real person in his horror scenario and had written to Gonda about actually "doing it."

He was now a free man.

Or was he? The government still had one more option: They could appeal Judge Cohn's ruling.

In November 1995 Christopher Yates exercised that option. Presumably he hoped that a three-judge appeals court would take a more conservative line than Avern Cohn. Mullkoff, Baker's defense attorney, seemed convinced that this wasn't going to happen. "I think the government is grasping at straws," he told a reporter. Still, he had to wait till the appeals court considered the case, which was still pending as of June, 1996.

Meanwhile, Baker was doing his best to retreat back into obscurity. He withdrew from the University of Michigan and started attending a community college in Ohio.

One question he had never really answered was why he'd written the stories and posted them publicly in the first place. A Net user named Phil Watson, who lived in Virginia, shed some light on this when he was questioned by reporters from the *Ann Arbor News*. Watson had traded his own series of e-mail messages with Baker. He claimed that Baker had stated at one point, "I have never hurt anybody, and never plan on hurting anybody." According to Watson, Baker had said that he wrote his stories "to rid myself of the overwhelming anger I feel."

If this was true, then the stories were a form of therapy. Probably they would have been ignored and forgotten if they hadn't been circulated via the Internet, with its awesome power to reach out and frighten just about anyone, from vulnerable young women to federal prosecutors. But frightening people wasn't necessarily a crime.

At the beginning of his opinion, Judge Cohn quoted a statement from a case dating back to 1886: "It is not the policy of the law to

punish those unsuccessful threats which it is not presumed would terrify ordinary persons excessively; and there is so much opportunity for magnifying or misunderstanding undefined menaces that probably as much mischief would be caused by letting them be prosecuted as by refraining from it."

Of course, this opinion was written in the rougher, tougher environment of the 1880s, but maybe it has new relevance to the frontier world of the Net, where "magnifying or misunderstanding undefined menaces" has become a growth industry for legislators and journalists alike.

Anarchy online does indeed create situations that make a lot of people nervous, but if we accept Judge Cohn's opinion, laws to suppress the anarchy could cause more "mischief" than the anarchy itself.

Naturally, people in law enforcement disagree. During Baker's hearing, Judge Cohn asked Christopher Yates: "What's the great social significance of this case?"

Yates had an immediate answer. He said that the case had two social values: "specific deterrence" and "general deterrence." Specifically, Yates hoped that if Jake Baker was punished for what he'd done, he'd be less likely to do it again. And generally, *every* Net user might think twice in the future before posting sadistic stories or swapping conspiratorial e-mail. If Baker was put in jail, it would tend to discourage "this sort of planning across computer networks."

Here was a federal prosecutor admitting what a lot of Net users had suspected all along: He wanted to fight fear with fear, even if this had a chilling effect on free speech.

In the Jake Baker case, a liberal, highly literate judge was ready to block this tactic. Next time, though, it might be different. It seems a short leap to imagine Internet service providers being intimidated by federal prosecutors, just as BBS users in Cincinnati were intimidated by the local sheriff. After all, this would be the simplest possible answer to the problems of content, distribution,

and access: throw a couple of people in jail, publicize the case in all available media, and create such a climate of oppression that most people will *censor themselves*.

The Pursuit of Privacy

Jake Baker chose to surrender his archives of e-mail when federal agents asked for it. What if he had said no? Could police have tapped his Internet connection and intercepted his messages to Arthur Gonda? How easy is it to monitor message traffic on the Net?

An anonymous member of the "cypherpunks" online mail list contributed the following message early in 1996:

In the 1960's-1970's when international cable traffic was in its computer infancy, access was had to EVERY CABLE MESSAGE passing through the message switches of U.S. common carriers. This means not only every international cable message originating from or destined to a U.S. point, but also included every message ROUTED THROUGH the U.S., such as Europe <—> South America.

There was no great skullduggery involved—the common carriers simply made copies of their own log tapes and handed them to messengers from the, ah, FCC (ahem). It was on the operations checklist and no one thought twice about it. It may be urban legend to some, but I've seen it with my own eyes, handled the tapes with my own hands.

If anyone else wishes to move this from the status of urban legend to something more solid, all they have to do is locate and ask people who worked in message switch operations at RCA Global Communications, ITT World Communications, or Western Union International, the three common carriers of that time.

Knowing this, I would assume something similar was done at overseas locations of the same carriers and at such other access points as could be

compromised. An organization such as NSA that viewed this as SOP [standard operating procedure] would have to be brain dead not to be doing the same thing with the Internet. The only question in my mind is how far they have gone beyond Usenet and the newer, fertile ground of web sites. Are they vacuuming packets and reassembling email? Just how many laser discs have been filled with coherent traffic?

Time to exercise those plain, brown envelopes.

In other words, the only secure defense that citizens have against this kind of surveillance is encryption.

Cryptography used to be an obscure little backwater of mathematics, a black art whose disciples did most of their work for national governments under conditions of secrecy.

When microcomputers became widely available in the 1980s, it became theoretically possible to create encryption software for the masses—but most programmers didn't know enough about it, and many important techniques were restricted by patents. Software publishers were also discouraged by the total lack of an export market, because selling strong encryption to foreign countries is a federal crime. The mathematical techniques are classified as "munitions," putting them in the same class as nuclear secrets. Consequently, by default, the government maintained a decades-long monopoly on high-powered code making.

In June 1991 a man named Phil Zimmermann changed all that when he released a program called PGP, which stands for Pretty Good Privacy. In fact, PGP was much better than "pretty good"; even the largest supercomputer would have to work nonstop for many years to break a single encrypted message.

The idea behind PGP originated back in 1976, when Whitfield Diffie, then at Stanford University, proposed the concept of a "digital signature" to authenticate text messages. In very simple terms, the concept works like this. Suppose I run a simple program that adds up the bits and bytes of my message and turns them into an identification number. Now suppose my program encrypts that

number. The result is a digital "signature." If someone alters my message, the signature won't match anymore. If someone tries to send a fake message under my name, they won't be able to put a valid signature on it, because they won't know the key to my encryption system. Therefore, my text is secure.

The system is actually more complicated and relies on some facts about prime numbers. A prime number always leaves a remainder when it's divided by any number smaller than itself but higher than 1. For instance, when 5 is divided by 2, 3, or 4, there's a remainder every time, and therefore 5 is a prime number. By comparison, when 6 is divided by 2 or by 3, there's no remainder. Therefore 6 is *not* a prime number.

If you take a couple of very large primes (call them A and B) and multiply them together, you get an even larger number (call it C). This multiplication is easy for a computer to do, regardless of how big the numbers are.

Now suppose you take the large number, which we called C, and challenge someone to discover A and B, the two primes that it contains. Basically, the only way is by trial and error. The simplest approach would be to try dividing C by 2 to see if there's a remainder. Then you try 3, 4, 5, and so on. If C is big enough, this process can demand more computing power than exists in the whole world.

This principle underlies modern systems of "public key" encryption such as PGP. You publicize your very large number, C, and people can use it as a key to encrypt messages that are sent to you. When you receive the message, in effect you use your prime factors (A and B) to decode the message. Since no one has enough computing power to calculate A or B, and since you don't tell anyone what those numbers are, you're the only person who can read encrypted messages that are sent to you.

When Zimmermann released PGP in 1991, suddenly a privilege that had been reserved for national powers was available to anyone with a cheap personal computer. Moreover, Zimmermann didn't even charge anything for his product; he was giving it away.

He did this to combat an ominous trend. "Before telephones were invented," he says, "no one could listen in on your conversations at all. That's where our expectations of privacy should be based. When the Constitution was framed, there was no need to put the right to privacy in the Bill of Rights, because every conversation was private. We should have the same privacy when we speak over the phone as when we speak face to face. An accident of technology should not require us to give up our privacy."

Zimmermann started out as a computer scientist specializing in designing small computing devices for consumer goods. At first he treated cryptography as a hobby. He began studying it more seriously in 1984, while he was also making a reputation for himself as an anti-nuclear-weapons activist. "I was involved in civil disobedience at the Nevada test site," he says, "and got jailed a couple of times, once with Carl Sagan and Daniel Ellsberg—in fact, there were so many of us, they couldn't hold us all."

He speaks carefully, precisely, and sounds slightly shy. Behind his soft-spoken manner, though, he seems to have a very stubborn streak; and his record implies that he has a deep distrust of government.

"*Moi?*" he says, laughing.

Does he think of himself as a radical?

"No, my background is more in a sort of quiet middle-class activism. I used to teach a class in military policy; I trained lobbyists for the nuclear weapons freeze campaign. I also served as a military policy advisor for some House and Senate candidates."

Eventually he went into cryptography full time, and PGP was the result.

It was distributed via the Net from a computer at MIT. If someone from a foreign country tried to download it, the MIT system sensed this and blocked the call. Still, there were easy ways to get around that. In effect, Zimmermann had released something that was guaranteed to escape around the globe. Didn't this mean he had

effectively violated the law against exporting munitions? Federal prosecutors saw it that way, and an investigation was initiated against Zimmermann in 1993.

That same year, the Clinton Administration unveiled plans for the Clipper Chip, a preprogrammed component to be built into every telephone, modem, and fax machine. Supposedly this would *increase* everyone's privacy by encrypting all communications on a routine basis. There was a catch, though: Each Clipper Chip would have a code number embedded in it, which would be kept in escrow by an appropriate government agency. If law enforcement obtained a court order, they could demand the code number and would then be able to monitor all messages that passed through the phone or the modem containing that particular chip.

The government seemed to be saying, "We think it's a great idea for all your communications to be private—so long as they're not private from *us*."

Officials were genuinely puzzled that anyone would object to this. The FBI already had the power to intercept mail or monitor phone calls if a court order authorized them to do so. They saw the Clipper Chip as just an extension of the same principle.

Ultimately there were four main objections to the Clipper plan.

First, it opened up nightmarish opportunities for government inter-ference. As Zimmermann put it, "By building an infrastructure that's required to meet government standards for wiretapping, you're building something that is optimized for surveillance. If we don't fight this, the government will make it law. And that is like requiring you to make it easier for them to search your house."

Second, no criminal in his right mind would rely on encryption provided by the Clipper Chip, knowing that the government could listen in anytime. Therefore, Clipper would be inflicted only upon law-abiding citizens.

Third, American electronics manufacturers would have a hard time exporting "Clipperized" products because foreign customers wouldn't want to own phones that could be tapped by the U.S. Government.

Fourth, many people wondered if the escrow system would be abused. Would the agency that held the decryption keys really remain independent from other agencies? Would the keys be properly protected from theft?

In a *Time*/CNN poll, two thirds of those sampled felt it was more important to protect the privacy of phone calls than to preserve the ability of police to place wiretaps. When Clipper was explained, eighty percent opposed it. In a rare display of solidarity, libertarian activists and lobbyists from large electronics corporations formed a united front of opposition.

In February 1994, after nine months of public debate in which almost everyone criticized and objected to the plan, the Clinton Administration announced that Clipper would be used by all government agencies for their own unclassified communications, but it would remain "voluntary" for the private sector.

Some activists concluded from this that Clipper was effectively dead. They were wrong. In August 1995 a second version was proposed, very little different from the first. "Clipper is a vampire policy," says David Banisar of the Electronic Privacy Information Center in Washington, D.C. "You keep shooting bullets into it, but it keeps on going. The only way to kill it is by driving a stake into it, and I don't know if there's one big enough."

Meanwhile, PGP had circulated throughout the Net, people had started using digital signatures to authenticate their messages, and Phil Zimmermann was still waiting to find out if he was going to be indicted for treason, a crime that carries a three-to-five year sentence and a $1 million fine. This didn't cause him to back down, though. He released a new version of PGP and counted more than 75,000 downloads from the primary site where it was stored. Many of those copies went to other Net sites for further free distribution. He then developed a totally new product to encrypt spoken-word messages for transmission as data over the Net. (The software can be obtained from MIT at http://web.mit.edu/network/pgpfone.)

Despite these provocations, in January 1996 the Department of Justice finally released a short, terse statement announcing

that Zimmermann was not going to be indicted after all. No reasons were given, and the document made it clear that no reasons *would* be given.

Naturally, Zimmermann was relieved. "I'm just really pleased that the Sword of Damocles is not over me anymore," he told a reporter from the Associated Press, "and I wonder why it took so long."

Simson Garfinkel, who wrote a book about PGP, wasn't so positive. "It seems to me," he told a journalist, "that all the U.S. Attorney is saying is that they don't want the public-relations nightmare of prosecuting Philip Zimmermann, but they still want everyone scared so that they won't exercise their constitutional rights."

Meanwhile, the future status of encryption remained unclear. A Freedom of Information Act request by EPIC revealed that as long ago as February 1993, the FBI, NSA, and Department of Justice were arguing for a national policy that would outlaw unapproved encryption. A briefing document titled "Encryption: The Threat, Applications and Potential Solutions" was sent to the National Security Council. It contained the following paragraph:

> Technical solutions, such as they are, will only work if they are incorporated into all encryption products. To ensure that this occurs, legislation mandating the use of Government-approved encryption products or adherence to Government encryption criteria is required.

Clearly the "voluntary" version of Clipper was of no interest at all as far as law enforcement was concerned. But would a compulsory version be constitutional? Conversely, if other forms of encryption were outlawed, wouldn't this violate rights to privacy? Even now, no one knows the answer to these questions. Most likely a test case will be needed before we find out.

Encryption has already made a difference in some countries. "PGP is being used a lot in human-rights activities around the world," Zimmermann told one journalist. "Opposition groups working in Burma are training their people to use PGP on portable computers in jungle training camps. Before, captured documents might lead

to the arrest, torture, and death of entire families. PGP is used where lives are on the line."

Inevitably many governments see this kind of thing as a threat. France has prohibited secure encryption, and police can arrest the author of any message that seems to be in code. The Australian attorney general's office has announced that it wants to follow the French example. The Council of Europe has drafted plans to outlaw any products using strong encryption if they fail to make keys available to law enforcement. Great Britain has a law allowing police to obtain a warrant requiring a suspect to produce all information on his computer "in legible format."

These laws, however, may be hard to enforce. There are many ways to hide a message in a stream of data flowing through the Net. For instance, a totally innocent picture can be digitized using twenty-four bits, or binary digits (ones and zeroes), to specify the color of each dot. When the whole picture is transmitted, it becomes a long string of bits. Now suppose we take a text message and turn it, too, into a bit stream. We can use the picture to hide the text message by replacing every twenty-fourth bit in the graphics stream with a bit from the text stream. In effect, we have fractionally modified the color of each dot in the image, but this will be virtually undetectable—as *Byte* magazine demonstrated when it illustrated the technique many years ago.

This code system is properly known as steganography, and there are various programs available (most of them free) that will do it for you right now. For further information check out

http://www.iquest.net/~mrmil/stego.html

There's also a Usenet discussion group named alt.steganography.

There are other, similar ways to hide a message inside another message. Suppose, for instance, the Clipper Chip is made mandatory. A user can still encrypt his message with some private scheme before passing it through Clipper. Now suppose a law-enforcement agency intercepts the message and strips away the Clipper code with a master key. The second level of encryption is still there to hide the original message.

Will law enforcement accuse the user of obstructing justice by applying her own private encryption system? How can the FBI prove that the message really is encrypted and is not some other form of data? Who will decide whether an unreadable set of bytes consists of software, graphics, encrypted text, or data that has been scrambled by an error?

Outlawing encryption raises still more questions—some of them bizarre. Writing via an anonymous remailer to the alt.privacy Usenet newsgroup, "John Shore" suggested a list of questions for the attorney general of Australia after that office announced its plan to ban private use of strong encryption online. Would the ban extend to disks sent via ordinary mail? If so, would it also be illegal to mail a printout of an encrypted message? How about transferring the message by courier? Or by fax? Could someone be arrested for reading it aloud, one character at a time, over the phone?

Shore took this a step further. He pointed out that a random-number table can create a code that is almost unbreakable so long as it is used for only one message. Would this mean that random numbers should be illegal, too?

A former officer of the Australian attorney general's office, who was jailed for allegedly hacking into their e-mail system, suggested a more practical approach. "I doubt that anybody is truly interested in decrypting or reading messages flying around the Net," he wrote. "Rather, I imagine that police or other agencies wish to be able to read the contents of hard disks and message files once they make an arrest and/or seize possible evidence. If you've encrypted anything dodgy, then so long as you've hidden the key, no evidence is forthcoming." And as Scott Charney of the Department of Justice has confirmed, the owner of encrypted data in the United States can refuse to divulge the key by citing his right against self-incrimination under the Fifth Amendment.

Moreover, sensitive material can be stored in ways that make it very hard to find. Modern hard drives have a huge capacity, making it easy to conceal an important document among thousands of "junk messages." Even very simple tactics may be effective if police

conduct only a cursory search. A document can be disguised with a seemingly innocent filename or given a file creation date that makes it seem too old to be of interest.

Police hoping to find evidence on computer systems or on the Net are thus faced with a needle-in-a-haystack problem. Moreover, the haystack keeps getting bigger, and the needle can be so cunningly disguised that it will evade every possible attempt to detect it. This is bad news for law enforcement and good news for privacy activists—and for those who want to evade the law.

Total Privacy

Suppose there's no conclusive way to stop citizens from using encryption, short of taking away their microcomputers or cutting their phone lines. Consider the ramifications when every message can be totally private. Conversations cannot be overheard. Phones cannot be tapped. Even financial transactions become impossible to monitor. No one knows where money goes or who it comes from. Will law enforcement be rendered impotent? Will taxation be problematic? Will crime run totally out of control?

The FBI thinks this is a very plausible scenario. Speaking at the American Law Institute in 1994, FBI director Louis Freeh warned that "there will be disastrous consequences . . . federal law enforcement will be crippled and the national security endangered."

History, however, tells a slightly different story. As Phil Zimmermann points out, a century ago privacy used to be an everyday fact of life. Wiretaps didn't exist. The idea of your bank revealing your activities to government agencies on a routine basis would have been unthinkable. Financial transactions used to be private regardless of whether you paid in gold, with paper money, or by check.

Why shouldn't we still have this degree of privacy today? Because, according to law enforcement, the dangers are now much greater. "Suppose we believe that two people are communicating about

blowing up an airplane," says Scott Charney at the Department of Justice. "If they're using encryption and we don't have access to the key, we will not be able to intercept that message, and as a result, 400 people may die. There are those who say that's the price of privacy. But you have to be able to live with the choices you make, and I'd rather save the 400 people. I like to think that if a judge orders access to data and it satisfies the Fourth Amendment test, it should be permitted."

So far as Charney is concerned, law enforcement should be able to listen in on computer communications on exactly the same basis as they use to justify searching a private residence. "If a judge says we can go into someone's home, this is to protect society, which means we're protecting the rights of many people at the expense of the rights of an individual. If you buy a bigger lock, we'll bring a bigger sledgehammer. But cryptography is a lock so strong, society cannot penetrate it at all, unless we are allowed access to a key."

David Banisar vigorously disagrees. "They're spending millions on automatic fingerprint identification technology," he points out, "and more millions on DNA databases. There are plans for automatic intelligent highways enabling them to track any car going anywhere. They can even peer through people's walls with forward-looking infrared radar. And now they need to be able to monitor the Net as well?"

Phil Zimmermann takes a slightly more moderate position. "I think that the government does have some reasonable points to make," he says. "Criminals *can* use this technology to hide their activities. . . . I think the debate on cryptography is not an open-and-shut case."

Why, then, did he give away a program that puts so much power in the hands of the people?

"The government would like to be able to get information about you. They want to be able to read your mail, listen in on your conversations—and if they can do those things, it puts them in a much more powerful position. It means that political opposition

groups cannot function as effectively, and I'm speaking of any government around the world, including countries such as Burma or [those in] Central America."

Consequently, Zimmermann feels confident that he did the right thing. "I have no doubts or misgivings," he says about giving the power of strong encryption to the citizens of the Net.

Electronic Money

In America today, it's easy to compile an electronic dossier on someone by using data from mail-order purchases, tax payments, bank loans, health records, car rentals, and all the other trails we leave as we move through the world. Almost all of this data is ultimately linked with one ubiquitous form of identification: the social security number.

Writing in *Scientific American*, David Chaum suggested a better idea. What if a person could give a separate, different (but verifiable) ID number for each transaction or personal interaction?

Digital signatures would make this possible. But Chaum took the concept farther. He proposed DigiCash, a form of electronic money that would be as untraceable as real cash. Every transaction would be private and secure. Instead of using one credit-card number again and again, creating the obvious risk of someone stealing the number, each DigiCash payment would use a separate ID number, just like serial numbers on dollar bills or travelers' checks. DigiCash would mean that our spending habits would become private again, just as they used to be.

Chaum is chairman of a European Union project to combine integrated circuit cards and software-only money. He has published over forty-five original technical articles on cryptography and founded the International Association for Cryptologic Research. He is also managing director of DigiCash, which he established as a corporation in 1990. Unlike most mathematicians, Chaum has worked to put his theory, and his ideals, into practice.

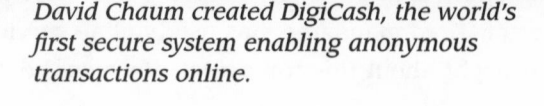

David Chaum created DigiCash, the world's first secure system enabling anonymous transactions online.

He first started thinking seriously about electronic privacy when he was a graduate student at Berkeley in the late 1970s. "I remember visiting one of my professors," he says, "sitting in a hot tub in his backyard, and talking about my research . . . and how to maintain anonymity in a network situation."

At that time the digital revolution was so young, few people shared Chaum's concerns. "I felt like I stumbled on a possibility for preserving the core values of our society as we make a transition into the computerized world. And I felt it was incumbent on me to push that forward, because I was really the only one who was aware of it."

At first Chaum imagined that if he merely publicized his ideas—as in his article in *Scientific American*—other people would put the ideas into practice. But it didn't happen, so he started his own company—even though he claims not to have strong personal feelings about privacy. "I'm not a privacy advocate," he says. "That's not it at all. . . . I just think I have a responsibility to give this technology a chance to be adopted to the extent that people really want to adopt it. I'm really committed to this. I wouldn't say running a business is what I find the most fun, or it's what I'm particularly good at, but I'm willing to do it."

The concept of anonymous electronic money is important not just for reasons of privacy but also to sustain economic competition. You can't have a truly free market if one business knows what many other businesses are doing. For example, Chaum points out that "if you're a phone company and you know what everyone is selling on the Net, and how much it costs and where the growth areas are, and you're also allowed to compete with everyone, you'd be able to compete unfairly." He refers to this as "data fascism."

Of course, digital money raises a very real possibility that almost all commerce could soon be conducted online. Some commentators fear it would erode the educational, noncommercial values of the Net and turn it into a giant shopping mall. Kevin Kelly, executive editor of *Wired* magazine, has used online services since 1982 and has thought about this topic a lot. He sees the danger but argues for a middle path.

"There's a great attachment within the Net for the gift economy," he says, "where things are swapped and offered without money. But I think that for network civilization to occur, there has to be money—secured and encrypted, authenticated money—because otherwise it's not going to happen. The danger is that we become completely

monetized and there is no more place to swap or have gifts. I think you need to have both."

DigiCash took its first small step into functionality in October 1995, when the Mark Twain Bank of St. Louis, Missouri, started issuing money online using Chaum's system. Five other competitive systems have also been developed, although not all of them are open for business yet: Cybercash, First Data/Netscape, First Virtual, Open Market, Inc., and Wave Systems. Two other systems were also announced: a joint venture by Visa and Microsoft, and a collaboration by Mastercard and Netscape.

Some of these systems merely take existing methods of credit card purchasing and digitize them, using the Internet instead of a phone line to convey conventional financial data. In other words, instead of calling an 800 number and reading your card number to an operator, you dial a remote site via your modem and type your number at your computer keyboard. A program on your computer encrypts the number so that no one else can read it. At the remote site, the number is decrypted.

This provides some security and convenience, but it isn't radically different from the way we do business today. By comparison, DigiCash is far more private and secure.

In principle it is a *debit system*, like travelers' checks, where you must pay for the money before you can spend it. By contrast, conventional credit cards are a *credit system*, allowing you to spend now, pay later.

How does DigiCash work in practice? Suppose you want to buy goods and services online. First you have to get some e-cash. You open an account with a bank that participates in the DigiCash scheme, and you deposit old-fashioned money the old-fashioned way: by credit card, check, or wire transfer. Subsequently the bank sends you a disk containing the DigiCash control program that has to be installed on your computer. You copy it onto your hard drive, get it running, then tell it to call the bank and transfer some e-cash from your bank account to your computer. At this point, some rather special code numbers are stored on your hard drive.

Now you're ready to go shopping. Suppose you want to buy a music CD from an online store. You use your modem to get to the store's home page. You find the item you want, and you tell your DigiCash control program to pay the store for the CD. This just means clicking your mouse button a few times and typing some numbers on the keyboard.

The control program transfers your e-cash to the store, and the store puts your CD in the mail—or maybe it transfers the digitized music to you electronically, over the Net.

Does this sound a little risky? Well, it's important to remember that transactions between banks are *already* electronic. We write checks with a pen and receive our bank statements on paper, but the balance is a number on a computer somewhere. DigiCash is just an extension of that system into the home.

Also, because the DigiCash system uses strong encryption, it's actually safer than older methods for protecting transactions. Here's what really happens inside the computer and on the Net when you make a purchase with DigiCash.

First, when you withdraw electronic cash from the bank, this is really a two-step operation. Your computer creates a random number that will be used as your own secret ID. This number is now "blinded." In other words, it's transformed mathematically into a different, public ID in such a way that no one can figure out what your secret ID was. The principle here is similar to public-key encryption. The public ID is sent to your bank with a request for e-cash.

The bank makes a note of the public ID. It issues e-cash that carries a serial number, just like dollar bills. The bank keeps a record of this serial number, links it with your public ID, and validates the cash.

Your computer receives the message from the bank and "unblinds" your original ID number. The bank knows that you ordered and received some e-cash, but the bank does *not* know your secret ID. This means that the e-cash is truly anonymous. After you spend it, no one will be able to prove that it was yours.

What's to stop you from spending it many times over, by sending the cash's serial number to many different merchants?

When a merchant receives e-cash, he transfers its value to his own bank account, and your bank receives a message telling it that the serial number for that cash is no longer valid. If you now try to spend that cash a second time, the merchant who receives it can check with your bank to find out whether the cash is valid before trying to deposit it.

The privacy advantage here is obvious—but there are also some potential pitfalls.

First, if you pay a merchant who fails to deliver the goods, you have to reveal your secret ID in order to prove that you sent the cash. This is the only way you can get your money back. The same applies if your electronic cash is lost or stolen.

Second, the bank that issues the money has to have its own private ID to generate and validate the code numbers of its cash. If this private ID is stolen, someone else can generate counterfeit cash, which means that the bank must invalidate all the money that it previously put into circulation and must issue new money using a new key.

Third, after you withdraw some e-cash from your account, it doesn't accumulate any interest. It gradually depreciates, like real cash stuffed under a mattress. By comparison, when you pay a bill using a credit card, your money remains in your bank, earning interest, till days or weeks later, when you settle your account with the card company.

Fourth, the anonymity of e-cash has caused some people to speculate that it could be used for criminal activities. In a case of bribery, for instance, totally anonymous electronic cash would stop anyone from proving that money changed hands, because the payment would be untraceable.

The current version of DigiCash avoids this problem by not being totally anonymous. The person who receives a payment doesn't

know where the money came from—but the person who makes a payment can choose to reveal it, and the system will provide complete authentication. This reduces the possibilities for crime so much that Chaum now claims it's safer than ordinary cash. "I've come to the realization," he says, "that the country would be far better off if there were no paper money and it was all electronic cash, because paper money is readily usable for criminal purposes: extortion, bribery, and black markets." He claims that on a recent tour of federal agencies in Washington, D.C., officials agreed that his product would make their jobs easier.

There's still the possibility, though, that someone else could introduce a competing form of electronic cash that *does* allow total anonymity. Chaum refers to this as "underground electronic cash" and fears that it may emerge if we take too long to establish the safer standard.

Totally untraceable electronic cash opens up some scary possibilities. Suppose there's a subversive group of anarchists who believe that all politicians should be assassinated. One of them circulates a petition calling for contributions to pay someone to kill a government official. Naturally, the anarchist passes his messages through anonymous remailers.

The more hated the government official is, the more people will pay to get rid of him. Supposedly this means that well-loved figures will be allowed to live, while bad guys will get what's coming to them. To the anarchists, this sounds like poetic justice.

Farfetched? Maybe so, but it was seriously proposed on a Usenet newsgroup. The inventor of the scheme claimed that "the goal is not primarily to cause deaths: The goal is to dismantle government permanently. It is NOT necessary that each and every one of these targets actually die to achieve that. In my plan, the main targets initially will be the agencies that make the most enemies: IRS, DEA, FBI, CIA, and various others. Once the IRS is demolished, none of the other organizations will have any money to pay the other employees, and everybody (government employees) would be on his own."

It's hard to imagine a more extreme use of digital cash. There have, however, been other proposals that seem moderate by comparison. Among them is DigitaLiberty.

Bill Frezza and one-time hacker Bruce Fancher are the prime architects of this initiative, which seeks to dismantle government by more peaceful means. "DigitaLiberty does not seek to educate or influence politicians in the hope of obtaining legislation favorable to our constituents," says Frezza. "We plan to make politicians and legislators irrelevant to the future of network-based commerce, education, leisure, and social intercourse."

Like many libertarians, Frezza feels there has been a scandalous retreat from the ideals on which the United States was founded. He sees the federal government as a parasite feeding off its people. "The Sixteenth Amendment," he writes, "passed in 1913 to empower the federal government to collect a tax on incomes, has since fueled the growth of a bloated leviathan, unleashing unchecked inquisitorial powers that are used to pry into the most intimate details of our lives. Not too long after our incomes follow our economic activity into cyberspace this inquisition is going to end."

Frezza doesn't underestimate federal power. In "the physical world" he sees no chance of citizens disentangling themselves from the web of taxation, assistance programs, agencies, and laws. "But we do believe that liberty can and will prevail in the virtual domains we are building on the Net and that national governments will be powerless to stop us. . . . We believe that no one will hold sovereignty over this new realm because coercive force is impotent in cyberspace."

His vision requires two future developments. First, manufacturing will be so highly automated that almost everyone will be employed in information industries. Second, communications, products, and transactions will all be encrypted. According to Frezza, "Encryption is to the Information Revolution what the Atlantic Ocean was to the American Revolution. It will render tax authorities as impotent in projecting their power as the ocean crossing did to King George."

Should we take any of this seriously? Does anyone in government take it seriously?

Maybe they should. Frezza's slightly less radical partner in DigitaLiberty, Bruce Fancher, suggests that the first step toward freedom from taxation could be just around the corner.

"Suppose an offshore bank starts selling electronic cash," says Fancher. "You will be able to send and receive messages *and* money in such a way that the government won't be able to detect

Ex-hacker Bruce Fancher now co-owns an Internet site that pushes the limits of online speech. [Photo by Erico Narita.]

the sender, the recipient, or the sum being transferred. This suddenly makes tax collection very difficult."

Doesn't Fancher see a downside to this? After all, many people depend on government subsidies and services.

"I think that government's only legitimate function is to protect its citizens from force and fraud. The IRS is more of a criminal organization than the Mafia, who don't mess with you if you don't mess with them. Anyway, there'll still be enough revenue from real-estate taxes to maintain police and fire departments on a local level."

But if everyone becomes anonymous and untraceable, this doesn't just create problems for government; it interferes with everyday transactions. When people hide behind digital signatures, how can anyone be trusted?

As a partial answer to this problem, Fancher foresees "trust brokers" who will rate the integrity of an online identity in much the same way that brokerage houses rate municipal bonds. The broker will take a percentage fee, and you'll be able to buy insurance against deals that go bad. To express his belief in anonymity, Fancher proposes setting up an anonymous remailer at his own Internet site, MindVox. "We believe that people should be able to express their opinions without fear of retribution from governments or private institutions," he says. "Some people complain that an anonymous person is free to libel anyone without fear of getting sued, which is a problem, but I don't see it that way. When someone sees a message from an anonymous person, it's going to be taken less seriously than a message that someone chooses to sign. The culture will adapt to this kind of thing."

MindVox has already drawn attention to itself as a repository for all kinds of information and discussion, including topics such as drugs, bombs, and perversion. Isn't Fancher taking a risk by starting an anonymous remailer service as well?

"No, it's a civil right to be anonymous. I would love to get busted for it." He sounds totally unconcerned. "Let them come and try."

Rolling Stone Revisited

Anyone who reads Usenet can't help noticing that many Net users show an antiauthoritarian mind-set. It's especially obvious in signature lines—such this one from a post in talk.politics.libertarian:

> You can test my urine when you pry my penis from my cold, dead fingers.

Is the online world just a refuge from reality where rebels can strike a pose without the hardship and risk of following through? Or is there a genuine spirit of rebellion that will create hard-core resistance if legislators try to eradicate anarchy online?

The Net was built originally by computer nerds who tended to be loners and misfits, not so different from early phone phreaks with their alienated, "fuck you" attitude. This free spirit has persisted to the present day, and even newcomers seem partially infected with it—perhaps because there's such a feeling of power and liberation in mastering a computer and exploring the vast resources of cyberspace.

The "don't tread on me" attitude is mirrored in *Wired* magazine, which the *New Yorker* has described as "the official organ of the digital generation." (I am a contributing writer for *Wired* and have sold more than a dozen articles to it, so my evaluation of it may not be totally objective.) Early in its history, *Wired* ran a big feature praising "cypherpunks" and condemning plans for the Clipper Chip. The magazine repeatedly has ridiculed any government attempt to interfere with the Internet.

Since *Wired* has been compared to *Rolling Stone*, there's a natural tendency to think that it's promoting an updated version of 1960s antiestablishment ideology. Editor and publisher Louis Rossetto denies this. "There's no concrete ideology that we're trying to get across," he says. He does admit, though, that he is biased against authoritarian systems. "Basically we feel that individuals are the best people to decide the important issues in their own lives.

Charles Platt

Louis Rossetto, editor-in-chief and cofounder of Wired
*magazine, believes that centralized political power
will be steadily undermined by the network economy.*
[Photo by F. L. Avery.]

Society works better if people have freedom than if they're being
directed. We also believe that markets work, and micro decisions of
the market are better than macro decisions of the government."

Taken together with Rossetto's known dislike of censorship, this
sounds like a low-key definition of libertarianism—but he dislikes that
word. "I shy away from libertarian or any other political label. I think
we're entering a period that's postpolitical. We need to develop a
new language and way of thinking about it."

Does he have any influence in that direction? Perhaps because
Wired has been accused of arrogance, Rossetto downplays this, too.
"We started a little magazine here," he says, "and it's still a little
magazine. I try not to think about power. I'm just trying to examine
the issues I care about and reflect the issues that matter to the
people we're writing for."

Yet when he does start talking politics, he can sound surprisingly similar to hard-core rebels such as Frezza and Fancher. "The twentieth century has been the century of statism," he says. "The dreams of statism have been played out, both on the right and on the left—and all of them have turned into nightmares. The statist ideology has now been proved to be bankrupt. There's no real discussion of the future anymore among statists because all the statist futures have been disasters."

According to Rossetto, government is already losing its former power. "Central authority is flowing away, acceptance of the need for national security is evaporating, acceptance of the welfare state is evaporating also. President Clinton's historic mission, as inheritor of the Roosevelt New Deal tradition of the left, has been to reconcile himself to the reality that that model no longer applies."

Yet government still has the power to make laws and enforce them, using weapons if necessary. How, precisely, is this power going to "dissipate"?

Rossetto seems to feel that as the network economy spontaneously evolves, many functions of government will simply become irrelevant. This may not be a painless process, though.

"I think there can be two ways we move into the future. One is by a gradual undermining of inefficient institutions. The market will determine how to deploy human and capital resources—and this is successfully transforming our society right now. On the other hand, some social structures are rigid, and they end up collapsing, which is what happened in the USSR. My sense is you'll end up with both things happening, though I hope for the former."

To Rossetto—and to many people who write for his magazine—the future is full of promise. These techno-optimists feel that almost everyone will benefit, one way or another, from major social upheavals in the years to come. "The network economy is the best way to use human and physical resources, and it'll make for a much more materially satisfying existence for almost all the people on the planet. I think we can also see a flowering of the arts,

because there'll be a lot more outlets for individual and eccentric voices. I think we can also see the final collapse of state-run education and the rebirth of real learning, as capital starts to get invested in what we really need to help our children become part of modern society and help us stay on top of the changes that are occurring. I think we'll have a much better-educated populace than we have today."

Why is he so optimistic while millions of people are fearful about the future? Rossetto suggests that this is a misconceived question, because people are not so much scared of technology, they're more scared that no one's in charge anymore. "I'm pretty sure that the future won't be any more violent or chaotic than what we have now," he says. "It will just seem that way because we will no longer have the illusion that some central authority is guiding everything."

Supposedly we will gradually adjust to the concept of distributed power—or "distributed being," as *Wired*'s executive editor Kevin Kelly refers to it in his book *Out of Control*, which describes many systems that run peacefully and efficiently without anyone in authority.

Does Rossetto have fears about this future? What's the downside?

"Well, a networked society is susceptible to massive collapse. Everything going online could be susceptible to viruses, terrorism, electromagnetic pulse weapons, other things. We're creating a monoculture that doesn't have the richness or the redundancy of the natural world, and this could be dangerous."

He doesn't sound as interested, though, in the gloom-and-doom stuff—partly because it's unproductive. If we want a better future, our task is to create it. "Despite the horrors of the twentieth century," he says, "and the pessimism of the so-called intelligentsia and progressives, the future is not bleak, it is positive—and we'll have a much better chance of achieving it if we think it's going to happen than if we just sit around moaning and wailing."

Nightmare Net Scenarios

In a roundtable discussion sponsored by *Harper's* magazine, John Perry Barlow, cofounder of the Electronic Frontier Foundation and prophet of connectivity, faced some self-described Luddites who called for a retreat from technoworship and a return to human values. Barlow referred to himself as an "old hippie" and claimed he sympathized with the Luddite point of view. "I love the physical world," he said. "I spent seventeen years as a cattle rancher in Pinedale, Wyoming. . . . I actually did go back to the land, unlike many old hippies. And after seventeen years I recognized the historical trends that nobody can do anything about, any more than the Indians could do anything about the historical trends that changed their society."

In other words, the digital revolution is coming to town whether you want it or not, and when it messes up your life, you'd better learn to like it—because there's not a damn thing you can do to stop it.

People who distrust technology are outraged by this take-it-or-leave-it attitude, and Barlow may be wrong when he says that they're powerless to resist. Right now, citizens who hate or fear the digital revolution can express themselves very effectively. They can lobby for legislation to cripple the Internet, they can elect state district attorneys and local sheriffs who will bust a few BBS owners and intimidate the rest, and they can present these actions as a sensible response to a situation that is totally out of control.

This is the basic conflict that I've tried to explore and analyze in *Anarchy Online*. So far, however, I've taken the situation at face value. What are the underlying motives that rouse such wild passions?

I believe that the conflict is rooted in fear and power. Doomsayers fear the power of technology to remake the world; they want the power to stop it. Likewise, fundamentalist Christians and political conservatives fear change and want the power to resist it. Government is traditionally the ultimate form of power, so naturally its members want to extend their control to a new environment—

especially when a bunch of technoanarchists starts claiming that "statism" is obsolete. (Time to teach those weirdos a lesson!) Finally, there's one more primal ingredient: the traditional need of adults to exert power over children.

Meanwhile, on the other side, millions of Net users have a new power to do neat things with their hardware. Many of them have also found new business opportunities through technology. Nerdy types who were beaten up, ridiculed, and rendered powerless at school now find themselves miraculously transformed, helping to mold a whole new sociopolitical system—and for them this power is a sweet form of revenge, a chance to run things *their* way for a change.

This is the subtext of the debate over netcrime and netspeech: a massive power shift from elder statesmen, adults, and law enforcement to teenagers, everyday citizens, and computer nerds.

Of course, some people are sincerely concerned about their kids being corrupted by netporn or their computers being raided by hackers. But what's the source of these fears? Almost always it turns out to be a group that is traditionally powerful and sees its power threatened by the decentralized, libertarian, self-governing nature of the Net. All the dire warnings are motivated to some extent by self-interest.

If we deafen ourselves to the hysteria and look at the online environment rationally, it is safer than any urban street, even safer than a rural meadow. No one gets mugged online. No one is punched in the face, bitten by snakes, or marooned by floods.

Unfortunately, though, journalists need to write stories that have maximum shock value, which makes the media a perfect tool for any group seeking to maintain its influence by scaring people. Legislators are well aware that if they publicize a threat, then "solve the problem," they will increase their chances of reelection. Special-interest groups know that the first priority in any fund-raising campaign is to portray a threat, then ask for help in overcoming it.

It shouldn't be surprising, then, that all attempts to impose legislation or "clean up the Net" have come from antagonists outside the online community. Aside from the Guardian Angels (who constitute a tiny minority), no group of Net users has called for decency laws or extra police to combat hackers. Netizens are generally satisfied with the online status quo. In fact, they have circulated petitions and waged angry campaigns demanding that the Net should remain uncontrolled.

These petitions have been totally ignored, for a very obvious reason: They are just another attempt to exercise power by a group that has scared people by seeming to have too much power already. So long as Net users are a feisty minority threatening to reform the status quo, they're not going to get anywhere by demanding more freedom. In fact, the louder they shout for liberty, the more scary they'll seem, triggering harsher backlash from traditionally powerful groups that want to keep them under control.

This, I believe, is the current situation.

And what of the future?

Most often, the Net has been portrayed as a way to chat with strangers and view pornography. This, of course, is a gross trivialization—although it may have been helpful in a way, since governments might be even more alarmed if they realized the *real* implications of global connectivity.

"It's much bigger than terminals with keyboards," says Kevin Kelly. "I'm talking about everything we manufacture being connected to everything else: cash registers, soil sensors, satellites, all kinds of devices sending information into this network where people are communicating with each other. The real Net is all of this data swishing around, this soup of information. It's bigger than we can encompass in our own minds. It has a collective smartness that is of a wavelength that we can't perceive, because it's too big."

Compared with this, the "threat" posed by a few dirty pictures is absurdly trivial. The online world is already much more than an information exchange; it's a full-featured commercial, artistic, and

social environment that is developing its own culture and customs and will soon possess its own financial currency. In many ways it can become a substitute for institutions, businesses, and social relationships in the physical world.

Kevin Kelly foresees two possible dangers. "One bad scenario is that commercialization proceeds at such a pace that it hinders and constrains the range of options, so that there is an atrophy of civilization, there is not enough elbow room for the kind of civics that we need to make this a really open development. In the land rush to develop the Net, we may not allow enough room for the online equivalent of parks, sidewalks, and open space."

Kevin Kelly of Wired *magazine expects to see less freedom online as the net becomes more civilized.*

But Kelly is equally cautious about excesses of freedom. "It could become so anarchic, so uncommercialized, such a ruthless frontier, there's not enough incentive for the domesticated stability that is required to have networked civilization unfold."

Consequently, he feels there may be some need for restraint. "I think that there should be limits to freedom on the Net, just as any society has to have limits to freedom. That is the definition of civilization: It is a consensual surrendering of certain freedoms that individuals theoretically have, as individuals, and they give those up because the advantages of doing so outweigh the cost. As the Net becomes more civilized we should certainly expect to see more of that, and I would go so far to say that until there are some freedoms surrendered, it won't be civilized."

But consensual may be the key word here. No society should be *coerced* into giving up its freedoms—least of all by hostile outsiders who don't live there.

As we enter the last years of the twentieth century, the Net is like a rebellious eighteen-year-old, still with a lot to learn but in some ways smarter than his parents. This precocious adolescent has a head full of utopian dreams and feels quite capable of making his own decisions, yet he's confronted with authority figures who want to take away his car keys and keep him grounded—because, they claim, neighbors have been complaining about his bad language and "immorality."

As any parent knows, this kind of clampdown doesn't always work. It can cause tantrums and hard-core defiance.

Bearing in mind that many Americans have become steadily more skeptical and hostile toward government, will traditional centers of power really manage to maintain their authority and keep the Net under control? Federal agencies have successfully regulated every other mode of communication, including the postal service, the telephone network, radio stations, broadcast TV, and cable TV. Will they regulate the Internet, too?

The following scenarios assume that some sort of federal decency

legislation is eventually enacted, and is judged constitutional. What would the consequences be?

Large Internet service providers would obviously bitch about it, but American corporations always complain about their regulatory burden. So long as they can turn a profit, regulation is a cost of doing business that they are usually willing to put up with. Some businesses actually prefer a certain amount of regulation because it saves them from trying to guess what's legal and what's not.

Smaller service providers may be less willing (or less able) to obey a decency law—and as a result, some of them will be busted. This crackdown will be widely publicized, causing other small service providers to censor themselves, and users will feel a need to be discreet for fear of getting into trouble or losing access to the Net.

Of course, they'll still be able to use encryption. But suppose encryption also falls under government control. In this nightmare Net scenario, legislators make it clear that they are absolutely determined to eradicate anarchy online.

Two scenarios are now possible.

1. Widespread rebellion.

Radical Net users stir up a groundswell of protest. They're ornery, resourceful, and combative. Thousands or millions of everyday Americans insist on defying the decency laws, just as millions of heartlanders chose to break the law in the early 1990s when they used illegal decoders with satellite dishes to steal TV programs.

Now what? Will federal legislators admit that they made a mistake and repeal the legislation that they just passed?

This would be unprecedented behavior. More likely, conservatives will demand additional funds for law enforcement to crack down on the rebels and "clean up the Net" as originally planned.

This means, of course, a full-scale "war on indecency." Result: sources of pornographic material move offshore; the U.S. Government tries to persuade other countries to adopt its standards; small nations are threatened with import tariffs or trade sanctions

if they refuse to control Net content. Meanwhile, in America, Net sites must obtain a license to operate and will lose that license if they violate decency laws. Rogue sites are traced and shut down by the FCC. Hard-core rebel users are randomly arrested and jailed.

The war on indecency ends up like the war on drugs: It can never be won, but so many dire warnings have been made about threats to American values that no one in government wants to lose face by backing down. Millions of everyday citizens violate the law to a minor extent on a daily basis. A minority are arrested and jailed. It's a huge waste of resources, and it ruins some people's lives.

This may seem to be the ultimate nightmare, but now consider the alternative.

2. Minimal backlash.

A few rebels defy the new law, but they gradually find themselves becoming isolated, like leftover radicals from the 1960s. One by one, service providers quietly impose controls and stop allowing access to controversial material. Filtering software becomes increasingly sophisticated, and law enforcement uses it to perform random samples of message traffic. There are high-profile busts of Net users who are punished for trying to use encryption.

Ultimately, hardly anyone is willing to risk being fined or jailed for the sake of free speech online. As a result, the Net becomes a dead, dull environment: a place to go shopping and swap totally inoffensive memos and business communications—although many businesses will now prefer regular mail for important messages, because secure encryption is outlawed and there's always a chance of surveillance online.

Similarly, individuals prefer not to use the Net for anything personal or private because they have the uncomfortable feeling that Big Brother may be watching. Cyberspace is now supposed to be safe for kids, yet children are discouraged from using it because their parents can be held responsible if a child uses four-letter words or says anything that seems too suggestive.

The Luddites rejoice. Anarchy online has been eradicated. The concept of a new era of wealth through connectivity is mocked as a silly technofantasy of the nutty nineties. Net usage diminishes, and people look back on the brief years without regulation as a bizarre quirk. "It could never last," they say. And they were right.

Are these two scenarios a realistic prediction of what may happen if there's a serious federal attempt to control netspeech? I'd prefer not to think so, yet they are quite consistent with previous examples of bad social legislation. A law may be widely despised and disobeyed, but it can still be rigorously enforced. This happened during Prohibition; it's still happening in the war on drugs; it happened on a more trivial scale with the 55 mph speed limit; and of course it happened during the Vietnam War, which was one of the few occasions where public backlash became so widespread that government was ultimately forced to compromise. Of course, thousands of young Americans had to be killed overseas before this resolution was reached.

I'd like to think that the need to preserve free speech could also rouse national passions. I'm hoping that millions of people who want to express themselves freely online won't allow a few thousand censors to stop them. I'd like to see legislation that derives from rationality and a sense of proportion rather than a mindless desire to maintain a traditional imbalance of power. I'm hoping that as more and more people get online, they'll see that there's nothing to be afraid of and no need for government controls that will cripple the medium they're supposed to protect. I'd like to believe that legislation to restrict online speech will be ruled unconstitutional, and a rich, egalitarian networked society will evolve, free from oppression by those who fear change.

But this will happen only if we fight to make it so.

Epilogue

Life After Exon

The telecommunications deregulation bill was
voted on by the Senate and the House of Representatives on
February 1, 1996, exactly one year after Senator James Exon first
proposed adding his decency amendment to it. After virtually no
debate, the huge piece of legislation was approved by overwhelming
majorities in both houses. President Clinton was expected to sign it
into law a few days later.

Most of Exon's original wording survived intact in the final law.
Ann Beeson at the ACLU reminded everyone that it would "subject
first-year college students under 18 to two years in prison and a
$100,000 fine if they engage in overly salacious dating patter online
(even in their private e-mail)." The ACLU's executive director,
Ira Glasser, also warned: "This law . . . places the free speech and
privacy rights of all Internet users in permanent jeopardy. It will
criminalize otherwise protected speech in cyberspace, impose
new censorship controls on television, and destroy the diversity of
media ownership. For a Congress that says it wants to get big
government out of people's lives, this law represents the most
extreme hypocrisy."

The day after the bill was approved, some newspapers reported that Senator Henry Hyde had made a hasty addition to the decency amendment just before the final vote. Hyde's text updated the 1873 Comstock Act, named after postal inspector Anthony Comstock, a notorious decency crusader who spent most of his life combating salacious pictures and immoral practices such as birth control. Many parts of the Comstock Act had been repealed over the decades, but one section outlawing communication about abortion was still on the books. It had been unused for decades and was a clear violation of the First Amendment, so why had Hyde extended it to include messages sent via computer networks? And why did he then issue a statement (quoted in *USA Today*) claiming that "nothing in the bill suggests any restrictions on discussions about abortion"?

More mixed signals came from President Clinton, who publicly assured Net users that the whole decency amendment was unconstitutional—even though he fully intended to sign it into law. Why would any President tell the world that the legislation he was about to create contained a provision that was illegal?

Perhaps there was a pattern here, a hint that on some issues legislators were more interested in looking good than in creating good laws. Henry Hyde could tell conservatives in his home state of Illinois that he had concocted an amendment to stop abortion referrals online—and if a court refused to allow it, well, that was beyond his control. Bill Clinton could tell liberals that he hated the decency amendment as much as they did and he was certain it would be ruled unconstitutional. Therefore, no one should think badly of him for legitimizing it with his signature.

Maybe most of the senators who originally voted for the decency amendment had a similar outlook. They cast their votes to prove they were "tough on porn," even though they knew the legislation would be unconstitutional.

At one point, when the Exon amendment was going through the committee process, there had been an excellent chance to limit its scope. Committee members had nevertheless voted for the most

extreme form of the amendment. Were they, too, deliberately creating a monster while confidently expecting it to be euthanized by the justice system?

One thing was certain: Hardly anyone in Congress cared very much about the impact of decency legislation online. They weren't Net users; the decency amendment wouldn't affect their lives or the lives of their families, and it seemed unlikely to have an economic impact, either. If it meant that people couldn't swear online, so what? That was a trivial matter compared with the rest of the telecommunications bill, which deregulated vast industries worth billions of dollars.

Many Net users seemed disillusioned by the cynicism they sensed in Washington. Voters Telecommunications Watch had organized a protest in December 1995, prompting an estimated 50,000 calls and faxes to legislators who were then debating the decency amendment during the committee process. The barrage of protests had no effect at all, causing some netizens to start comparing themselves with American colonists suffering taxation without representation. There was talk of staging more militant protests, maybe even trying to shut the Net down.

Meanwhile, Bill Clinton signed the telecommunications bill in the Library of Congress. Ironically, this criminalized the very institution in which he sat. The complete library catalog is available online, including many book titles that would horrify Senator Exon. A quick search on the day after the decency amendment became law turned up the following titles:

```
B06+Fuck//(TITL=1)
B07 Fuck (The English word)//(SUBJ=1)
B08 Fuck journal//(TITL=1)
B09 Fuck off, unless you take off that mask//(TITL=1)
B10 Fuck you (])//(TITL=1)
B11 Fuck you heroes//(TITL=1)
B12 Fuck you(]) Underground poems//(TITL=1)
```

The Library of Congress has not taken any steps to prevent this listing from being viewed by children all over America. Therefore, the library is now in violation of federal law.

Naturally, Clinton's signature was barely dry before the ACLU filed for injunctive relief, just as Ann Beeson had promised they would. One week later Judge Ronald Buckwalter, a Bush appointee with a conservative reputation, granted a temporary restraining order prohibiting any prosecutions under the indecency provisions of the telecommunications deregulation act until a three-judge panel had time to evaluate the ACLU petition along with a response from the Department of Justice—which had argued against decency legislation a year earlier but was now compelled to defend the law. When free-speech activists read the statement from the Justice Department, they were dismayed to find that it contained data derived from Martin Rimm's study. Even now, his Traumatic Statistic lived on.

Everyone assumed that the amendment would be ruled unconstitutional. In the meantime, Attorney General Janet Reno signed a legal stipulation pledging that she would not "initiate any investigations or prosecutions" under the provision. Still, if the amendment turned out to be constitutional after all, the Justice Department would be able to take action against anyone who had placed indecent material on the Net during the moratorium.

Reactions of Net users ranged from compliant to defiant.

An Internet service provider in Oklahoma started blocking access to about ten of the most "controversial" Usenet groups.

A former judge named Steve Russell wrote a diatribe for an online newspaper, deliberately violating the decency law and inviting prosecution. His opening sentence: "You motherfuckers in Congress have dropped over the edge of the earth this time."

On Usenet, in the alt.tasteless.jokes newsgroup, some people started cautiously using euphemisms for four-letter words.

On alt.censorship, users vowed to violate the law as often as possible. A netizen named Henry posted the following rant:

> i intend to toss 'fuck' liberally into every Subject: line i touch until the dumb motherfuckers come to get me. i intend to flagrantly defy this law and spit on it until it is overturned by the obvious supreme court judgment.

> i am well aware that the dipshits who passed this
> law, deliberately spitting on the first amendment,
> are completely informed and know that it's a
> malicious violation of the first amendment.
>
> however, these scumsucking pigfucking freaks
> don't give a fuck about the constitution they swore
> to uphold. they're faith-breakers, liars and traitors
> to the united states, and any nation that valued its
> liberty would declare them traitors and have them
> shot at dawn.
>
> bob dole ought to be castrated and burnt at
> the stake.
>
> senator exon ought to be ripped to shreds by wild
> boars and left to the vultures, buried at dawn with
> donkey dicks in each eyesocket and a stake
> through his chest.
>
> (i'd say 'through his heart' but obviously we're
> discussing a man without a heartbeat.)

And Henry finished with a new signature line that he planned to append to all his mail in future:

> fuckfuckfuckfuckfuckfuckfuckfuckfuckfuckfuckfuckfuckfuck
> f   f
> u   "When you can't say 'fuck,' you can't say   u
> c   'FUCK THE CDA!'—Lenny Bruce rephrased   c
> k   k
> fuckfuckfuckfuckfuckfuckfuckfuckfuckfuckfuckfuckfuckfuck

The CDA that Henry referred to was the Communications Decency Act, the formal name for the Exon amendment.

Some netizens started figuring out practical ways to evade the law, in case it somehow survived the ACLU's challenge or was rewritten and reintroduced in some new form that turned out to be constitutional. Jaron Lanier, the inventor of virtual reality, proposed that indecent images or text could be broken into tiny pieces, none of which would be illegal on its own. The pieces could be distributed at dozens or hundreds of Internet sites. Special software could then retrieve and reassemble them in the privacy of a user's computer. Within days, Lanier said he was hearing from people who liked the

proposal and were "busy creating the program with the idea of distributing it freely."

Other rebels describing themselves as "electronic guerrillas" launched a Web page for discussing defensive tactics. Their URL was http://www.onworld.com/MUT

An organization named Offshore Information Services (OIS) started offering totally uncensored Net access for $50 a month from its base in Anguilla, a tax haven in the Caribbean with strict privacy laws. The OIS press release promised netizens that "setting up an offshore e-mail identity can be as easy as changing the POP [point of presence] server name, user name, and password in their mail program. Using this new identity they can again have free speech on the Internet." A Web page at http://online.offshore.com.ai/ offered additional information.

An internet user known only as Henry chose to violate the Exon amendment in the worst possible way. [Photo by the author]

Overall, it seemed that the Internet community was in no mood to knuckle under—at least, not in this first tentative skirmish. And the mood of rebellious euphoria intensified still further in June when a Philadelphia appeals court unanimously ruled that Exon's amendment was, in fact, unconstitutional. (At the time of writing, it is not known whether the ruling will be appealed to the Supreme Court.)

The decency activists were bruised but unbeaten. They naturally vowed to try again—and again—with as many different legislative approaches as necessary to end anarchy online. Suppose that one of their attempts is eventually successful; will we see a massive populist backlash, with numerous net rebels risking jail time?

During the great legal battles against literary censorship in the 1950s, there were no massive populist uprisings. The struggle was waged by a tenacious minority of writers and publishers, while the general public seemed unconcerned or even hostile to the idea of sexually explicit free speech.

Online, though, the situation is different. Everyone is a writer now, and anyone can be a publisher. Technology has given Net users a new sense of power and freedom that they will be reluctant to surrender. As a result, free speech may seem more personally important to a larger number of people today than it did forty years ago.

When some sort of decency legislation ultimately becomes law— perhaps a more limited, revised version of the Exon Amendment— the courage and concerns of Net users will truly be tested. At that time some cynics in congress may be in for a surprise.

Appendices

1. The State of Your State

Has your state been passing new laws restricting free expression? Have these laws been applied, yet? The chart on pages 202-203 gives guidance based on an exhaustive search of legislation in all fifty states. Note that the chart concentrates mainly on laws affecting freedom of speech; it doesn't deal with other instances of computer crime, such as hacking. Also, the chart lists only state laws, and lists only laws that *specifically* mention computers or networks. There have been cases where old, general legislation was successfully applied to computer crimes, but we chose to omit these cases and emphasize areas where legislators have targeted free speech in the online community.

You may approve of some of the laws that we found. For instance, laws against child pornography or child solicitation seem like a good idea to many people. But is it really wise to turn someone into a criminal if he or she possesses *any* picture of a person under eighteen in a sexually provocative pose? And who decides whether the model really is under eighteen? (Some states make their own estimate, then require the defendant to prove otherwise. In other words, the defendant becomes guilty till proven innocent.)

Laws can also damage innocent people in unexpected ways.

Suppose someone sends you a piece of kiddie porn—by error, or maliciously. You save the image, then view it, and as soon as you realize what it is, you erase it. But your computer's operating system only removes the filename; it does not touch the actual data, which is still on the hard drive. If your state makes it illegal to possess a single piece of child pornography, you are now technically guilty of that crime. Police technicians would be able to recover the data, and you might have a hard time proving that you received the picture unintentionally. Moreover, if you try to erase the file, you are destroying evidence—which is another crime. The only legally safe option would be to turn the picture over to the police, which could create other hassles for you.

Overall, computer crime laws are an attempt to control an environment so new and so different that we don't even know what it will look like and what it will be used for ten years from now. Some of these laws seem premature at the very least. Laws that punish Internet site owners for online content, for instance, are almost certain to inhibit free speech generally. And a mosaic of differently worded state laws is obviously a nightmare for access providers, who can have charges filed against them in any state where the data comes from or is sent to.

Remember, if you look on the chart and find that your state hasn't created any legislation, this doesn't mean you're safe. If you send something "offensive" through the Net, you can still be prosecuted at the receiving end.

Remember also that if your state hasn't passed any computer-specific laws, there may be old laws that are worded so generally that they can be applied to computer networks. In Florida, for instance, it's a crime to allow children to read "accounts of sexual excitement, or sexual conduct" where there is no redeeming literary or social value. The account can appear anywhere—on paper or on a video screen. This means that if a seventeen-year-old samples Internet Relay Chat, the site owner who provided access could be arrested for violating Florida law. Also in Florida, you can't send a message that "facilitates or encourages sexual conduct with a

minor." This means that teenagers who are old enough to have legal sex are still not allowed to make a date online. The law doesn't mention the Internet, but it's so broadly worded, it doesn't have to.

Crime Categories

The chart splits computer crime into five categories.

1. *Harassment.* Existing laws make it a crime to harass someone over the phone. Some states have now broadened these laws to include computer communications. This means that bad behavior such as spamming, flaming, or bad language may now be illegal.

2. *Juvenile access.* These laws may make it illegal to make adult material available to minors online. Since minors can gain access to all public areas of the Net, these laws would effectively reduce the whole Internet to a level suitable only for children.

3. *Kiddie porn.* Under these laws, you may not distribute child pornography electronically or store it on your hard drive. In some states, digitally retouched simulations can count as kiddie porn.

4. *Child solicitation.* This means enticing a minor online to indulge in sex or an indecent act.

5. *Other laws.* Michigan, Oklahoma, and Virginia have general obscenity laws that now mention computer media. Georgia has an antiterrorism law (see "Hot Spots," below).

Weighting

Some laws are more sweeping than others. We attempted to gauge the effect of each statute and indicated this with a cluster of black squares ranging from 1 (little effect) to 4 (disaster area). The total number of squares in each row is the overall rating for each state.

If a state has a history of criminal cases, this increases the state's overall rating, because it indicates that prosecutors are ready to make active use of computer-crime laws. Civil cases (in which one private party sues another private party) are included, because legal

Computer Crime Laws in the 50 States

	OVERALL RATING Low score means less legal activity	Laws Passed Against Use of Computer for:						Laws Pending	Cases So Far:	
		Harass-ment	Juvenile Access	Hacking/Piracy	Kiddie-porn	Child Solicita-tion	Other Crimes		Civil	Criminal
HIGH activity										
California	6							■■		■■
Connecticut	6	■■■■						■■		■■
Georgia	9	■■		■			■■■		■■	■■■
New Jersey	9	■■■■		■			■■■	■	■	■■■
New York	7			■	■■				■	■■■
Oklahoma	8		■	■	■	■		■	■■	■■
Tennessee	6									■■■■
Virginia	9		■■	■	■■		■■■	■■	■■	■■■■
MEDIUM activity										
Alabama	3	■		■				■	■	
Colorado	2			■						
Florida	5			■	■					
Illinois	4			■	■■					■■
Kansas	4	■■■		■	■					
Maryland	2		■						■	
Michigan	5			■			■			■■
Minnesota	5			■					■	■■■
Missouri	2			■					■	■■
Montana	2				■■					
Nevada	2									
New Mexico	4			■	■			■		■■
North Dakota	5	■■■■		■				■	■	
Ohio	5							■		
Pennsylvania	4			■	■			■■		■■■■

State	Activity
South Dakota	4 ■■■■
Texas	3
Washington	2
Wisconsin	2

LOW activity

State	Activity
Alaska	0
Arizona	1
Arkansas	0
Delaware	0
Hawaii	1
Idaho	1
Indiana	0
Iowa	1
Kentucky	0
Louisiana	0
Maine	1
Massachusetts	1
Mississippi	1
Nebraska	1
New Hampshire	1
North Carolina	1
Oregon	1
Rhode Island	1
South Carolina	1
Utah	1
Vermont	1
West Virginia	1
Wyoming	1

Key: ■ Little effect   ■■ Moderate effect   ■■■ Major effect   ■■■■ Disaster Area

action of this type is usually reported in local newspapers and may give rise to copycat actions. For example, if someone recovers substantial damages, this may encourage someone else to bring a similar suit. Generally speaking, however, the chart gives civil actions a lower weighting than criminal actions.

Laws currently pending are weighted according to the number of laws and the effect they may have if they are passed.

Harassment laws are heavily weighted because they criminalize speech that most people assume is legal. If some of these laws are actually applied, they might be declared unconstitutional on appeal—but who wants to be a test case?

Some juvenile access laws received a relatively high rating because if they are enforced, they would effectively block adults from accessing constitutionally protected materials. Also, these laws seem to hold the Internet service provider or BBS owner liable for material that the owner may not know is on the system.

Hot Spots

California has a bill pending (871)which states that anyone merely possessing more than ten copies of the same obscene picture is guilty of wholesale distribution. Think twice about making eleven copies of that graphics file as a gift for your friends! California has also seen two recent civil actions, one brought by Scientologists, the other by an AOL user who disputes their billing procedures. Also, a nineteen-year-old boy who offered shares in his eel farm over the Internet was faced with criminal charges by the SEC.

Connecticut has made it a criminal act to send online communications that are "likely to cause annoyance or harm." If you flame someone who finds your behavior annoying, you're flouting this law (Connecticut Statute s53a–182(b)).

Connecticut has also used its new kiddie porn law to file an additional charge against a child molester, because he possessed sexually explicit computer images.

Georgia, *Kansas*, *New Jersey*, *North Dakota*, and *South Dakota* have laws against "lewd speech" or "indecent communications."

Georgia passed Act 332 in April 1995, which made it a crime to spread "information designed to encourage, solicit, or otherwise promote terroristic acts." Yes, Georgia has achieved what some U.S. senators only dream of. Another Georgia law can make a BBS owner criminally liable if obscene images are available to children online. (Georgia Code 16–12-100.1).

In *Maryland*, *Oregon*, and *Washington*, Net-related bills were introduced but were defeated during 1995, partly through efforts of ACLU affiliates. In the future we may see new versions of these bills from legislators who don't like to take no for an answer.

Minnesota's state attorney general has used state and federal fraud and advertising laws against some individuals who advertise on the Internet. A "make money fast!" pyramid scheme and an herbalist offering home remedies were among the targets.

New Jersey has a new squad of "cybercops" in the Consumer Affairs Department, and their first major action was aimed at twenty people who spammed Usenet with chain-letter Ponzi schemes. New Jersey also has one of the most sweeping kiddie porn laws; it includes any kind of visual depiction, not just photographs, and it even mentions video games.

Illinois, Montana, and *Nevada* have similar kiddie porn laws that can send you to jail for possessing a *simulation* of the real thing. In Nevada, at least one year of jail time is mandatory. In Illinois, if you own more than one copy of any one image, the state assumes you're in the distribution business and applies higher penalties.

In *New Mexico*, law-enforcement officers cunningly inverted a new computer law and applied it to an ordinary case of long-distance telephone fraud. The state argued that since the telephone system is a kind of computer network, the Computer Crimes Act was backward-compatible.

New York legislators approved a bill in January 1996 that would prohibit the knowing dissemination of material depicting "actual or

simulated nudity" via computer networks if it might be "harmful to minors." The law might also criminalize information such as safe-sex guides, and could require Internet service providers to monitor everything passing through their systems or face prosecution. At the time of writing, there was no way of knowing if the governor would sign the bill into law. Meanwhile, existing New York laws have been applied to two criminal cases, one against an accused child molester, the other against a contractor who shut down a client's phone service when he claimed they failed to pay him for his programming work. In addition, three civil suits have been fought, and new legislation is pending. New York came close to passing an online indecency statute in 1995 (in the face of heavy lobbying by the ACLU and other groups), and the sponsors of that bill will probably try again.

Ohio has been a hotbed of legal action. In the Cincinnati area, Sheriff Simon Leis's computer-crimes task force seized five bulletin boards suspected of harboring obscene material. The SEC filed criminal charges against a company that posted a "make money fast!" scheme on the Net. Writer Brock Meeks was sued by a direct-mail company after he accused them of misleading trade practices; the case was settled with Meeks paying a $64 court fee after he had already incurred more than $25,000 in legal costs.

In *Oklahoma*, a CD-ROM distributor was jailed even though identical products are distributed by mail through national-circulation magazines. A bill that would have specifically prohibited obscene bulletin boards was rewritten after pressure from organizations such as the ACLU, but BBS owners were warned that if they don't clean up their act, they'll be faced with stricter legislation next year. (This legislation is not actually pending, but since it has been threatened, Oklahoma rates one mark in the "Pending" column.)

In *Virginia*, existing state laws already banned a very wide range of erotica. These laws have been extended to include the viewing and transmission of images online. Also, the state can assume that a young-looking model in a sexually explicit picture is underage, leaving the defendant with the task of proving, somehow, that the model is over eighteen. (The New Jersey kiddie porn law follows a similar "guilty till proven innocent" logic.)

2. Useful Web Sites

Search Engines

http://www.yahoo.com
http://www.webcrawler.com
http://www.altavista.digital.com

Sources of Information

American Civil Liberties Union

http://www.aclu.org/siteindex.html

Anonymous remailers—
general information

http://www.well.com/user/abacard
http://www.cs.berkeley.edu/~raph/remailer-list.html
http://www.replay.com/staff/usura/chain.html

Anonymous remailers—
do-it-yourself Windows program

http://www.c2.org/~winsock

Jake Baker

Archives c/o Peter J. Swanson:
http://krusty.eecs.umich.edu/people/pjswan/Baker/Jake_Baker.html

Case and court transcripts:
http://www.umich.edu/~mttlr

Judge Cohn's opinion:
http://ic.net/~sberaha/baker.html

Boardwatch magazine
(an authoritative online guide)

http://www.boardwatch.com

Center for Democracy and Technology

http://www.cdt.org/

Christian Coalition

http://cc.org/

Cincinnati

Free Speech, c/o Scott Madigan:
http://w3.one.net/~smadigan/free/newsidx.htm

Computer Professionals for Social Responsibility (CPSR)

http://www.cpsr.org/home

Computer Underground Digest

http://www.soci.niu.edu/~jthomas

Congress

Information:
http://policy.net/capweb/congress.html

Names and personal e-mail addresses:
http://www.vtw.org/congress/

Cyberangels (online division of the Guardian Angels)

http://www.safesurf.com/cyberangels/

Digicash

http://www.digicash.com/

Electronic Freedom Foundation

http://www.eff.org/

Electronic Privacy Information Center

http://www.epic.org/

Federal news and links to other federal sources
http://www.fedworld.gov

Joel Furr home page
http://www.danger.com/index.html

Hoffman and Novak, critics of Rimm
http://www2000.ogsm.vanderbilt.edu

Libertarian Party
http://www.lp.org/lp/

Library of Congress card catalog
http://lcweb.loc.gov

Netiquette guide (by Brad Templeton)
http://www.clari.net/brad/emily.html

People for the American Way
http://www.pfaw.org/

PGP (free software for secure conversations)
http://web.mit.edu/network/pgpfone

rec.humor.funny, archives of the Usenet group
http://www.clari.net/rhf/

Rimm, Martin

Case history and commentary:
http://www2000.ogsm.vanderbilt.edu/cyberporn.debate.cgi

Carnegie-Mellon University censorship information:
http://www.cs.cmu.edu/~declan/

Satellite TV information

Legal:

http://www.nmia.com/~roberts/

Illegal:

http://www.hackwatch.com/

Steganography
(hiding data in digitized pictures)

http://indyunix.iupui.edu/~emilbran/stego.html

Voters Telecommunication Watch

http://www.vtw.org/

Web information, including directory of sites

http://www.internic.net/

Wired magazine—
Hotwired, and *Wired* back issues

http://www.hotwired.com/

3. Prayer for
a World without Porn

Full text of the prayer recited by the Senate Chaplain, immediately before debate of Senator Exon's Communications Decency Act:

Almighty God, Lord of all life, we praise You for the advancements in computerized communications that we enjoy in our time. Sadly, however, there are those who are littering this information superhighway with obscene, indecent, and destructive pornography. Virtual but virtueless reality is projected in the most twisted, sick misuse of sexuality. Violent people with sexual pathology are able to stalk and harass the innocent. Cyber solicitation of teenagers reveals the dark side of online victimization.

Lord, we are profoundly concerned about the impact of this on our children. We have learned from careful study how children can become addicted to pornography at an early age. Their understanding and appreciation of Your gift of sexuality can be denigrated and eventually debilitated. Pornography disallowed in print and the mail is now readily available to young children who learn how to use the computer.

Oh God, help us care for our children. Give us wisdom to create regulations that will protect the innocent. In times past, You have used the Senate to deal with problems of air and water pollution, and the misuse of our natural resources. Lord, give us courage to balance our reverence for freedom of speech with responsibility for what is said and depicted.

Now, guide the Senators when they consider ways of controlling the pollution of computer communications and how to preserve one of our greatest resources: The minds of our children and the future and moral strength of our Nation. Amen.